RELATED TITLES FROM PRENTICE HALL PRESS

THE MEDICINE WHEEL: EARTH ASTROLOGY
by Sun Bear and Wabun
THE BEAR TRIBE'S SELF RELIANCE BOOK
by Sun Bear, Wabun, Nimimosha
THE BOOK OF THE VISION QUEST
by Steven Foster with Meredith Little

A **SUN BEAR** BOOK

THE PATH OF POWER

Sun Bear, Wabun, and Barry Weinstock

PRENTICE HALL PRESS

New York   London   Toronto   Sydney   Tokyo

Published in 1987 by Prentice Hall Press
A Division of Simon & Schuster, Inc.
Gulf + Western Building
One Gulf + Western Plaza
New York, NY 10023

Originally pulished by Bear Tribe Publishing, Spokane, WA

PRENTICE HALL PRESS is a trademark of Simon & Schuster, Inc.

Library of Congress Cataloging-in-Publication Data

Sun Bear (Chippewa Indian)
  The path of power / Sun Bear, Wabun, and Barry Weinstock.
    p. cm.
  "A Sun Bear book."
  Originally published: Spokane, Wash.: Bear Tribe Pub., c1983
under the title: Sun Bear, the path of power.
  Bibliography: p.
  ISBN 0-13-653403-1 (pbk.): $9.95
  1. Sun Bear (Chippewa Indian) 2. Chippewa Indians—Biography.
3. Chippewa Indians—Religion and mythology. 4. Indians of North
America—Religion and mythology. I. Wabun. II. Weinstock, Edward
B. III. Sun Bear (Chippewa Indian). Sun Bear, the path of power.
IV. Title.
E99.C6S92   1988
970.004'97—dc19   88-22570
                                                       CIP

Book Design: Nimimosha of Gaiagraphics, Spokane, WA

Manufactured in the United States of America

10 9 8 7 6 5 4 3 2

THIS BOOK IS DEDICATED TO ALL OF
THOSE HUMAN BEINGS — BOTH
NATIVE AND NON-NATIVE — WHO WANT
TO REACH FOR AND FIND THEIR OWN
PATH OF POWER

CONTENTS

BOOK ONE
MY LIFE

BOOK TWO
WALKING THE PATH OF POWER

When we complete the circle, the hoop of the nations will be rejoined, and the great visions of Black Elk, Sun Bear, Sweet Water and others down the ages will be implemented so that, at last, our grandchildren, who are the promised land, may play together in love and harmony on the many planets in the universe; and our Mother Earth will be healed and come to her full glory.

PROLOGUE

Who is Sun Bear? He is more than a man. He is also a shield that he carries with him, a presence that goes wherever he goes. This shield proclaims him to be Sun Bear, warrior of the rainbow, brother of peace, keeper of the Medicine Wheel. His vision shines forth from his shield and is seen by the people. Those who know him personally are deeply affected by his shield. Those who come to his gatherings are invariably touched in ways difficult to describe except in words like love, healing and unity. His vision is of such quality that it never is devisive, mean, or self-serving. His vision is of the caliber of a great shaman or teacher.

Sun Bear is a rainbow spirit dwelling within a red man's body. Not only that, but he seems to be many different kinds of American Indian rolled up into one. Hence, he is a *representative* Indian, as opposed to Sioux, Chippewa, Paiute, Cree, etc. Undoubtedly, his traditional medicine training has much to do with who he is. But he has not been one of those Indians who, like religious fundamentalists, have held unswervingly to his tribal way. His visionary path has led him into the modern world and the contemporary expression of culture known as America. Sun Bear's vision is not only Chippewa. It is Native American in the broadest sense.

Actually, the human meaning Sun Bear represents is more than just America. It represents the entire human experience. His message is found in every major human religion. The native people of America, and the earth, have *always* dreamed of peace and unity on the earth, for all people. Sun Bear is a messenger from our sacred ancestors. His message is: We are all one and the earth is our mother. He activates this message by bringing people together, regardless of their color or religious persuasion, to celebrate their oneness with each other and their mother.

As his influence expands, Sun Bear will encounter a good deal of criticism. Much of it will come from other Indians who resent his ingress into the white man's world. They will accuse him of selling medicine secrets or of cheapening his own traditional ways. These same voices are raised against anyone who consciously chooses to take the risk of bringing good medicine to modern America. Certainly, Indians have reasons to be forever bitter. And as long as there are bitter Indians, there will be guilty white men. Sun Bear seeks to heal this vicious cycle of bitterness and guilt that keeps both down. He does not use band-aids. He uses the simplest and most powerful of all kinds of healing.

The effects of this healing are feelings and emotions, positive in nature, involving deeper respect for and understanding of American Indian ways, and a new, yet old, recognition of the use of ceremony in modern life. Benefits are experienced by all kinds of people who gather to identify with and celebrate the vision of Sun Bear. But the bitterness runs deep. There are some American Indian "medicine men" who would forever withhold good medicine from the white man, hoping that he will eventually expire in a trap of his own devising. This kind of sorcery is foreign to Sun Bear. It is foreign to his personality. Sun Bear is a practicing warrior of the rainbow.

Steven Foster, Meredith Little
Directors, The School of Lost Borders
authors of THE BOOK OF THE VISION QUEST

★ ★ ★

"Sun Bear makes full use of the four 'H's' — Humility, Honesty, Humor and Harmony in all of his encounters. The story of these encounters is a warm human document which has a direct and deep impact on the reader. Whether he is a stunt man employed by the leading studios in Hollywood or a model prisoner in Lompoc for desertion during the Korean war, or the organizer of a project to enhance the dignity of his people in Nevada, Sun Bear is one of the *bridge builders* of the 20th century whose passage through life has altered whole strata of different societies.

"But it is his simple profound teachings and the example he sets of letting his light shine on all around, that makes this book a must for readers and seekers of the new era. Here is the authentic Ring of Greatness.

"I believe this biography of Sun Bear will take its place among the great Twentieth Century classics of American Native literature.

"It is brilliantly written by the only one who could do it justice, Wabun ... along with Barry Weinstock.. With Wabun's writing skills and bridge building disciplines and her long and close association with Sun Bear, she is the channel those of us who know them both would have joyfully chosen for this work.

"Wabun and Barry bring Sun Bear directly to us — the man, the prophet, the healer, the warm-hearted friend. Thousands carry Sun Bear's teachings in their hearts and try to show them in their lives as they struggle to complete the rainbow circle. Half of this circle is given by the Creator, and we make the other half through the living of our lives. When we complete the circle, the hoop of the nations will be rejoined, and the great visions of Black Elk, Sun Bear, Sweet Water and others down the ages will be implemented so that, at last, our grandchildren, who are the promised land, may play together in love and harmony on the many planets in the universe; and our Mother Earth will be healed and come to her full glory."

Evelyn Eaton
author, THE SHAMAN AND THE MEDICINE WHEEL;
SNOWY EARTH COMES GLIDING; I SEND A VOICE

"Sun Bear is one of those few great American Indians who are surviving the so-called civilization of the United States. He is a proud example for the generations to come. He shows our young people how the great people of the American Indians used to live, how they used to be in harmony with nature, how they understood the healing power, and how they taught how to stay healthy rather than to cure illness.

"Sun Bear is a great teacher and a good friend. I am proud that I have lived at the same time as this great, warm, loving, and caring person."

Dr. Elisabeth Kubler-Ross
author of ON DEATH AND DYING
★ ★ ★

"The life story of Sun Bear is a living example to every human of a way of knowing and being that is not only inspiring but also necessary as we approach the year 2000. This is an important and beautifully-written book."

Joan Halifax, Director, The Ojai Foundation
author of SHAMANIC VOICES;
SHAMAN:THE WOUNDED HEALER
★ ★ ★

"Sun Bear has very powerful visions, and is one of the only people I know in the world today who is living his visions fully. I sincerely believe that if more people would come into the circle of his vision it would be the saving of the world. I give him, his vision and his books my fullest support. He has been like a grandfather to all of us in the most exalted sense of the word *grandfather*.

Tom Brown, Jr., Director, The Tracker School
author of THE TRACKER; THE SEARCH;
THE FIELD GUIDE TO WILDERNESS SURVIVAL
★ ★ ★

"During these times of great change, Sun Bear's vision seems particularly appropriate. What a pleasure to study with a teacher whose teachings come from a past that proves the problems of today can still be solved with living the simple way. Sun Bear's life and vision call for a unity amongst people and the earth upon which we live. What a different world it could be if we listened to this man's teachings, then turned them into reality."

Page Bryant (Bright Bear Woman)
author of THE EARTH CHANGES SURVIVAL HANDBOOK
★ ★ ★

"The story of Sun Bear's life-journey is a fascinating tale — and an important lesson for modern society. He teaches us how to 'walk in balance on the Earth Mother' through the wisdom of his Native American traditions presented appropriately for western culture. His medicine power is authentic and hard-won; his caring wisdom is real. Sun Bear is one of the quiet heroes of our time."

John White
author, POLE SHIFT;
PRACTICAL GUIDE TO DEATH AND DYING;
EVERYTHING YOU WANT TO KNOW ABOUT TM.

ACKNOWLEDGMENTS

So many good people have helped me to walk my path of power over the years that I hesitate to write these acknowledgments. I have a great memory for faces, but a bad memory for names. So my first acknowledgment is to all of you who have helped me, whether or not I remember you here by name. This includes all of those friends, lovers, acquaintances, apprentices, supporters, students, teachers, and detractors who have helped me to become the person that I am today. Thank you all for your contributions, large and small, to my path of power.

Next I wish to thank all of you who have helped me in fulfilling my visions through supporting or being with The Bear Tribe, and through attending and working on the Medicine Wheel Gatherings.

A very special thanks goes to all those people who are now members of The Bear Tribe, or have been in the past, and to those of you who will come in the future. Special thanks to Shawnodese, Wabun, Nimimosha, Raven, Cougar, Yarrow, Elizabeth Davis (Earth Seeker), Michelle Buchanan (Odayinquae), Donna DuPree (Singing Pipe Woman), Casey, Elisabeth Robinson, Ruth Stafford (Blue Camas), Gaia, Simon Henderson (Corn Man), Gail Buckner (Morning Wind), Saundra Crombie (Path Weaver), Cheryl Crombie, Matt Ryan, Erika Verdugo, and Regina Kerr. Also deserving of thanks are the four-leggeds who live with us and help us remember our connection to the animal kingdom.

I want to thank Wabun and Shawnodese for all of the work they did to organize the original Medicine Wheel Gatherings, and Glenn Schiffman for his work with these early Gatherings. Particular thanks to Singing Pipe Woman for all her superb work coordinating the Gatherings we have held since 1983. Thanks also to the people who have been the local organizers for the Gatherings.

I want to thank Shawnodese, Wabun, Odanyinquae. Cougar,

Raven, Nimimosha and the Tribe members for all of the work they are doing with my Apprentice Program. I also want to thank all of you who have become apprentices.

I want to thank my uncles for the teachings they bestowed upon me in my youth, and I also thank all of the other Native teachers who helped me learn about my people and their ways.

I've been fortunate to know many strong women who have helped me, loved me, and taught me. I appreciate all of you.

Many people around the country have given me much hospitality and kindness throughout the years of my travels. I wish to thank all of you.

This book has taken many years to complete, and has involved quite a number of people. Wabun originally came to the Tribe to write about me. That was in 1972. We have a file drawer full of outlines and early efforts that did not seem quite right to either of us. When my medicine told me that this book needed to be published soon, Wabun suggested that we bring in Barry Weinstock. In the summer of 1982 he came to live at the Tribe for several months. While seminars, vision quests, and apprentice programs were underway, while Howard and Sue Lamb, Nadja Glassy, and other organizational development people were helping the Tribe deal with our rapid growth, Barry taped and typed and brought our early efforts into a coherent whole. After a year more, and several rewritings, we were ready to publish our first edition.

This book has two godparents who were a source of constant encouragement. One of them is Oscar Collier of Collier Associates in New York. Oscar has, at various times, been both agent and editor for us. The other is the late Evelyn Eaton, a great and famous writer, as well as the spiritual grandmother of the Tribe and hundreds of other people. She read the almost-completed manuscript in the last week of her life, and even found the strength to comment upon it in her own hand. Her assistant, Edith Newcomb (Willow Woman) of the Rainbow Bridge (formerly Draco) Foundation, has also been a source of continuing encouragement.

Thanks to all of the Tribal people, especially Nimimosha, Shawnodese, Matthew, Ruth, and Cougar for reading and commenting on the book; and to all of the friends who added their ideas, particularly Glenn Schiffman, Page Bryant, and Morning Star.

Thanks for the book design to Nimimosha, and to Barbara Sailor for her advice.

I wish to thank the following people for their financial support of Bear Tribe Publishing's first edition of this book: J. Edward Babbington, Margaret Batsel, Adrian and Cher Cairns, Donna DuPree, Carolina Elliott, the late Margaret Hawkins, Roberta Hoots, Wes and Judi House, Carl E. Ogren, Rosemary Stratton.

A special thanks to Bill Thompson of Prentice Hall Press. His

understanding of the earth, and of our work, were instrumental in bringing
THE PATH OF POWER to a wider audience.

As always, I give thanks to the Creator, the Great Spirit, for the
gift of life. I give thanks to the beautiful Earth Mother for sustaining my
life, and the lives of all of my relations.

SUN BEAR

SUN BEAR
THE PATH OF POWER

Thank you Creator, thank you for my life. Thank you for the Earth Mother, and for all the beauty that I see in the things around me.

photo courtesy of Valley Newspapers, Kent, Washington

INTRODUCTION

The Native man stood naked upon a hill. His long dark hair blew gently in a southwesterly breeze. His face was drawn.

He prayed in the old way.

"Great Spirit" — he looked skyward — "Show me direction; renew my vision. If I have gone wrong, show me what to do. This one has tried, Great Spirit This one has tried ..."

He sank to his knees, his hands clasped over his heart. "Show me the way, Great Spirit. Send me a sign."

He kneeled against blue sky; the sun was ready to set. His eyes glistened. He gazed up at the sun, then he glanced to his left, toward the movement that he sensed.

Slowly, from the south, a golden eagle circled. It flew above the hilltop, circled lower and lower, closer to him. He raised his hands and watched the circling bird; it seemed the eagle's eyes were so close he could see into them, into the soul of this holy messenger.

"Thank you, Gitche Manitou. Thank you for sending brother eagle. What is your will?"

The bird flew even closer; soon, it seemed that their eyes were fused. The eagle circled, circled. The Indian prayed for guidance. He gave thanks for this holy sign; then, the eagle began to fly away. It circled higher and higher, and the man's face grew pained once again.

The eagle disappeared. The man was thankful for the messenger; yet, the message still eluded him. He knew the eagle looked into his soul, even as he had looked into the bird's. He prayed again for direction, for another sign.

From the southwest a great cloud materialized and moved towards him. The rest of the sky was clear. The Indian watched as the cloud grew in mass, in height, and hovered in white and dark texture above the hillside. The cloud sailed toward the northeast, and a small puff of it separated off from the rest and started to spin. It whirled faster and faster, and, as the Native watched it, his mind began to spin, back, back, back to the beginning, back to the beginning of the vision that brought him to this time and place.

Like one who is drowning, he saw his life pass quickly before him. It took courage to see all of the joy, the pain, the mistakes, the things done rightly, the people loved, hurt, found, lost — and to know when this review of his vision was complete he would have to come back to this world, and continue on.

The small cloud continued to spin, seemingly caught in a whirlwind of the heavens. It spun like his mind had a few minutes before; then, it separated in two. One piece evaporated into the sky; the other returned to the large cloud. The man knew this was his answer, this was how his vision would go on to fulfillment. His first attempt to form a tribe of medicine teachers who would help to bring balance and harmony back to the Earth Mother, seemed to have failed. He knew now, however, that in time it would succeed.

The man put on his jeans, his cowboy shirt, his black hat, and walked down the hill to his vehicle, a recycled police car he had purchased in Los Angeles. The year was 1971. The place was a hillside above Vacaville, California. The man with the courage to renew and live by his vision was Sun Bear.

★ ★ ★

Because of his courage he has been called "perhaps the wiliest man in America", an "Indian who is ten years ahead of all of the others", a saint, and a con man. He has been supported and attacked by notable people of many racial and religious backgrounds. Over the years, some of the same people have been both supporters and detractors, depending upon the political climate of the moment.

I first heard about Sun Bear in California, in early 1971, when I was there researching a book. From what I heard I deduced he was an old Indian medicine man putting together a tribe of people who thought they were reincarnated spirits of Indians from the past. I was at the point in my life when I wanted to find my own spiritual path, and his ideas didn't sound any stranger to me than the ones I'd been hearing from Hindu, Tibetan, Sufi or Russian mystics. It certainly seemed worth a story. I contacted the Bear Tribe and offered Sun Bear my apartment to stay in while he was in New York City, with the idea of interviewing him while he was there.

I met Sun Bear in the summer of that year when he was travelling across the United States to tell people about his vision and his tribe. I opened my apartment door not to a decrepit old man wrapped in a blanket and leaning on a stick and the arm of an assistant, but to a handsome, virile 41-year-old man dressed in cowboy shirt, jeans and his ever-present black hat. He had more charisma in his big, broken

Indian nose, (broken, I was later to learn, by a white man who didn't like Indians), than most people had in their whole beings. With him was Morning Star, a slender, blond woman, with love beaming from her eyes ... not the big Native man I had expected Sun Bear to have as his assistant and bodyguard.

In that first moment I was hooked, though I wouldn't admit it for quite a while. This, too, I would learn later, is a very common reaction to meeting Sun Bear. He has a presence that goes right to the core of many people, and begins to shift them, challenge them, shake them from their everyday view of the world. I had not experienced enough people of vision, at that point, to even know what hooked me. I thought I was in love with the man. I didn't know I had taken the first step toward becoming committed to his vision.

Like a good reporter, I tried to interview him about his past, his ideas, his plans. Like a good sacred teacher, he told me all about his vision, and how it was being fulfilled. He spoke of the earth as though it was a living being. He spoke of the prophecies Native people had about this time of the Cleansing of the earth, when the earth would heal herself of the sicknesses man's poisons had caused. He had the nerve to tell me how I fit into his vision.

I was frustrated because he wouldn't cooperate with the interview. I was confused by all of this *vision* business. I had never read Native American literature or met a living man of vision before, and I just didn't know how to fit this concept into my world. It didn't matter to Sun Bear that I felt confusion. His vision showed him where I could fit in, and his vision had me hooked. It was only a matter of time, he knew, before I realized that. He could afford to dance with my mind until I saw my path clearly. While this mental dance went on, he and Morning Star showered me with so much love that my heart felt like it would burst with joy.

I joined Sun Bear and what remained of the Bear Tribe in early 1972, after spending four months in New York finishing up my writing projects, and wondering if I had gone crazy. I was, after all, preparing to give up my comfortable life, my promising writing career, my friends, to move to the wild west and become part of a contemporary vision. The idea of cults wasn't popularly-known back then, so I and my friends and family wondered just what kind of strange group of people I was becoming involved with. As it turned out, when I came to understand what cults are and how they work, the intellectual/spiritual group I had been with in New York came a lot closer to fitting that definition than the Bear Tribe ever would. It was that New York group that implied I had left the true path of enlightenment to join the Tribe, while Sun Bear or Star never put any pressure on me, but rather, supported me in whatever I felt I should do.

Since 1972 I have been Sun Bear's student, his apprentice, his medicine helper, his co-author, his confidante, his instructor in certain areas of the white world, editor of his magazine, director of his community and its businesses, and at times, his worthy opponent.

I know Sun Bear as a medicine man, a friend, a teacher, a shaman, a magician, a brother, a father-confessor, a business partner, a man of mystery and a man who eats, sleeps, dreams and burps just like all the rest of us.

During the first few years I spent working with him, I watched everything with the loving eye of a new believer. He showed me how to see the earth as a living being. He taught me how to see the magic of all of her children — the rocks, the plants, the animals, the clouds, the waters — and I wondered how I ever lived before without seeing all of this beauty. I learned about Native American culture, and for a time, rejected my own background as a white, middle-class, educated writer.

I watched Sun Bear enchant thousands of people, and every dog and cat that sniffed at his jeans. I watched him call in the thunder beings, and marvelled at the rain that would follow them. I saw him heal people of broken hearts, divided souls and sick bodies. I watched him exorcise people beset by spirits that belonged elsewhere. And I wondered about the strange scars on his back that would only appear sometimes when he talked about a particular vision.

I was with him when his first attempt at fulfilling his vision failed, and when he began his second, successful attempt at building a tribe of teachers. He came to tell me about his new vision of the return of the ancient medicine wheels, and together, we wrote of this vision, and began the Gatherings that are bringing it to fulfillment. He came to Shawnodese and me to tell us of his vision of lights springing forth on a darkened earth, and together, we have begun the apprentice program that allows living humans to become these lights.

After the first few years, I found my own balance and my own visions, and learned how to incorporate what I was learning from Sun Bear with the lessons I had already learned. I began to realize what a wonderful spirit path I was on, even though I knew it was fraught with danger. I had become, like Sun Bear, a bridge person, one walking between two cultures and looking for the connections that could bring unity and understanding.

Ever since the first European set foot on this continent, this Turtle Island, the white race has been seeking to understand the red race that they mistakenly called Indians. From Rousseau's concept of the "noble savage" to Custer's practice of killing Indian women and children because "nits make lice", there has been a veil of mystery and separation between Native Americans and their often ungrateful European guests. That veil still exists today, now kept in place as much by some Natives as it has been, and is retained, by some European Americans. Around that veil, there is and always has been a lot of curiosity, that forerunner of understanding.

The veil hangs heaviest around the Native concepts of medicine and vision. European philosophies would have us believe that Native medicine is comprised only of strange-looking sorcerers dressed in feathers and hides, shaking rattles, making remedies out of snake's tongues, frog's legs and other exotic ingredients that either kill or cure the poor ignorant patient. Others have taught that Indian medicine is "the work of the devil": evil, undermining, and dangerous to all the civilization that the white man has built. Medicine men have been painted as heartless savages, bound upon a course of human sacrifice, and as ignorant heathens who pray to the rocks and the trees. People of vision are often portrayed as dangerous lunatics.

Because many Europeans were determined to destroy all the medicine people and practices they could, Native people went underground with their medicine. They had no choice. No one wanted to hear what medicine people really knew or practiced; they were killed if the European religious leaders found out that they practiced any medicine at all.

Today, when there are many people from the dominant society who wish their ancestors had listened to the Native medicine people, some Natives don't want to share those things they still remember, or the visions they are having now.

Sun Bear is a notable exception.

He feels that Native medicine is the correct philosophy for this land which we are living upon, and that if Natives are unwilling to teach the pilgrims upon Turtle Island how to correctly take care of her, there is no one else who can. Knowing the spirits of this land, he follows their direction to share knowledge with others who really want to learn. Thus he fulfills that main function of Native medicine people: that of sacred teacher, one who can communicate with the many realms of reality and bring understanding.

Medicine people (for both men and women served in this capacity) also served as healers of bodies, minds, souls and hearts. They fulfilled the functions of the people that we today call ministers, priests, rabbis, doctors, lawyers, psychologists, psychiatrists, midwives, family counsellors, teachers, masseuses, body workers, meditation teachers, and breath specialists. They also fulfilled some duties we have lost until recently: they designed and carried out rituals and ceremonies that marked the changes in the lives of people and of the planet.

The longer I worked with Sun Bear, the more I came to respect his courage in daring to rend that veil of separation, to say that we all are brothers and sisters no matter what color skin we wear. He tells people we have to learn to come together in love and understanding, in order to heal the earth of the many sicknesses we have given her in our times of separation and arrogance.

His courage has often been tested. I mentioned the time his nose was broken by a white man who didn't like Indians; a few years after I joined him he came home from a pow wow looking strange. Upon close inspection I noticed his nose looked quite a bit broader. It had been broken again — this time by an Indian who objected to Sun Bear's working with whites.

Despite declarations of support or communiques of attack, Sun Bear has steadfastly stood by his first vision that told him we must all come together in love and harmony upon the Earth Mother. I've never heard him criticize people for their beliefs, or their being. Sometimes he's objected to someone's actions, especially actions that hurt other people, but he still manages to love that person with compassion, if not with respect.

The longer I know the man, the shaman, the more I understand that love is the magic he uses and teaches: not merely romantic love, nor "tough" love that teaches through discipline, nor cold love of abstract humanity, nor love of service that overlooks the individual, but a combination of all these, and more. I have told many audiences that Sun Bear is the most generous-hearted individual I have ever met. He is.

There have been times when that generosity caused him much more pain than pleasure. He is the type of person who not only brings home wounded dogs, cats, snakes and birds, but also wounded humans, often ones that need a lot of healing. His first effort at building a tribe failed because of his generosity. That caused him some months of despair, and taught him lessons in discrimination, but he never lost his generous heart.

I've seen Sun Bear sit down to talk with prisoners, with priests, with psychologists, doctors, scientists, garbage collectors, factory workers, actors, dishwashers, mental patients, bereaved individuals, dying children, and confused parents, and get up with the other person feeling that he or she had just spoken to the one person in the world who could truly understand. He has a gift for being with another person, no matter what that person is experiencing. That gift among others is what makes him a healer.

I've watched Sun Bear come out looking good on some business deals that were so bad they would have ruined anyone else. It's his medicine that takes care of him. His isn't only a medicine for healing, it is a medicine for living, and he is willing to share the principles of that medicine with anyone who sincerely wants to learn … another trait of generosity that gets him into trouble with people who think you should only teach the *right* people such principles. Depending on the criticizer, *right* might be defined by color, sex, national origin, intellectual ability or degree of affluency.

Sun Bear says if a philosophy or religion *doesn't grow corn* — meaning take care of its proponents every day of their lives — he doesn't want to hear about it.

His medicine does *grow corn*. The Bear Tribe began in 1969 with a trickle of students from the community around the University of California at Davis, where Sun Bear taught Native American studies and journalism. Today that trickle has become a tidal wave. Daily, growing numbers of people call, write or visit the Bear Tribe. Their goal is to learn a better way of life. In addition, Sun Bear, and some other tribal members travel worldwide, offering seminars, workshops and Medicine Wheel Gatherings. They have taken our message to England, New Zealand, Germany, Austria, Switzerland, and to every corner of the North American continent. Each year, Sun Bear estimates, he travels close to 100,000 miles. Among our students are people from every conceivable profession and way of life.

What is it about this half-breed medicine man with an eighth-grade education, that draws doctors, lawyers, dentists, army officers, housewives, hippies, and banking executives to study his teachings?

Sun Bear explains, "I have been given the power to heal. I am a teacher. I see as a great part of my mission on the Earth Mother the need to impart to others, those who may be sick-at-heart or out of balance, the knowledge that they too can develop medicine power and heal themselves. They can center themselves. They can draw from their own souls, as part of the Great Spirit, the knowledge and power to use their energies in good ways.

"The medicine that I believe in and offer through the Bear Tribe is not a medicine of the Sioux of yesterday or the Chippewa of yesterday. It is a medicine of today, as well as a medicine of tradition. This is the kind of medicine that will bring balance between the races on the Earth Mother."

Sun Bear's medicine is based upon the teachings of many tribes. Yet, it is larger and more universal than any of the separate ways he has been taught. His medicine comes from the Creator and the Earth Mother through his dreams and visions. He does not tie himself to any particular tradition or ritual, but incorporates what he has learned into medicine that is truly all-embracing. What else could a bridge builder of the rainbow path do?

A part of the medicine is self-reliance on the land. Much of what the Bear Tribe teaches combines spirituality with good practical skills: farming, herbology, foraging, hunting, building, beekeeping, butchering, canning, preserving, food storage, water maintenance, waste removal, composting, bartering, and survival economics. Students don't, however, just learn how to raise and then kill a chicken. They learn how to raise it with respect, and take its life with the proper prayers and ceremonies. They don't just learn how to identify herbs; they learn how to speak to the spirit of the herb. As well as learning how to find water, keep a spring or well flowing and clean, they also learn how to pray to the water spirits every time they wash their hands, dishes or clothes.

Another part of that medicine is communication. Sun Bear believes in the prophecies of many Native people, which tell of this time in history as a time of clearsing upon the Earth Mother: a time when the earth will shrug off the poisonous aspects of technology, and also the way of life which tells people they are separate from the rest of creation.

In our travels, we teach people about these prophecies, about this time, and how they can help in the healing of the planet. Knowing that we cannot travel far-enough, fast-enough, we also communicate this message through *Wildfire*, which Sun Bear founded in 1961 in Los Angeles as *Many Smokes* magazine, through media appearances, and through our books.

Sun Bear has authored AT HOME IN THE WILDERNESS, which is a guide to living with the earth, and BUFFALO HEARTS, a book of Native American philosophy and biography. We have co-authored THE MEDICINE WHEEL: EARTH ASTROLOGY, which tells of the return of the medicine wheels, and of the way of self-knowledge that he saw in his vision; and THE BEAR TRIBE'S SELF RELIANCE BOOK, with Nimimosha, which tells about self-reliance, spirituality and community.

Since 1980 we have also sponsored numerous Medicine Wheel Gatherings. These are large gatherings which many teachers and medicine people attend to celebrate the earth, and to pray for her healing. An average of 900 people have attended each gathering. They are held in different locations around the United States, and we have brought them to Europe and Hawaii. Wallace Black Elk, the grandson of the revered Sioux holy man Black Elk, Whose vision has been immortalized in the Native classic BLACK ELK SPEAKS, has called the Medicine Wheel Gatherings "history in the making".

Blossoming from Sun Bear's vision, the Bear Tribe is a realization, in part, of many Native prophecies. Most striking is a parallel with the great Hopi prophecies, as well as a coinciding with the prophecies of the Midewiwin Medicine Scrolls. Both foretold the coming of a time of great purification, a time when the earth would shrug off technology, and the sons of white men would come to Native leaders, asking for guidance.

Beyond this, the Bear Tribe is also a community, a living example of people striving to learn balance within themselves, with each other, and with the earth and all of her other children. We live outside of Spokane, Washington, on a mountain that has been used for hundreds, perhaps thousands of years, for seeking vision, and other medicine practices. Our neighbors, these days, are people who share our vision, and we hope, in the near future, to build the Vision Mountain Center, which will allow us to expand the number of people who will be able to visit, learn and work with us.

Sun Bear's medicine has given him an abundant *corn crop*, and there are many seeds he has planted that are just now beginning to sprout.

Sun Bear, like many traditional people of old, is a *doer*. Following the outlines that his visions have given to him, he spreads seeds in many areas, and watches to see which ones will grow.

He is a living testimonial to the power that comes from opening yourself to vision, to medicine, and then following the directions that that medicine gives to you. He is doing this today, in the 1980's, not back in the 1600's. More importantly, he is telling me, and all of you, that we have the same power to have vision, and to let that vision guide our lives.

Sun Bear is a living prophet, advocating a religious approach that is responsive to people, the planet and the changes that are a part of all life. He comes from a tradition of living prophets. The Native religions of Turtle Island, when they were practiced freely, always kept themselves open to changes that would come from new dreams, new visions, new communications from the Creator.

Theirs was not a religion carved in stone, unchanging for thousands of years. It was, rather, a religion of constant renewal and growth.

In my years of study with Sun Bear I have realized that many people, from all levels of society, hunger for just such a religious approach. They want to know that the Creator is alive, and that they can communicate directly with this force. Sun Bear, through his words and living example, proves that they can.

If Sun Bear had been educated as a psychologist, his autobiography would probably be called: THE PATH OF POWER: HOW TO WIN IN ALL LIFE SITUATIONS. The book would break medicine down into all of its component parts, then tell you how to fit them into your own life situation. How much fun you could have evaluating, analyzing, thinking! Chances are, you'd come away from reading it with a whole new logical framework, one that could keep you away from feeling for a few more weeks, months, or years.

Luckily for us, Sun Bear is not an evaluator. Believe me. I spent years trying to get him to explain logically what he was doing, to no avail. It took me two years to begin to understand what medicine meant. It took several more, and a couple of really powerful experiences that defied logical explanation, before I had a glimmering of what vision was. When I first began "hearing" Native chants, alone, with no one singing, and went to him thinking that I was now a strait jacket candidate, he just told me to relax and listen more closely.

Native teachers, traditional teachers, from what I have since learned, always teach the real lessons by demonstration and example. They don't outline what they are going to teach, teach it, then have a review. You watch patiently, listen quietly, and learn truly. And when the rain clouds come, or the plant talks back to you, and you wonder whether you are going a little crazy, they just smile and tell you that it is good.

I finally understood enough to tell Sun Bear that if there were petroglyphs (picture writings) of modern people, they would have giant heads, little sticks for bodies, and tiny dots for hearts, just like the stick figures we teach our children to draw. He liked that, because he knows people today think too much and feel too little.

Sun Bear's books reflect his way of teaching in person. His teaching is laden with lessons about life, and about how to better your own life, but they are told, most often, subtly, in stories or circular terms. This way of the circle is another of the Native mysteries that he can help to unveil, if you'll allow your mind to float freely.

His words and his stories are eloquent, in the great tradition of Native orators, but they are rarely direct. This is a book in which you'll have to read between the lines.

I've been working on Sun Bear's story since that first, fated meeting in 1971. I've completed five book outlines, along with numerous shorter proposals, and several sample chapters. When it became apparent that it was the right time to share Sun Bear's teachings with the world, it also became apparent to me that I was so enmeshed in both his life and the vision of the Bear Tribe, that I could not pull back sufficiently to sort the years of material which I had into a book of reasonable length and clarity.

The vision that wants this story to be told sent me a helper. Barry Weinstock wrote to the Bear Tribe for help in researching a young adult book on medicine men. We began to correspond and he volunteered to help with any projects that needed help. At that time we had a novel that Bear Tribe Publishing was thinking of bringing out, and he spent many months editing it. In the course of that editing, I noticed that his style was compatible with both Sun Bear's and mine. We never published the novel, but we invited Barry and his family to spend the summer of 1982 at the Tribe, helping with Sun Bear's book.

He came and began to pull all the notes, chapters, outlines and quotes into sequence. He taped interviews with Sun Bear, myself, and most other members of the Tribe. While we had two Apprentice Screenings, many seminars, work with organizational development people who were helping to re-organize the tribe, several speaking tours, and copious visitors, he wrote away, drawing it together. Then he gave the manuscript back (a difficult *giveaway* for a writer) to Sun Bear and I for whatever revisions we felt were necessary. Barry has done a wonderful job of maintaining Sun Bear's voice, and presence, throughout the book.

We offer this book to you now as our giveaway, knowing that only in emptying oneself through the giveaway does one make space for new knowledge, new power, new medicine to come.

Marlise Wabun James Wind

BOOK ONE
MY LIFE

You begin your Path of Power when you wake up in the morning and you thank the Creator for being alive.

CHAPTER ONE
EARLY VISIONS

<u>1932, NEAR FOSSTON, MINNESOTA:</u>

The full moon draped the pines with its arms of light; the light advanced toward a small log cabin in a clearing. Inside, a woman and two men relaxed around a woodstove.

"A ya ya, a ya ya ya!" There were sounds of a war cry.

"Do something, Louis," the woman said, "your son is dreaming again."

The cries grew louder.

Louis La Duke moved towards a corner of the cabin, where his three-year-old son slept. The boy, Vincent, was sitting stock-straight, eyes shut, mouth wide open. In the moonlight the child's face seemed ancient, worn, as he chanted in a rising pitch. The face was fevered, that of an angry war-chief.

"I was so young that I remember little," Sun Bear says. "I remember, vaguely, chanting and my father standing before me, sort of transfixed.

"Then, I remember someone chanting back at me, in a voice so soft it was drowned out by my own war whoops. Gradually they tell me, the other person's chant rose and mine receded, died."

Abruptly, there was silence.

"There was the sweet smell of cedar smoke; in those days we didn't have sweetgrass. Somebody smudged the room. He blew smoke over me, and spoke in Ojibway".

'Not yet, little bear. Your battle will come, later.'

"All of this is vague, now. I was only three."

The girl saw her young brother lying on the ground. She knelt down by his prone figure, touched his face; he burned with fever.

She ran into the cabin to get her mother. The woman carried the boy in, stripped him down and put him in a pan of icy water. She was worried; she knew diphtheria was going around.

"I was in another place," Sun Bear says. "I didn't feel the water. Where I was, it was all blue. The sky was bright blue, the ground was the color of the Great Lakes on a cloudless day...blue, rippled with black.

"I felt good being in this blue place, secure and happy.

"I saw on the horizon, what looked like a giant red ball, so red it was almost hard to see.

"The ball rolled toward me and I reached out, wanting to play with it. It rolled past me and I was sad. Then, a brighter red ball came by and I reached for it. It rolled on, followed by an orange ball, a yellow, a green, a dark blue and a violet one.

"I couldn't catch a single ball. They all rolled past and I was sad; then I looked behind me. The balls were all in a line.

"I reached out, touched the violet ball, and the others began to roll around me. They rolled faster and faster, until finally they blended; they formed a rainbow sphere around me. It was so beautiful, I didn't want to move.

"Outside the sphere, I saw a brilliant light, brighter even than Father Sun. Through the light, an animal walked toward me; it seemed very large, and bright as the holy light. As the animal came closer, I saw it was a bear, a large black bear surrounded by the rainbow of color.

"The bear walked once around the sphere, then stopped in the west and sat and looked at me. I stared back at the bear and, after awhile, it stood on its hind legs, put its paw through the sphere and touched me gently on the hand.

"Then I woke up. I saw my mother bending over me, looking very worried.

" 'It's alright, mother', I told her. 'I can come back now. I'll stay with you.' "

"It was a very powerful thing which happened to me, this vision, although I didn't know it at the time. I was four years old. I did have diphtheria. I had gone through some convulsions, and the Great Spirit let me live.

"From time to time now, I can return to the power place of that vision."

In gentleness there is great strength. Power most of the time can be a very quiet thing.

photo: Philip Liebman

CHAPTER TWO
THE RESERVATION

So many things in life to me are good and holy and sacred. If you're planting corn, that's good. If you're hoeing your garden, that is good. If you're getting up the wood for winter; if you're helping somebody else; if you're making love ... all of those things are very good.

Everything's part of the circle of life; everything is part of the song of the Great Spirit. That's the way I see things; it's probably the biggest difference between Native philosophy and the non-Indian philosophy, where ideas and actions are put into little boxes, where some things, some days, are thought of as holy, while most other things are not.

That is not the Native way. In sharing with you the experiences of my life, I want you to understand why I do the things I do, and feel the way I feel. You need to realize that I see the holiness in everything, in the dramatic and the daily humdrum. That is a part of my vision, of my dream.

That's why all things give me power, and I can take that power and grow stronger in my medicine every day. The term *medicine* as I use it means many things. It is the power to heal with herbs, to heal using spirit forces, to work with the sweatlodge and other ceremonies, to make prayers for rain to bless the crops, to share power and teachings with people, and much more. With the Creator's help, through my medicine I can tap into the life force and I can channel it for many kinds of healing. My medicine, like anyone's, is not all mine to keep. There is one good way to give away your power; when you've reached a strong point in your medicine you can give it to other people, by teaching them. You can help them to learn they too have very strong medicine inside themselves. That's one of the reasons for this book.

I don't speak about medicine in the name of all Native people; I won't do that, nor will I speak for a single tribe. I can only speak of the teachings that my vision has given me.

Other Native medicine people, of course, have their own dreams and visions, and that is why there are so many little differences in Native ritual from region to region. But you will notice, too, great similarities because the visions have all come to these people from the same source, the Great Spirit.

Everything of importance to a traditional Native person, every ritual and prayer, is the result of some person's vision: the teaching may be how to build a sweatlodge, and why to shape it like a turtle and face it to the east; how to do a pipe ceremony; the sacred sun dance; the peyote medicine. None of these sacred rituals were invented out of the imagination; they were sent to individuals, we believe, through sacred visions.

My visions and my work are for today, for the people who are here now, and that's why I don't stick to any particular old way ritual, but incorporate whatever my medicine calls for, from everywhere. It's not really a traditional view that I hold, and yet it is. I don't believe that technology is a bad thing; if I want to communicate with a lot of people I'll pick up a telephone, use a computer, or go on a radio or television program. Technology in itself is not a bad thing; it's the greed and misdirection of its users. The Bear Tribe Medicine Society, as my subchief Shawnodese is fond of saying, is not going back to the stone age; it's going into the new age.

So, as we go along, I'll be sharing with you my vision of what to do today, and how to survive tomorrow, with or without technology.

I know how to live both ways myself.

I was born on the White Earth Reservation in northern Minnesota, on August 31, 1929. Two months later the stock market crashed. I always wondered whether my birth had anything to do with that, and with the depression that taught me and many others how to make do with a lot less than most people in the United States have today.

My father, Louis, was a Chippewa or Ojibway Indian with some French blood, and my mother, Judith, came from German/Norwegian stock. My mother was born in a sod hut near Gladstone, North Dakota, a *sod shanty* they called it, and she grew up surrounded by Native Americans — so I guess she was used to tall, dark, handsome men like my father. It wasn't as noteworthy as people think for Indians and non-Indians to get together back then. It happened a lot. There was a family near my mother's whose members were good friends of Sitting Bull; my mother used to tell how, one winter, those people had no food and Sitting Bull rode by and dropped a deer on their doorstep. He was just following the Native way of taking care of those who needed food or help, but I guess non-Native people then didn't act in the same way, so this deed of Sitting Bull's impressed my mother enough that she often remembered it.

My Native grandmother worked a lot with herbs. When I was a boy she would sometimes take me with her to find medicine. That was the Native way of teaching, silently, by example. There was one herb that she would pick and then let sit in a warm, shady place by a stream until it would grow a green mold that was used to cure serious illnesses, just as penicillin is today. She used to lace up her moccasins with swamp grass, in the old way, and utilize as many natural things as she could. She would only talk to me in what she called "The People's languages", meaning Ojibwa or French. The French people had always mixed pretty well with the Natives. They did not try to totally change the way that we lived our lives like some later emigrants did.

My grandfather was an *engagee*, or *voyageur*, for the Hudson's Bay Company. He was one of those hardy guys who paddled enormous trade canoes through the wilderness, sometimes twenty men to a canoe, singing songs, stacking furs, and eating eight or nine pounds of meat a day.

I had ten brothers and sisters in all, though only one, LaVonne, is my full sister. The part of the White Earth Reservation where we lived was checkerboarded with Indian and non-Indian families. The land had been allotted to Native Americans originally by the U.S. Government, but many Indians sold their land to whites, or traded it for cars or farm equipment. My dad, though, kept his parcel of land, and later added to it by buying surrounding plots. Eventually, we had eighty acres.

I remember the Depression very well. Winters were freezing, sometimes thirty-five below zero. Summers brought the Dust Bowl when swirls of dust got into everything and burned your eyes. Men would come to the Reservation and ask to chop wood in exchange for a meal. My brothers and uncles travelled out west to look for work, riding on freight trains.

We heard about the soup kitchens in big cities, about all the people committing suicide because they'd lost their fortunes. But we got along. Other than the men coming by looking for a meal, I don't think that things were much different then than they had been before. News of how bad things were elsewhere came to us by word of mouth, through an occasional newspaper, or through a radio set my uncles listened to with a set of earphones.

When I was seven, my mother read me a book called LOST IN FUR COUNTRY, and it really whetted my appetite for outdoor adventure. Throughout my youth of course, my uncles and brothers had been teaching me wilderness lore. What a treat it was in the winter, to go to the ice house and fish with my uncles. We could look right down through the hole in the ice and see fish.

We had a big garden and raised cows, sheep and chickens. I used to help with chores — chopping wood and hauling water from the time I was seven years old. I also ran a trap line which was twenty-five miles long, and I caught weasels, muskrats, raccoons. My brother Howard taught me how to run it. The first animal I caught was a weasel, and the pelt was shipped to Sears-Roebuck along with some others. I think I got paid 35¢. Although that was a very exciting event then, I don't believe in trapping today. There are far too few four-leggeds left. At that time, however, trapping was part of my family's survival, and I never wasted any part of any animal I trapped.

I had a .22 rifle in my hands about the time I was nine, and provided much food for the family. I was taught early that the rifle was a valuable tool, never a toy. I hunted a lot of grey squirrel, and ruffed grouse. I also hunted with a slingshot, and got many rabbits that way. In the fall, the rabbits — especially the snowshoe rabbits — would turn white before the snow fell on the bare ground, and they'd think they were hidden against the snow. But of course the pure white rabbits showed well against the dark background.

My dad worked with some wood cutters and trucked wood to sell in surrounding cities. He used to drive eighty miles to take wood to Armour and Company, a big meat-packing plant in Grand Forks. Sometimes he traded wood for honey, sometimes for apples or cabbages. During the winter, the wood business was hard. The old truck would freeze up. We'd have to build fires, and put pans of coals underneath the engine block, to warm it up enough to turn the engine crank, and get the wood moving into the cities.

The thing I loved most at White Earth was the land. The gently rolling hillsides were very green in summer, and snow-covered in winter. I loved to sit under the trees, to watch the snow come swirling out of the clouds. The fall was beautiful with all the red oak trees, and when we walked through the woods, kicking up the leaves, we'd see the grey squirrels scurry up into the branches. I remember looking at the cornfields on an early fall day, the cut cornstalks lined up in corn shocks like tipis, pumpkin and squash fat everywhere, and a great flock of blackbirds soaring overhead.

To me, that is true wealth ... sitting on the Earth Mother ... seeing, smelling, tasting the freshness of it all.

It was at that early age when I first realized what nature is all about. I realized that the Earth Mother is a living organism ... always changing, always growing. Some part of me knew then that someday, like the Earth Mother, I would have good medicine and that my medicine, too, would not be static. It would be organic, growing, changing, flowing like a river to the sea that is the Creator of all things. Even then, my vision continued to come to me a bit at a time, and as time began to pass, that vision grew stronger, always clearer.

Later in the Depression, we moved around quite a bit while my Dad looked for other work. We went off the Reservation, to Idaho and then to Clarkston, Washington. There were months of dirt and drought; I remember how good a rainshower felt. I liked all of the travelling. It was exciting to see new places and meet new people, both

Indian and white. I got to learn a little about Native culture in other places, although at that time, there wasn't much difference between the cultures, in my mind. I just saw people as people, as I still do.

In 1937, we returned to Minnesota. The trip back across the country was a sadly memorable one; livestock were dying and wells were drying up everywhere. Farmers stacked Russian thistle, a kind of wild fodder — really a weed — to feed their cattle. It was that way all through Montana and the Dakotas. It made me sad to see the land that way. Later in life, when I would hear the word "savages" I would always think of the wheat savages: those farmers who raped the land and turned it into swirling dust.

I started my schooling then at the La Duke School (named after my father). I walked to school, and I enjoyed the walk a whole lot more than the classes. With the neighbor kids I'd get out under a tree, either before or after classes, and we'd share our lunches under the branches, watch the snow fall during the winter, and just enjoy the good feeling that we had being there.

★ ★ ★

Two of my uncles at White Earth were prominent medicine men. One was *Bo Doge*, which is Chippewa for *Like the Wind*. Uncle Bo Doge gave me the name *Gheezis Mokwa* (Sun Bear), but I didn't use it until I was grown up. He was a little man, about 5'7", and he lived way out on the Reservation. My dad would take me to visit him from time to time. His knowledge was of herbs, and he was a very good healer with them. I think I had a basic knowledge of what he was doing, even as a young boy, and I was fascinated by his medicine. Eventually, he taught me a few things; among others, I learned some of the songs and chants he used.

My other uncle, my dad's half-brother, was a very powerful medicine man named Bill Burnett. People had great respect for him; they knew he had the power to do many things with his medicine. He worked primarily with the elemental forces. He wasn't so much a healer as he was a shaman who could materialize objects and make things happen.

When Uncle Bill and other medicine men on the Reservation would go into their lodges and start singing, the lodges would start to vibrate and shake. That is a very ancient thing with the Ojibway — the tent shaking — and some of the earliest explorers and missionaries were amazed by it. They'd even tie up the shaman before he went into a tent, so he couldn't do anything to shake the tent poles (they were too massive to be moved by a single man anyway), and still, when the medicine man began to sing, the tents would vibrate and shake like they were sitting in the middle of an earthquake.

Many times Forest Rangers would come by Uncle Bill's or other medicine men's places. They'd be looking for somebody who was lost, maybe hurt, and the medicine man would tell them exactly where to find him.

Uncle Bill could also tell you where to find game if you were hunting. He would never hunt himself, but he'd say to one of his sons: "Well, you go half-a-mile southwest and there's a buck sunning itself behind a brush pile. You go and get him; he's for us today." Sure enough, the buck would be there.

What Uncle Bill would do would be to make prayers, and his spirit guides would tell him where the game was.

The medicine of the *Midewiwin*, the Grand Medicine Society of the Ojibway, comes in different degrees. Some Midewiwin people work only with herbs, for healing; some work with the knowledge of the sweatlodge; and some work with the knowledge of the spirit realm. They are very powerful healers and teachers and you don't mess with them.

There was a man who came out to Cass Lake Reservation one time, when they were doing ceremonies there. The man was non-Indian, and he started bad-mouthing what was going on. He was drunk and said, "This is a bunch of humbug!"

The medicine men gave him the eye. They pointed their medicine bundles at him — that's called "shooting them with the medicine" — and he fell down, completely paralyzed.

He was taken to Rochester and other places, to try to get him healed, but nobody could help him. Finally, the doctors gave up on him, so his people brought him back to the Midewiwin men. He apologized; they took the medicine off, and he was healed.

My people's medicine is very similar to the medicine of the *Kahuna* in Hawaii, also to that of the Australian aborigines. It can be *very* strong.

There are a number of ways we come into our medicine: through visions, through training with another medicine person, or through a combination of those two. I respect Midewiwin medicine, and I work with it when I need to. Although I'm not totally involved with it, I do regard myself as a Midewiwin practitioner. I work with whatever kinds of medicine are shared with me, although I mainly follow my own vision. I've learned the medicine of the sweatlodge; I've been with the peyote people, and they've taught me and given me the right to practice their medicine. I guess you'd have to call me a *universal medicine man*; I don't claim any one label, except that of my own vision and dreams. Most of these are to heal the earth and bring about a balance between the rest of creation and the human race.

There are a few of us around now who don't just follow the visions of 1880. This is the latter part of the twentieth century, and one of the big differences between the Native religions and others is that we know that the Creator is always alive, and gives visions today that are just as great and valid as those given long ago.

Another difference between Native American life and contemporary living is we had a lot of old-timers back then who just kept sticking around. When I was a kid, I remember some medicine men living well past their hundredth year. There was an old man in my tribe named John Smith. What most people called him was "Chief Wrinkle Meat", because his skin was leathery and shrivelled. He was at least 137 years old when he died. He'd had seventeen wives during his lifetime, and when you asked him where they all were, he'd say: "Some of 'em died, I guess, and some of 'em just took off."

He was a happy old guy, Chief Wrinkle Meat; the railroads gave him a free pass because he was so old, and he'd ride trains everywhere. The reason he died was that when he fell and hurt his hip, they took him to the U.S. Public Health Hospital on the Reservation, and he caught pneumonia. Otherwise he might still be around.

When we see problems that require new answers, think of the Power that created the Universe.

CHAPTER THREE
MOVING ON

One of the pastimes in northern Minnesota was going to weekend dances, either at the school house, or at the Flowing Well Tavern. These happy occasions would usually end up with a roaring fistfight. My father gained fame one time by taking on seven men, six of them brothers, who'd decided they would jump my Uncle Charles.

My dad wasn't all that big; he weighed 185 pounds, but he'd been working as a lumberjack, and he was all muscle. He had a way of grabbing a man by the shirt with his left hand, pulling him toward him. At the same time, his fist would come crashing forward. The result would be a collision of knuckles and face that not too many men walked away from.

Well, Dad took on seven men and left them lying on the floor. He was still in the mood to play, but he couldn't find any more takers.

Twenty-five years after that brawl at the La Duke School, I met a man while I was buying wild rice.

"I know you," he told me. "Your dad knocked the hell out of my father and my five uncles!"

When I asked Dad to teach me to fight, in my early teens, he refused.

He said, "Son, you have too good a head to use it for a punching bag."

My dad fooled around with more than fighting, and when I was nine or ten, he and my mother separated. We called it "splitting the blanket".

I lived with my mom and my sister La Vonne. We planted a big garden every year; I remember how much I enjoyed pondering over the seed catalogs, thinking about the spring.

One of the most beautiful spring smells, to me, was the aroma of fresh earth released from the winter's snow. The smell was mixed, then, with the smell of pines and the soft aroma of woodstove smoke.

I liked walking the creeks at night; you could almost hear the fish. I had a trapper friend named Skunk Martin; he showed me how to make a pine torch by putting pine knots into a wire basket. You tied the basket to the end of a long pole, and if you held it over the water after dark, you could see the fish just laying near the surface. We made spears out of old hay forks and easily filled our baskets with fish. We'd spear suckers, mostly, because they wouldn't bite at the hooks. We'd take them home and smoke them or fry them in cornmeal.

There were lots of good times back then. Most whites and Indians there got along real well, but you couldn't get away from prejudice completely. There was a neighbor boy, when I was eight, who'd just moved up from the south. He hated blacks and I guess he transferred that hate to Indians. He was seventeen or eighteen.

He pushed me to the ground one day and pissed in my face.

"Remember," he told me, "that's what the white man has done and always will do to Indians. Piss Face!"

I felt a lot of anger about being helpless, but I never told anyone about the experience; I guess I was too humiliated. I got even with the kid later, though, in my own way.

When I was older, I had a pet skunk. I named it James, after him.

★ ★ ★

When I was fifteen, I went to a tribal council meeting and tried to tell the members how I thought they could manage the tribal resources better. They had a 20,000 acre ranch which they were leasing to a banker for $3000 a year. I knew that if they managed it themselves it would bring in more money and put some of my tribesmen to work. In some of the visions I had received after my childhood bout with diphtheria, I had seen the time when Native people would have to be more self-sufficient and I tried to communicate that to the council.

They told me I was too young to understand such things.

Twenty-five years later, my own and twenty-one other Chippewa and Winnebago Bands paid me to tell them the same thing. I was then considered an economic development specialist, so they listened that time.

At that first time, at fifteen, I decided that if a prophet couldn't be recognized on his own reservation, it was time to try my wings. I said temporary goodbyes to the White Earth Reservation, and with several neighbor boys, began my young man's odyssey. We hopped all over the map during the warm months, usually returning to White Earth every fall to hunt, trap, and cut wood.

It was growing up time, and we worked our tails off. First, we travelled to Devil's Lake, North Dakota, where we worked in the fields hauling wheat, barley, and oats. In those days the wheat grass was cut by a machine called a grain binder, which would not only cut the stalks; it would bind them into sheaves. The sheaves, in turn, would be set together with their heads up, into shocks. We got paid 85¢ an hour. We ate well, slept in the barn with our work horses, and were up everyday at 4 a.m.

After threshing time that first year out, I went back to Minnesota, and that winter my brother Howard and my sister Mercedes cut sixty cords of firewood. We all pitched in, shed our coats in below zero weather, cut all the wood with a bow saw and axe, and split it by hand with a splitting maul.

Summer came and went; it was haying time. The following fall we went to Grand Forks, North Dakota, to pick potatoes. It rained too much that fall; the potato picking was very slow, and our bellies were very empty.

I met a hobo Sioux Indian, who taught me a few survival skills. He wore a big overcoat lined inside with pockets, like the one Harpo Marx used to wear in most of his movies. He'd go into a market and come out empty handed, but his coat would be brimming with goodies … meat, bread, even butter. From there, we'd go over to the warehouse to pick up whatever produce had fallen off of the delivery trucks. We ate delicious *hobo stews*. Although I never tried this man's overcoat trick, I have often checked in the garbage bins of warehouses and grocery stores for produce that they have thrown away. Some of it has been delicious.

That winter, I returned to White Earth again; we had some record snowfalls. Blizzards hit, and the wind drove snow sheets high on the hills. Half of the time, I'd saddle up a horse to ride out for supplies, and have to turn back, my horse lunging and bellying through high drifts. It was so cold so clean; I remember the snow being so deep one time, that I rode my horse over a railroad trestle, without even seeing it. The gully that it crossed had all but disappeared.

★ ★ ★

During the next few years, I worked and travelled all the time. I worked in a cemetery in Grand Forks, in a bakery in Moorhead, Minnesota, and as a cook on an extra gang crew for the Great Northern Railroad.

After that, I visited friends in Los Angeles; then we drove to some other places in the country. We visited Yellowstone. We brought our own Old Faithful geyser. It was the radiator on our Model-A Ford. I think we fed it more water, going up hills, than we ate food.

Los Angeles was okay, but the loud noise of the sirens drove me out. Native people have a hard time getting used to loud noises.

We believe that one should walk quietly, as part of being in balance upon the earth. Old time hunters used to know how to go so silently that they could get within touching distance of an animal. After Los Angeles I decided no more big cities for awhile. I hitch-hiked north and worked at a ranch near Sprague, Washington. After that, it was home to see the family, then on to Fargo, North Dakota.

Fargo proved to be an important place for me; there were many turning points. For a time , I was a real estate salesman, selling property for Dakota Realty. At the tender age of nineteen, I had a reputation for being quite a salesman. I could unload anything, they said. "If you want to sell your property, go see that Indian boy."

In the late spring I'd sell houses along the Red River; the view was beautiful, but they'd flood out once a year. So every spring, when the river rose, my buyers of the previous year became sellers. These people knew the river would flood, but they bought the houses anyway. I had a self-perpetuating market. I didn't feel any stranger about doing this than I did about selling land in general. Native people have always believed that you cannot own the Earth Mother. It follows that you can't buy and sell her. In my heart I feel like the old-timers, but I recognize that we are living in a society where land is bought and sold. I think, at that time in my life, like most young men, I had to prove that I could survive well in the wheeling and dealing of this society. Though selling land seemed strange to me, I was good at it, and I was proud of that manly ability to survive and provide. I was also proud to be able to "make it" in the white world.

There was an old house in Fargo that wouldn't sell, because it faced on the main street (North Broadway) and the taxes were enormous. So what I did was I had the front entrance boarded up, and I knocked a side door into it, facing on Sixteenth Street. The taxes dropped in half, and the house sold real quick. I also sold ranches and resort property, and was working nights on a contract, building government grain bins.

It was about this time that I joined an Indian club called the White Buffalo Council. It made me feel good to find other Native people in Fargo who were interested in finding out more about their Native heritage.

I was a hustler back then and busy, but not too busy to be feeling frisky, looking for my first taste of love. I found it while I was in Fargo. I remember the lady well, and fondly. She taught me that love can be sweet, and also sour. When the sour overwhelmed the sweet, I went to Louisville, Kentucky, where I worked for a few months for the American Tobacco Plant.

When I came back home from Fargo, the Korean war was happening. The U.S. Army, it seemed, had ideas about where I ought to spend my next couple of years. The draft seemed unavoidable, and I had friends and relatives buzzing in my ears about how, if I enlisted, things would go much better. So I did it. I signed enlistment papers and went off to basic training at Camp Chaffee, Arkansas.

That was really a hard thing for me to do; I liked my freedom, and I didn't believe in killing senselessly, which was what the army seemed to be doing. Killing for meat was one thing — you could go about that with the proper prayers and ceremonies — but taking a human life was quite another. I felt that there was something dirty and unnatural about that act. I'd gone to the draft board, and told them I was a conscientious objector but they hadn't been impressed. There were few legal routes to take back then (in 1952) to prove that fighting for the U.S. Army was against my traditional Native American beliefs. I guess the experience was okay for me, because later, when Vietnam came along, I was pretty well prepared psychologically to help out my Native brothers who didn't want to fight.

I took my basic training at Camp Chaffee, and had time to take a good look at myself and what I stood for. What I finally discovered was that I *didn't* want to be there, *didn't* want to go fight natives in their own country, and simply, just wouldn't do it.

I'd been taught how to fire artillery, how to use an M-1 carbine, and it turned me off. As a boy, I'd learned to hunt for meat, to live. This was different. There was no way that I could see that training with a gun would allow the circle of life to grow. It would only lead to death.

I thought of how my people used to do *battle*. When a young man wanted to prove his bravery, he'd steal horses from another camp. If he really wanted to prove his courage, he'd join a war party, ride out and count coup on the enemy. That meant, early on, simply touching your enemy with a stick.

Firing artillery didn't seem much like counting coup. You never hit your enemy, counting coup, you just *touched* him. You never tried to kill him. Killing made a warrior unclean; he would have to fast, and pray in a sweatlodge before returning to his village.

The idea of firing artillery at an enemy you couldn't even see, made me feel filthy. The more I saw of the military, of its approach to life and death, the more I knew I couldn't go to Korea, to be a paid patriotic assassin.

If I wanted to fight those who had taken my country from me, I wouldn't be fighting Koreans.

I headed for the hills.

I took off from Fort Smith, Arkansas, and went west to Oklahoma and freedom. I guess I was what you might call a "ninety-day wonder", but in a different sense than usual. I did my *ninety days*, and for the next four years the FBI *wondered* where I was.

From some of these pictographs I can gain knowledge to help others; some are secret, so I can't tell you much more about them.

CHAPTER FOUR
MEDICINE PEOPLE

My experience with the army forced me to figure out who I was. In that way it was good medicine.

Moving down the road, I decided it was time to learn more about my people, so the early 1950's became a time of learning, expanding, and studying the medicine of many Native American brothers and sisters.

I travelled through North Dakota, earning enough money to buy a car, then left for Omaha, Nebraska. When I arrived there, I was broke, and ended up on skid row (16th Street), where a lot of other Indian people were staying. Finally, I landed a job with a Hinky Dinky wholesale market, and there I met some Winnebago brothers. After a few days they invited me to come to a peyote ceremony. I'd heard much about the Native American church, the peyote religion, but had never experienced it firsthand.

The first night that I was supposed to go, I couldn't make it. They set up a spot on the floor for me anyway, and drummed all night to the empty seat. The following week I was again invited to go and that time I went.

Meetings were held in the house of Ballantine Parker, an Omaha Indian who was the local leader of the Peyote church. I brought him a wallet as a gift.

Both Winnebago and Omaha Indians were there. The ceremony began at about nine in the evening, and lasted until dawn.

The room was bare; the furnishings had been taken outside. We all sat down on the floor. There was a woman in the room, and

Ballantine Parker introduced her.

"This sister is very sick," he told us, "and she's asked us to pray for her."

A young man, called the "servant of the peyote", brought in a pan of hot coals and placed them in front of Ballantine who took cedar and tobacco, and offered it on the coals, making prayers.

I could feel the power rush into the room.

Now the servant came into the room with a cloth bag; it was filled with dried green peyote buttons, the sacrament of the peyote religion. The buttons were passed to everyone, in a sunwise manner. I took two, broke them open. Inside, there was a cottony substance which had to be removed.

We began to chew the peyote buttons; they tasted like bitter chocolate, only stronger. After we'd finished eating them, the servant brought us peyote tea.

A friend of mine, Hawk John, began to sway and chant; a man beside him beat a drum while Hawk John sang four chants. He held a rattle and a beaded staff in his hands which the peyote people call the staff of life.

Others began to sing. Some chanted; some just prayed, and the peyote sent us on a journey. It was a feeling of great expansion, a buzzing, a beating inside the center of the forehead.

When Hawk John finished his four chants, he passed the staff of life to the next man, sunwise. This was the way of the ceremony; each man would take the rattle and staff, and chant or pray. The man beside him would beat the drum in accompaniment.

The peyote filled me, gave me a sense of depth and dimension, a sense of opening, of oneness with the universe. Everything, the beadwork, the room itself, the faces of the others, grew visually intense; every detail came into focus. I became an eagle, soaring with the chant, over a lake of clear blue water. My veins filled with love, and the drumbeats entered, became one with my pulse.

The Great Spirit was everywhere. Time had stopped and we were ancient beings, without need of language.

After awhile, Ballantine Parker spoke.

"Me and my wife," he said, "are happy to share this meeting with our Winnebago brothers. We use tobacco and cedar here tonight, to honor both ways. And we welcome our Chippewa brother." He nodded at me.

The staff passed around the circle three times that night. It must go completely around, no matter how late it gets.

Some brothers prayed for loved ones in prison or hooked on alcohol; some praised the peyote for its healing power, for its vision.

The woman who had come to be healed seemed to be much better.

In the morning, we shared a ceremonial breakfast...first came a bowl of water, again passed sunwise. Each person took a drink, and thanked the Great Spirit for the water's gift of life. Next, corn was passed and we all ate from a common bowl, again thanking the Creator. The corn was symbolic of all grains on Mother Earth. Next, peaches were passed around, representing all the fruits and berries, and finally, we ate from a bowl of meat. Each dish, again, represented a separate kingdom of foods, which the Great Spirit had provided on the Earth Mother for us.

After this breakfast, we visited for several hours and then, at noon, we had a peyote feast. This meal signified the ending of the ceremony.

The peyote meeting was a meeting of hearts; all things had been done with love and humility. At other peyote meetings, which I've attended in California, the brothers would light a cornhusk cigarette filled with tobacco, to make a prayer. They would pass it around, each praying first in English, then in their Native language.

The first meeting, with Ballantine Parker, was a very powerful experience. Nobody celebrates peyote just to get high, or go tripping; the peyote brings power and energy into you. And what really brings power to that medicine is the all-night beating of the drum; you can hear it in your head, feel it pounding in your chest, for three weeks afterward.

The drum in a peyote meeting is a special kind; it's a small kettle drum that you can pick up and hold. Around the sides of the kettle there are seven small stones, and around each of the stones, the buckskin top is wrapped. The stones are wrapped with thong to stretch the hide tight, first, in a circular line, then up and down across the bottom of the kettle. When wrapped right, the thong forms a seven pointed star across the bottom of the drum.

The kettle is filled with water and when the drum has been beaten for about an hour, the hide "opens up"; that means its resonance improves. There is the beating sound then, like a heartbeat, and the whirring, reverberating sound as vibrations travel through the water. Sometimes, when the ceremony has been underway for a long time, the water in the kettle evaporates. When it does, you suck hard against the buckskin, thus creating a vacuum in the kettle; then you pour more water onto the hide. It goes right through, refilling the kettle.

Like your heartbeat, the drum becomes a part of you; it carries you, over and over. And people do change into animals sometimes, like I did, into an eagle. Castaneda s pretty accurate, in the Don Juan books; you can change into a crow, or a coyote, with peyote or other herbs, or without them.

The peyote is a healer both spiritually and physically; it has a quinine effect. I've made peyote tea for some of my people when they're feeling sick, and it always helps them. It's good medicine, but it is a sacrament and, I feel, should only be used ceremonially under the direction of people who have been properly trained in its use. Otherwise you don't get the full power of it. Taking it by yourself isn't the same, and I don't recommend it as a thing to play around with.

I met Willard LaMere, a Winnebago, in Omaha and we travelled together to Wichita, Kansas. Meeting Willard was a good thing. We both wanted to find out more about our people, we both liked to travel, and neither of us had that much money. I worked with an Indian pow wow club called the Wichita Warriors Club. We put on Indian dances twice a month, and I had an opportunity to meet many brothers from many tribes. There were a lot of Oklahoma Indians there, all good people.

Willard and I joined forces and traveled to Phoenix, Arizona, a few months later, in a 1939 Chevy sedan. We pulled a tear-drop trailer, and picked up soda bottles along the way to pay for food and gas.

When we got to Phoenix we lived on mourning doves, which we killed with slingshots, and fruit, which we picked off the trees. The only Indians we met at the Phoenix Indian Center were Christian churchgoers, so we just stayed a short while, eating potluck dinners at churches, and visiting Willard's relatives.

While he was visiting, I went down to the Papago reservation near the Mexican border with some other friends. We got caught up in a little battle, trying to keep people out of there who were bringing in heavy drugs and ripping off some of the older Indians in other ways.

Some of my friends and I got pretty strong in our insistence that these people leave, and a few of them caught me walking in the desert alone one day. They took me to a little wash, and hung me up by the thumbs from the branches of a mesquite tree, to "educate me", they said, so that I wouldn't be messing with their business anymore.

This was a very painful experience; I swung there for a long time, my toes barely touching the ground. Finally, my friends came looking for me, and they cut me down. That wasn't my Sun Dance experience, I'll tell you. There were no great visions, only pain, both physically and spiritually, knowing that there were such people trying to destroy a people and a culture that loved the earth and each other. If you look now, you can still see the scars of that experience on my thumbs.

From there, it was on to Las Vegas, Nevada. Willard and I went to work unloading boxcars, landscaping a cemetery, and washing cars.

You can see that my job experience covers a wide range.

We headed on to Reno; then Willard and I went separate ways. We stayed in touch, though, and sometimes our paths crossed again. Willard went on, later in his life, to be very active in Chicago Indian affairs. He also directed the American Indian Businessman's Association. I headed west to pick strawberries in California. In Sebastapol, California, I got a job at an apple cannery, dumping apples onto conveyor belts that took them up for canning and making vinegar. That job was a tough one; one of the things I had to do was to clean out the vinegar vats. I had to wear rubber pants and boots; I went into the vats through a side door, washing down what was called "vinegar mother", great slimy chunks of it that stuck all over the inside of the vats. The only way to get it off was with a fire hose.

I camped at a trailer park nearby, and met a family of Pomo Indians named James. The Pomo Indians live near the coast in Northern California. In the old days, it is said they had one of the most ideal climates and cultures. There was always abundant food and so the people had time to be very creative in all ways. The Pomos are known as great dancers, singers, and dreamers. One of the brothers became a good friend; he was an artist, and had a good knowledge of Pomo medicine, which he shared with me. We'd sit under a clump of pine trees, cooking on a fire, and he'd tell me Pomo hunting stories and medicine ways. He told me about the Bear Medicine Society. Bear medicine men, after special prayers and ceremonies, would run up to 150 miles in a single night. The ceremonies before the run, he told me, included abstaining from sexual intercourse, and not eating fatty meats. A Bear medicine man would wear a bear skin, and there was another group of runners who would wear coats made of wampum shells. Since the bear is my own medicine, I had great respect for these clansmen. Often, I was told, these medicine men would outrun horses.

They were healers, and the long run was part of their medicine, a way to vision. Each man went into his power in a different way; they sang their own chants, and they were secret. That's why I can't say anymore about them; other than describing them, I'm not at liberty to tell more.

Pomo Indians, my friend told me, never went hunting while their women were menstruating; it was said to be dangerous, to cause misfortune or death.

The Pomos, in the past, often dipped their arrow tips in menstrual blood and rattlesnake venom when they went on war parties. It was said to be deadly medicine.

During the time I spent in Pomo country, my love life improved. I'd been travelling around so much, that most of my contact with women had been wishful thinking; now, I met a Pomo girl and spent a lot of time with her. Her mother was a very active medicine woman, and she taught me some Pomo medicine.

I met California dreamers, medicine people whose healing power came to them in dreams, much like my own does. That is a very powerful way to heal, a very good one.

I met Elsie Parrish then, too, an outstanding Indian healer and suck doctor. She would do her ceremonies, make her prayers, then suck poison out of the body of a person who was sick. Sometimes she would bring forth bits of rancid flesh, or stones; it was a very powerful experience, to watch her suck the poison into her mouth, and spit it on the ground. Though her medicine was different from what mine seemed to be, I had very great respect for this woman and her power for good.

In the Feather River country of California, I met a medicine man named Calvin Rube, who was a servant of *Sasquatch*, the ones we call the "Bigfoot" people. He was a chief of the Wichipek tribe, and when we were learning about Sasquatch he'd go up into the mountains, make his prayers, and Bigfoot would come to him, either in person or in spirit. The Bigfoot would speak to him; he would teach him. You see, we Native Americans believe that the Sasquatch is a superhuman being, a spirit keeper who can change form or disappear. The Bigfoot has knowledge far beyond ours, and he is protector of the forest. Being around Calvin increased my knowledge of, and respect for, the power of prayer, and of the spirit realm.

At the time I was up there, a construction company was trying to cut a road through the area; the Bigfoot people came into the road crew's camp. They overturned tractors and heavy equipment. They threw oil drums off the side of the mountain the crew was camped on. There were footprints everywhere, and a friend of mine, Craig Carpenter, made a casting of a track.

The Bigfoot appeared to Calvin Rube; it told him that because the developers were molesting the Feather River country, there would be two big earthquakes...one on the California coast, and one in Alaska. Both of these Earthquakes occurred shortly after that.

Today, a funny thing is that the folks near the Bear Tribe Medicine Society have built up a legend that we feed the Sasquatch here, on Vision Mountain, near Spokane.

★ ★ ★

When I left California, I went east, to Reno, Nevada. I wanted to spend some time with the Nevada Indians, and learn some of their medicine ways. When I first got to Reno, as always, I had to find a job. I worked for a man named Fisher, picking potatoes and grading onions in a warehouse. I stayed with my cousin Dan, Uncle Bill's son, and I got a few more odd jobs, landscaping and painting.

During that time I started working with the Reno Sparks Indian Colony on a self-help program. Most of the Indians at the Colony were of the Washoe tribe, but there were also Paiute and Shoshone people.

I'd always been interested in Native American art, so I started classes at the colony. Art appreciation, I felt, and art expression, were things which could lift the morale of Native Americans. A man named Ed MacAmoil, with the Reno Kiwanis Club, helped get supplies for me, and we did a lot of good arts and crafts, as well as oil paintings, watercolors, hide paintings, and sand paintings. I'm a lousy artist myself, but I'm great at giving praise and serving coffee.

Our art class did real well; we even had an art exhibit in downtown Reno, after about five months. Later we exhibited at the University of Nevada. It was really gratifying to see the looks of surprise and appreciation on the faces of the local folks, when they saw how much talent there was at the Indian Colony. I actually heard a few people say they thought "all the Indians down in Reno Sparks were just winos and bums". They were not much on sensitivity.

I should explain that the Reno Sparks Colony was, in fact, a pretty destitute place; Indians who lived there worked at transient jobs, doing labor on farms during the right seasons, and little else. They didn't have much choice in the matter. They had been uprooted from their homes, their culture, their warm, extended families and now found themselves in shacks in the middle of a growing city. When I first got there, I saw 87 little clapboard shacks. There was no timber land, no farming land, no good way to make a living. There was little hope that things would improve, so many of the people just sat around and waited. It was 1956 and a lot of business establishments still had signs which read *"No Indians Allowed"*. You couldn't eat at the restaurants, and you couldn't cook in the kitchens. All of this made it feel doubly good to see some brothers and sisters working in a creative way.

There was discrimiration; I worked for a woman one time, doing some handyman work, and when lunch time came she handed me a plate and told me to go out and eat under a tree. Luckily, I liked that better anyway.

I had many white friends, too; there was Mrs. Claire Beatty, who was with the Nevada Historical Society. She helped me get a lot of arts and crafts supplies, and gave me work with the Society when I needed a few dollars.

During the winter, when things were really tough, I even made an arrangement with the Salvation Army; they gave me my meals, so I could continue working with the arts and crafts project, since there was no work available that winter in Reno.

I did a lot of hunting with my Washoe brothers from Reno Sparks, and learned a few new tricks. We'd go out on rabbit drives, five or six of us, and drive the rabbits ahead of us, towards a dry lake bed. Once they were there, there was no ground cover, and we'd bag our limit, shooting them with small caliber rifles. I loved the dry countryside, and felt that I belonged in the desert; I often went deer hunting with my cousin Dan. The longer I stayed there, the more interested I became in Nevada history, and the history of Native Americans there.

One day a man came by the Historical Society; he'd been out in the desert near Pyramid Lake, and near a cave he'd found a hand carved head of a jaguar. It was made of jade, and had no business being there; we finally decided that it was most likely of Aztec origin, or, if not, then definitely from Latin America.

With friends, I got a chance to do some exploring on my own. We went out to Lagamacino Canyon, between Virginia City and Reno, to a place where there was a half-mile of ancient Indian pictographs on the canyon walls. There were many burial sites there, and we found some *metates*: corn grinding equipment of the old Native people.

It was at Lagamacino Canyon that I discovered my own ability to read pictographs; it was nothing that could be learned, it came simply from the heart or mind. By studying the pictographs, or *petroglyphs*, I deciphered the fact that they represented four distinct tribal cultures. There were some very powerful medicine symbols; there was the spiral design which symbolized the continuing path of life; there were symbols to tell how many people were in each tribe; there were symbols representing medicine wheels; symbols showing the Aztec sunburst; and even one picture which showed an ancient woman who had just given birth. That picture was fascinating and very moving; it showed a woman with a newborn babe beside her... her hands clasped a stick which was braced across the back of her shoulders. She would push against the stick, the pictograph said, to give her pushing power to bring forth the child. It was beautiful.

When you go to the petroglyphs, if your power is strong within you, and you want to communicate with the spirit keepers, they will tell you the meaning of the rock paintings. You can feel their presence so powerfully that sometimes you think you can't move away.

The method of interpretation comes to you, as in all medicine; you can smoke your pipe, or just sit and listen. It's the same way when I do a ceremony, or make a prayer. The way of each ceremony depends on what the spirits call on me to do.

There are other pictographs, which I have seen since then. Many reveal past knowledge; others predict things to come.

I've studied the winter counts of the Sioux and other Plains tribes, which are painted on buffalo and deer hides. I've seen hides with accounts of battles, hunts, disease epidemics. The Midewiwin chants are recorded on birch bark scrolls.

From some of these pictographs, I can gain knowledge to help others; many are secret, so I can't tell you more about them.

I don't want to hear of any philosophy unless it grows corn.

CHAPTER FIVE

MY FIRST
SCREEN TEST

I not only learned medicine ways, during the fifties; I also learned to be an activist and an actor. In the spring of 1955, I left Reno and went to Los Angeles to find employment. The FBI was still looking for me, as AWOL from the army, and I figured it wouldn't be a bad idea to move around a little. The funny thing was, though, being in California and looking like an Indian, there was only one really good job for me; that was to get my face in front of a camera and do some TV programs. I figured that I was safe from the FBI; to the white man, it seemed, all Indians looked alike.

I also felt that if I could make some decent money, I could better help my brothers back in Reno.

In Los Angeles, I hung out with Native friends at the Los Angeles Indian Center and met a Jewish brother named Salty, who eventually introduced me to a man who wrote scripts for television shows.

At the time, I'd taken out a classified ad which read "used to hunt buffalo, now am hunting for a job", and I'd landed one at the Hollywood Spaghetti Kitchen. I washed dishes, and spent my spare time learning about my Native brothers who had come to Los Angeles from different parts of the country, like I had. Though nearly all tribes seemed to be represented in the L.A. area, there was a large concentration of Navajos, Lakotas and Blackfeet that I met. Many of them had come to Los Angeles through the Indian relocation programs because there were no jobs on the reservations. The relocation programs were basically another government land grab technique, where the BIA would tell unemployed Indians that they would move them to the cities where there were plenty of jobs. They hoped that the Natives, in moving, would be assimilated into the dominant culture and forget about their homeland and ways.

Eventually, Salty's connections paid off; I was introduced to Wallace Bosco, the assistant producer of CBS's "Brave Eagle" series. It was a funny thing, you know: I was only half-Indian, and the only one of my mother's children who looked Indian at all. Yet, I looked totally Indian, and later I would even feel badly about it for awhile, because I'd get jobs in TV and movies that other Indians couldn't get, because they didn't look *authentic*. I halfway-felt like I was taking a job away from them.

Anyway, Wally Bosco talked to me for a long time, and he was pleased and surprised to discover that I was so knowledgeable about Native customs. He asked me if I would like to work as a technical director for the "Brave Eagle, Chief of the Cheyenne" series. They really needed a technical director. The first pilot for the show had been called "Cochise", and they had paid $75,000 to make it. When they took it to New York for CBS to review, one of the producer's sons, a Boy Scout, sat in on the screening. At the end, he pointed out to the producer that Cochise, an Apache, would never have worn an eagle feather headdress. With that comment, the $75,000 pilot went down the tubes and "Cochise" became the "Brave Eagle" series.

Of course, I jumped at the opportunity to become a technical director of a television series dealing with Native people. I saw it as a real opportunity to educate people about authentic Native ways. It was a slow jump; just about the time I got the job, the Actor's Guild went on strike. So I took a deep breath and kept my job at the Spaghetti Kitchen. I paid my rent by painting rooms for my landlady on North Poinsettia Drive.

Finally, the strike over, I was ready to become a director. I told my boss at the Spaghetti Kitchen that I was going to work in television, and he said that he didn't know I knew how to repair them. I explained that I was going to be an actor, and of course, he didn't believe me, until I cashed a few paychecks with him later.

I went to work at the Goldwyn studios, and lived two blocks away. Every day, we'd ride out to Roy Rogers' ranch near Chatsworth, in the San Fernando Valley. That was the filming location. Most of the stars of the series were genuine Indians, I was pleased to discover. Keith Larsen, who's part-Cheyenne, played Brave Eagle. Anthony Nokema, (a mixture of Hopi and Klamath), played the part of Keena. Kim Winona, also a star in the series, was a full-blooded Sioux who'd been raised on the Rosebud Reservation, and the fourth starring role was played by Burt Wheeler. He was not an Indian, but he'd been a full-blooded comedian for many years.

It was exciting work, doing research for the series, playing bit parts, and hob-nobbing with the upper echelons of TV stardom. Sometimes I prepared scripts in the office and at other times I did my work right on the sets.

It was my responsibility to make sure that the series was as authentic as possible, so you can imagine how much I learned. I'd always check out the scripts to determine if the dialogue was consistent with Native American philosophy. I'd also look over the sets, as Leslie Lieber punned in his *Los Angeles Times* column, to make sure that the wigwams, the ceremonies, were "the real McChippewa". Puns were pretty common in publicity columns back then, and I don't mind telling a few, as long as I can't be blamed for them.

There was a whole rash of upcoming Indian TV shows back then, and one TV tycoon punned terribly, calling the industry the "brave's new world".

I'll never forget the first day I came out to a set, and they were ready to shoot a scene. J.C. Penney blankets were hanging all over the tipis, and there was a congo drum in the middle of the village. I told the prop men that it looked kind of tacky, that it didn't look authentic at all, so they ditched the flaky stuff.

I played bit parts all the way through the series. In one episode I played a medicine man, and in others I played dozens of different warriors. I had a good time and met many of my brothers who were actors or bit players.

I always knew when the script writers had run out of ideas; they'd come up to me and say, "Hey, Sun Bear, how about coming to dinner tonight?" I knew they had their mental fish hooks out, and I really enjoyed snapping up the bait. We'd go out, eat well, and kick a few ideas around. At that time the series ran a half-hour a show, and there were six writers, so I ate pretty well, and had the chance to help develop at least a half-dozen scripts.

I really thought it was fun, and funny, being out there sitting on a horse, playing an Indian. I used to tell people: "Most of us only get to play cowboys and Indians when we're kids. As for me, I was too busy to play then, but now that I've grown up I get to play the same, and I get paid for it." One time, I remember, one of the publicity men saw me standing in a phone booth making a call. I had on full regalia, and it must have tickled his funny bone. He took a picture of me, and it ended up on the wall in the CBS studio.

There were a lot of little problems shooting the "Brave Eagle" series, most of them having to do with civilization. Pollution was a real problem; every morning before we left the studio to go on location, a few of us said prayers to lift the smog. There was the sound of airplanes that had to be cut from filming, the chug and whistle of Southern Pacific Railroad trains, as they huffed their way to the Chatsworth Tunnel. Uncle Sam, too, had added to the confusion; the army had recently built a new missile site in the vicinity, and there was no telling when we'd hear the roar of an experimental test rocket. It was no fun.

During the filming of "Brave Eagle", over forty million viewers saw my face. All that time I was on the FBI wanted list.

After the "Brave Eagle" series was over, I went back to Reno to work with the Reno Sparks colony again. I had some good ideas about starting other self-help projects. I made connections with the railroad, and got some railroad ties for building material. I also got the lumber from some condemned houses, where the Sparks Nugget now stands, in Sparks, Nevada. We used the wood from these places to build housing in Reno Sparks.

By the late fifties, I was learning that getting help for my people meant sticking my toes into the lake of politics. I began speaking at private clubs and public functions. If you look up an article in the Reno Evening Gazette, in November of 1957, you'll see a picture of me at the Young Democrats National Convention, placing a war bonnet on the head of Senator Hubert Humphrey. I was trying to open up channels to help my Native people.

I went back to Los Angeles for awhile, and with the help of columnist Paul Coates, who wrote "Confidential File" for the *Mirror-News*, managed to publicize the fact that I wanted to paint the whole Reno Sparks Indian Colony.

The publicity worked.

The Paramount Paint Company in Los Angeles donated a huge amount of experimental paint. With donations of leftover paint from people's garages, and a few cash donations, we had our five hundred gallons. The Western Gillette Truck line in Los Angeles hauled the paint up to Reno for free, and with all those goodies coming in, local shop owners and members of the painter's union joined the fun; they donated brushes, ladders, whatever else we needed.

We had a paint orgy. We started at the south end of the Reno Sparks Colony and moved north, painting everything that didn't run away.

There's some humor in everything. I remember the minister at the Colony coming up to me when the work started. He said: "Well, Sun Bear, I hope you intend to paint the good people's houses first?"

I said: "Who do you call the good people?"

"The ones who go to church of course, " he replied.

I said: " No, sir, I'm going to paint my way from south to north. That's the best way."

Later, my friends and I developed a kind of proverb of our own about that, which was: "The paint falls on the just and the unjust, alike".

That's the way it was.

We gave of our time and energy; I used whatever money I'd saved to buy Cokes and sandwiches. We went for it and we painted all eighty-seven houses.

Some folks could paint their own places, but others were too old or sick, so we did it for them. There was one family of drunks that I remember. Though they kept on drinking, they wanted to join the work anyway. They did a good job, too; they got their house painted, also themselves, and their dogs. That was okay.

After that project was finished, I got the use of a truck, which was donated by a local attorney's wife, and we hauled out tons and tons of garbage. With the place looking so much cleaner, the town folks didn't look down on it quite so much; the *Reno Evening Gazette* even ran an article, calling the results amazing. My Native brothers at Reno Sparks picked up lots of good energy from the project. That's the way to do it.

We just kept on going; a Washoe friend of mine named Willy Astor donated the use of a piece of land and we built an arts and crafts center using donated concrete blocks. It was almost finished, and I was feeling the best I'd ever felt, when the FBI caught up with me.

I always like to expand kids' minds; make them question the ways of the world.

CHAPTER SIX
THE NINETY DAY WONDER

I was in Reno when they finally nabbed me. I was working on a job near Sparks, tearing old shingles from a building and thinking about the last rabbit hunt I'd been on with my Washoe buddies. Suddenly, I knew how the rabbits must have felt; two well dressed men came around the corners of the building, one from each side.

"We're FBI agents," one said. He flashed a badge.

I surrendered.

My medicine had told me they were coming soon, so I wasn't terribly surprised. I never discovered for sure how they finally found me, but there had been plenty of good clues for them. There was my work with the "Brave Eagle" series, and also, I had become increasingly politically active. In the late fifties, political activism meant an FBI file, whether you had one previously or not.

They took me first to the Reno jail. When my Native brothers in other cells — people who knew of my work with the Colony — heard that I was there, they all started chanting. It was their way of showing support for me and for the work I had been doing and it was really something, their songs and drumbeats on the walls and bars, echoing throughout the jailhouse. I think it shook up the guards; they weren't quite sure who I was, or what kind of hocus-pocus they had on their hands.

Needless to say, they transferred me rather quickly to Stead Air Force Base, where they locked me in the stockade. I felt pretty down at first, being caged like a zoo animal, but I'd been living by my principles, doing what I believed in. So after awhile it came to me, that when they put me in the first jail cell and turned the key in the lock, I was the free one. I wasn't in Korea.

The sergeant in charge at Stead was a pretty good guy. He seemed to like me.

"Hey, Sun Bear," he said to me one day, "I know you Indians hate to be locked up. There's a hole in the back fence, here; take a long walk, if you need to."

I thought about freedom again; I knew the hills around Stead; I had no doubt that once outside I could stay outside. But it would start the whole cycle over again, and I was tired of running on a treadmill.

"Thanks," I told the sergeant, "I appreciate your offer. I think I'll stay here, though, and pay my dues."

He shrugged in agreement.

Two guards came for me from Fort Ord, California. They took me by train, in handcuffs; that really bugged me, having my wrists shackled. After I'd done my time, I actually got a bill from the army, a charge for sending those two guards to fetch me. I really laughed at that one.

I gave the bill to a lawyer friend of mine and asked him to handle it.

"Write the government," I told him, "and tell them that when they pay for the land they took from my people in the 1880's I'll take care of my delivery charge. But make sure you tell them I won't settle for anything less than full compensation."

I never heard anything about the bill again.

Although I'd prepared myself emotionally for doing time, it was hard to accept it as a way of life. I had been in jail in Reno for about four hours, and at Stead Air Force Base about three days, but when they finally locked me in the stockade at Fort Ord it looked a lot more permanent.

Once the reality of steel bars and cold cement walls hit me, though, I accepted it; I determined to use the whole episode as a way of learning more about myself and the culture that had imprisoned me. After all, I told myself, the life force flows through everything, even prison walls.

I remember watching a fly go out between the bars. I knew then that I would be okay. I felt pretty well centered into my medicine by this time in my life, and I felt I might be able to slip my mind and spirit out beyond the bars like that fly, sometimes, if things got really bad for me.

I was restless while in prison, but never really despondent. A lot of folks do "hard time"; they tell themselves often how bad it is, and so they suffer. That's not my way. My life has never been really weighed down by despondency; there are too many good things to learn about.

I was impatient though. I knew I would get *some* time for desertion, but I didn't know how much. When I first went in and folks heard why I was there, their brows knit ominously; they estimated twenty years! "Good God," they told me, lots of them, "You deserted at the height of the Korean War, and you were anti-army." They shook their heads.

I didn't feel too great about their predictions; nobody was encouraging. I sat in the stockade for a month-and-a-half waiting for my court-martial.

I heard tiny sounds; I felt the sun go around. In a place where time goes by so slowly, any detail, any incident, takes on importance. I even memorized the number of my building; it was 4953, not my lucky number.

At the time, I remember, there was a disc jockey in Salinas called Frantic Fred. Every so often, he would play songs and dedicate them to men in the stockade. One of his favorites was "Please Release Me, Let Me Go...". We all got a bittersweet chuckle out of that.

The man in command at Fort Ord was a major whose first name was Richard. That's all I'll call him. So many inmates escaped while I was there that we nicknamed him "Open the Door" Richard. I think, deep down, he really hated seeing all of us locked up; that made me like him. Of course, he could never admit to having any such feelings, so he acted like a tough guy, striding, and hawking out commands.

He was acting that way one day, when a commanding general came on an inspection tour of the stockade. It was a bad day for Major Richard; it was a day when six of my compatriots decided to bolt for freedom. The major tried jumping all over the rest of us; he told us we were rotten, making him look bad that way in front of the general. He talked about how we mistreated him; he tried to sound angry and mean, but beneath it all I could sense a sadness.

It was tragically funny, yet touching. Here was a man who'd given his life to the armed forces; yet it was clear that he didn't like his own job. He was battling inside himself, and I felt free.

It was late December; as punishment for the escape of the others, he cut back on his Christmas clemency policy.

I met a lot of "criminal types" while I was treading water at Fort Ord; many of these folks were quite enterprising entrepreneurs. There was one group called the "Post Office Gang", and what they had done was pretty clever. They had been stationed together in Japan, working in an Army post office, and they had friends from the States send them loads of cancelled stamps. They'd slap the cancelled stamps on outgoing packages, then pocket the good stamps or the money that was paid for them.

There were thirteen in the Post Office Gang, and they'd racked up quite a few thousand dollars before they were caught and sent to Fort Ord.

Actually, they weren't *caught*; they were turned in. One of the thirteen was the squealer. The army knew he was in hot water with the others, but exercising their usual perverse sense of fair play, they sent him along with the bunch. It seemed as though the army officials involved couldn't decide whether to praise the stoolie for turning in the others, or punish him for ratting on them. The army ethic, after all, is to always stick by your buddies. Yet, another army by-law is never to break the rules. It was confusing, especially to the squealer whose buddies broke the rules.

The poor informant finally got his punishment; one night his *friends* gave him a blanket party. That means they threw a blanket over him and beat him to a pulp. The blanket is used as a precaution, so the victim can never testify as to who hit him.

It wasn't much like counting coup, where you faced your enemy eye-to-eye.

We had an old sergeant at Fort Ord, who was *making up bad time*, because he had stolen some military equipment and sold it back to the army before World War II. You made up bad time by staying longer than originally planned.

He was a grey-haired, crusty old guy we called Sergeant Satan. He acted tough, but really, he was a pretty good fellow. He used to say: "If you guys want to find out why they call me Sergeant Satan, just cross me once. You'll find out".

It was Satan who entered the cell block, right after the Post Office stoolie had been creamed; later on they questioned him at a court-martial inquiry about the blanket party, but he said: "I don't know anything about it. I came in and saw him lying on the floor. I thought he slipped or something".

He wouldn't tell them a thing, so nothing was ever done about the incident. I don't know who was right or wrong in the whole mess; nobody was right, according to Native philosophy. But then, the Indians didn't make confusing rules, which invited you to break them; and Native American cultures tried to establish systems where stealing wasn't necessary, where superficial desires would not arise.

There were a few more operators in our cell block. I remember a couple of brothers from a wealthy southern family. They were kind of spoiled; they decided they needed bigger allowances than their army paychecks, so they burglarized the company safe. They weren't too good at it, though; they worked on the safe for awhile, but couldn't get it open, so they threw it into a wheelbarrow and made off with it.

A few blocks away from the company office, they finally broke into it. There was only a thousand dollars inside, but at their court-martial they were accused of taking a whole lot more. It seems that their company commander had already been skimming the till; he must have been delighted to have some underlings to pin the crime on.

Another group in the stockade had been truck rustlers. They were stationed in Japan, and they would dress up as MP's. When a fully-equipped convoy came down the road, they would signal it off onto a side street, then tell the drivers to park and take a break at the local canteen. While the drivers were relaxing, the rustlers would sell off the entire convoy.

During their stay at Fort Ord, these guys would look over the motor pool every day, and they'd lick their chops. We were all on police duty one day, picking up cigarette butts and other trash, when I heard one rustler say to another: "Look at all those gorgeous trucks and jeeps. You know Papa-san, he'd pay a lot of money for that equipment".

So much for rehabilitation.

One good thing I can say about Fort Ord is that they fed you well in the stockade, and a full belly keeps me relatively happy. There have been quite a number of times in my life when there was no way for me to get my belly full. I wasn't used to being kept under lock and key, of course, and I could never really be content living that way, but I decided I ought to focus on the good things, so I ate a lot.

I worked at whatever details they assigned to me, mostly policing the grounds, and I did a real good job. I also did a lot of reading, going through all the books I could on Native philosophy, and then on other philosophies, and history. I enjoyed talking to my fellow prisoners. They taught me a lot about this American society. I think you can often learn as much from the supposed failures of a society as you can from the successes.

Finally the big day came — the time for my court-martial.

I began fasting, and continued to fast during the entire proceedings. I made my medicine and prayed that whatever happened, I would be able to continue to serve my people in the best way possible.

I spoke a little at the court-martial; told the commission my feelings in the matter. I quoted Crazy Horse and Sitting Bull. I tried to communicate the traditional ways of my people, how we felt about the land, about war, and about killing human beings.

I had good help from the Great Spirit; I was assigned a defense counsel, a major named David S. Panitz. When the proceedings began, there was hardly anyone in the hearing room; by that afternoon, however, the place was filled. Major Panitz had built me up as an *Indian Robin Hood*, and word had spread. He said I'd been doing such good work with my people, that my arrest and confinement was a travesty. The folks who came to listen really backed him, and me, and that felt good. Most of them were white folks.

It felt so good, in fact, to hear Major Panitz's summary, that I'm going to share some of it; I was surprised at the time that an official in the army could be so understanding:

> Let us take this man's background. He is an Indian born upon a reservation. He went to school on the reservation and stayed there until the age of 15. He came under the social and cultural environment of, actually, a group of foreigners. He was not an American up to that time because reservation life is not conducive to what we ordinarily call citizenship in

the United States. He was an Indian living as a tribal Indian. An Indian reservation is like ... a foreign territory to the United States ... He was just as far away from the American culture as if he had been on the moon.

What did he do during his absence (from the army)? Did he go out to make money and live comfortably? No, he did not. He went out to study the Indian problem and learn more about the minds of the Indians. Mind you, gentlemen, you are dealing with a man that thirsts for knowledge .... He did not want to use it to enrich himself or make himself famous. He went to Indian reservations to study his people ....

In his travels to the various Indian reservations, he came to Reno, Nevada. There he found the Indians in the lowest ebb. And he said to himself, 'Here is a place where I can do some good.' What did he do? He got paint to fix up the houses in the area... To us it is minor, but to an Indian it is important because he discovered the truth in his two years of searching and study. He found that to improve yourself you must have self respect. He knew the greatest secret of all learning ... and that is a great compliment to this man.

He started teaching them their culture ... He knew that if the Indians could learn to do the right things in their culture that they would get their self respect back and be able to meet the world...

Here is a man that claims to devote his life to his mission, that mission being to help his people ... and he did help the Indians ... He knows that in order to continue his work he must go back and face the charge of desertion or absence ... and have it settled and resolved.

Gentlemen, you have a great opportunity here today ... the way you handle this case will be reflected ... in the minds of a lot of people as to whether a person can get justice or not. You have to judge him in terms of his background, training, experience and way of life."

★ ★ ★

Many people I worked with in Reno had written letters in my behalf. The Rev. Felix Manley, of the Federated Church of Reno, had said:

I think Sun Bear's contribution to the community ought to get into the record at this trial. While justice must be done, society would be much better off with him at work helping his own people, than it would be with him vegetating in a prison cell.

There were letters from the Reno Sparks Tribal Council, from Brady Johnson, chairman of the Walker River Tribal Council, and many others. One letter, I remember, even made the statement that I'd done more for the Native people in a few years than the Bureau of Indian Affairs had ever done for them.

I was deeply touched by such strong support; it made me feel humble, as well as honored. The letter which touched me the most, I have to say, was a petition sent in by the people at Reno Sparks. At the top, it read:

> We have had promises of all kinds, from other people and organizations who said they would help us, but Sun Bear was the only person who ever really did. There isn't a person in the Colony who hasn't benefited by something he did.

★ ★ ★

It took the court-martial commission only fourteen minutes to decide, regardless of the support I had received, that I was guilty of desertion. Of course, *I was*. It took them twenty-seven minutes more to decide to sentence me to a bad conduct discharge, (rather than a dishonorable discharge), forfeiture of all pay and allowances, and confinement at hard labor for one year.

I was sorry, both personally and because of the precedent set, that the court-martial commission hadn't taken the opportunity to be more lenient, as Major Panitz had requested. Yet, I was relieved that the waiting was over, and in truth, my sentence *had* turned out to be relatively light. I knew of others at the time, who had received about five years for the same offense.

After the trial I was transferred to Lompoc Prison in California to complete my sentence. I had my own cell, number 18713, and I worked inside for a month, in the prison kitchen. Then I talked to a young psychiatrist there, who interviewed all incoming prisoners; we got along well, and he set things up for me so I could work outdoors, on the honor farm. That was great. From then on, I worked as a gardener around the officers' quarters. I was comfortable serving time that way; I enjoyed working with my plant friends, being able to feel the goodness of the Earth Mother on my hands again. I also enjoyed some extra benefits: the officers' wives always served me cake, ice cream and coffee while I was working. Some of them would talk to me, and it felt good having direct contact with female energy.

Sometimes, I would get the chance to talk to the officers' children, tell them about Native ways. I really liked that; I always like to expand kids' minds, make them question the ways of the world. These little ones really enjoyed learning, too; sometimes, they showed how much they wanted to understand. One time, I talked to the grandson of the army chaplain.

"How come," I asked him, "we're going off and killing all these people in different parts of the world?"

He told me they were the bad guys.

I said that I couldn't understand it, that sometimes the Germans were the bad guys, and sometimes they were the good guys. "How come," I said, "the bad guys are changing all the time?" He couldn't figure that one out.

During my stay at Lompoc, I met a few more entrepreneurs. One I remember in particular was in for theft; he worked out on the prison farm with me, and one day he made a phone call to his brother-in-law. A short while later, the brother-in-law showed up with an empty semi-truck. The two men proceeded to fill it with a cattle herd from the prison rangeland.

I continued with my reading while at Lompoc, read a lot of books about Native Americans, and I took courses that eventually led to a high school equivalency diploma.

I guess I looked pretty trustworthy for a prisoner, both at Fort Ord and at Lompoc. It seemed the guards were always leaving loaded guns around me. During the time that I was waiting for my court-martial at Ord, there was a guard who always marched me around. He carried a twelve-gauge shotgun, and during court-martial proceedings, he was my shadow.

One morning, he was pretty hung over from a big night on the town. We went into the latrine and I took care of my business, then dabbed water on my face.

"Here," the guard said, as he handed me his shotgun. "Hold onto this while I take a leak."

"You'd better be pretty careful, you know," I told him. "If you handed this gun to some guy pulling a lot of time, he might just turn it on you, and march you back to the stockade. You'd end up having to pull his time."

He sobered up quickly when I suggested that, and snatched the shotgun back. I'll bet he never did that again. He was lucky I didn't want to go anywhere; what I had told him, about pulling a prisoner's time, was one of the rules that was on the army's books.

At Lompoc, I painted the guard towers one day with another inmate. We asked the guard in one station to come down, so we could work up there. He did come down, and he left his carbine up there with thirty rounds in it.

I called him back, and handed him the carbine.

"Be careful with that," I told him. "I think it's loaded."

He's lucky the only coup I counted was touching his hand with the gun stock.

Later at Lompoc they actually gave me a .22 rifle. I was supposed to shoot badgers for them with it, but I never did manage to get one. The badgers had been creating problems, so the army wanted to get rid of them. Badgers can be vicious. If you corner one, he could chew your leg off. Because of the army's fear of these four-leggeds I became, for awhile, Lompoc's one-and-only armed prisoner.

In prison there were lots of guys who had pulled long, long

sentences. The first thing you asked new inmates was their name; the second thing you asked was how long they were in for. I remember one time I asked a guy about his sentence, and he told me he'd be there for 65 years, more or less.

"What did you do?" I asked him, in amazement.

"I killed a German, after the season closed," he shrugged.

Lompoc was, in fact, a place for long-term prisoners. Anyone serving less than a year there, like myself, was said to be taking a "camera tour".

★ ★ ★

I served six months at Lompoc Prison. By that time, the army had so many petitions demanding my release...from the Native people in Nevada and from friendly politicians...that they let me out on parole for the six months that remained. I found out later that Congressman Walter Baring (D-Nevada) had gone into the Pentagon, pulled my records and reviewed them. He decided I would be, in fact, more valuable outside the wall than in. So he pulled a few strings, I'm told, and I was free.

After they released me, I was flown back to Reno. My Native brothers and sisters met the airplane and we had a big celebration. There was a traditional feed waiting for me, and a huge cake that said "Welcome Home, Sun Bear".

Food never tasted so good, I'll tell you, and ladies never looked quite so pretty.

Being locked up with only male energy around me for so long had made me feel out of balance. The life force doesn't pulse as strong, without a merging of male and female energy. I enjoyed being back to normal, being around the good female vibrations, but there was one lady I needed to see much more than any of the rest.

The minute I could break free of the celebration, I drove into the desert. The moon was full and the air was clean. What a perfect setting, I thought, for our reunion. I got out of the car. I was in a remote section of the hills; the earth was abundantly covered with sage.

I stripped down naked; I made a tobacco offering and picked some fresh, strong-smelling sage. I rubbed it all over my body, from face to feet, praying that its cleansing power would remove all the negative energies the prison had filled me with. I felt the negativity drain away, and my balance being restored. I felt clean enough, now, to have contact with my special lady.

I laid down upon her, smelling her sweet earthy smell. I took some of her crust and rubbed it all over me; only then, did I feel my balance was fully restored. I gave thanks to the Earth Mother for her beauty, and her wonder.

I stayed with her in the desert until sunrise. As the sun father rose the next morning over the beautiful, spacious, free hills of Nevada, I made my prayers to the Great Spirit, that I might be worthy of the love and support that the Earth and my people had given to me.

I prayed that I might strengthen my path, my vision, my direction, so that I could help an ever-widening circle of people to walk the good road of the Creator, the path of respect for the love and splendor of the Earth.

Now I felt ready to continue my work with the Reno-Sparks Indian Colony; the time I had spent alone in the desert had drained me of the bitterness I felt. After blending again with the Earth, I felt a full sense of belonging, of being a part of all the natural forces around me.

I drove back to the Colony hoping, praying I could transmit that sense of balance, of harmony, to my people. There was a lot of work ahead of us, of *me*; it was work that seemed, always, to draw me closer to fulfillment of my larger vision, my lifelong dream.

Being an actor expanded my view of life; gave me a broad perspective.

CHAPTER SEVEN
PLAYING COWBOYS AND INDIANS

I stayed in Reno for awhile; I was hoping I could remain there to help my brothers and sisters at Reno Sparks. I had no money at all, though, and little know-how about raising funds quickly. I'd been working on my gambling medicine, but had not yet developed it to a dependable point, so things looked pretty hopeless.

I would like to explain here the Native feeling about gambling, because it is so different from the non-Native. I'll be talking more about my gambling medicine and I want you to understand what I'm saying.

The place today where a lot of Native gambling happens is at the pow wows that are held throughout the country, mainly in the West and Canada. These are big get-togethers where people come to dance, drum, sing, meet friends, buy, sell and gamble. One thing that is really big at the Indian pow wows is the hand games. It's a form of Native gambling that goes way back, and, in the old days, warriors would bet horses, weapons, even their women in the hand games. Sacajawea, in fact, was traded in a hand game, from an Indian to a very cruel man named Charbonneau. Later, she accompanied him on the Lewis and Clark expedition to the Pacific Ocean.

Anyway, the hand games go like this. There are two teams which compete, and each team has two bones. One bone is smooth, and the other has a mark on it. In addition, each team has six sticks, which are, I guess, an equivalent to card chips or any other markers.

One team member juggles the bones around in his hands; he puts them under his blanket, or hides them behind his back. All the time he is doing that, he's switching them from hand to hand, and in order to win a stick from him, his opponents must guess which hand the marked bone is in when he's finished juggling.

Each team has a set of singers and drummers, who chant and play to make medicine to confuse the other team. In order to win the cash in a pot, a team has to win all six sticks from its opponents. If you guess the correct hand, you get a stick. If you guess the wrong hand, you have to give one up.

The thing about the hand games is they can go on, and usually do, for the three or four days a pow wow lasts. They start early on the first afternoon, and just keep going on. The hand games, you see, let out good energy for my people; we don't have the same sense of possession the white man has, so if we lose our money or our belongings, then in a way, we almost feel a sense of freedom.

It's that Native feeling about gambling that takes me to Reno, even now, when I want to have some relaxation. Some old buddies from my Reno days are still around the casinos, especially the Cal-Neva and the Comstock. They arrange to put me up at the Comstock, right in the heart of downtown Reno, so I can walk around and check out the gambling action. It's against my medicine to play the hand games against my brothers and sisters, so I need the casinos to sharpen up my gambling — and my sense of freedom.

Sometimes, at a hand game, you'll find a couple of thousand dollars in the pot. Not only the players bet; but the singers, the drummers, even the people watching can place bets on a certain team. That's why the whole process becomes an exercise in group intoxication; it's really exciting to sit there with the drums beating and the singers chanting, and all that energy flowing around you. It's a very powerful experience and, like the peyote ceremonies, after you leave a hand game marathon, you hear the sound of the drums and chanting for weeks on end.

You'll often find old women, in their 70's and 80's, playing in the sessions; they sit themselves down in their cane chairs, and they sometimes outlast the younger players.

As I said, though, in the days following my release from prison my gambling medicine was not so developed, and I needed to make, not lose, money. After awhile I decided there was only one thing I could do; I could go back to Los Angeles, pick up the pieces of my TV career, and try to make more money.

When I took the job with the "Brave Eagle" series, I had no idea it would be the first of many acting jobs that would keep bringing me back to Hollywood. For the next eleven years, off and on, I would be working in TV and the movies, and, in my spare time, I would be working with the Native Renaissance movements. Acting was an enjoyable profession, and one that would bring me more "green energy" than washing dishes.

In 1957, I returned to Hollywood; I had the same room I rented before, the same old comforts. There was a hot plate, a sink and a bathroom down the hall. Now, though, after my Lompoc days, the place looked like the Ritz.

I was conservative with food; I ate a lot of bologna sandwiches and canned goods. If I felt rich after a job, I'd go to a cafe for a hamburger steak or liver and onions, or I'd go back to the Spaghetti Kitchen.

The industry was good to me. I could make a good living working only two or three days a week, so that left enough time to work on some other things. I was working with the Los Angeles Indian Center, and with Doc Spotted Wolf who was a very powerful medicine man.

In 1957 I landed a job with the "Broken Arrow" series, starring Michael Ansara, and filmed by Twentieth Century Fox. I had lots of fun with that.

Being an actor expanded my view of life, gave me a broad perspective; I worked with so many different types of people, and learned a great deal of history from researching scripts. I watched the actors and the characters they portrayed with keen interest.

I also watched my bosses; it was nice to know I'd never have the same one for too long. It was the nature of the business to move around, and I ended up working for every major studio in Hollywood. Eventually, I was a "two-card man". I belonged to both the screen actors', and screen extras', guilds.

I got my jobs through casting offices: Central Casting; Independent Casting; Allied Casting. I would call in every night, and if an office had a job I'd hear something like this over the telephone: "Sun Bear, seven a.m. Monday, Warner Brothers, playing an Indian. Wear make-up. Ride a horse." That was it.

If no jobs were available, they'd tell me to call back later, and I would. I'd call back later, and later, and later. I'd give them ten or fifteen minutes between calls, until, finally, I hit on something.

I was characterized in studio films as a "character, Indian, Western type", so I got a lot of jobs. One director said of me, "This guy looks so much like an Indian, you'd swear he just stepped off of the buffalo nickel." Another fellow named Foster Hood and I were called the "Gold Dust Twins", because we always managed to get ourselves hired.

The screen extra is the person who always walks around in the background, whenever a scene is being shot. If there's a big crowd scene in an Indian encampment, the Indians that are busy tanning hides, making jerky, are the extras. In a Western scene, the folks lined up at the bar before the big shoot-out are also extras.

What you do on-screen determines your daily pay. When I was working at it, an extra would get $24 for an eight hour day. Now, I understand, it's about four times that much. If you went over eight hours, you'd get more money. If you were in a close-up with an actor, you'd be called a silent bit player; that would mean a raise in salary. If you did something special, if you held a torch or shot an arrow, they'd call that "special business", and you'd get a "bump" or a "whammy", a few bucks more. There were also "double whammys".

As you can see, there was a lot of room for juggling on paychecks. It was an assistant director's job to interpret pay — to see that the studio got as much as they could out of an extra for the least amount of money. Some studios were tighter with money than others, and so were some assistant directors.

I remember one time, working on a "Wagon Train" segment for Universal Studios, I'd done a few extra maneuvers in front of the camera, so I expected at least a non-speaking part role. At the end of the day, the assistant director walked toward me, put his arm around my shoulder confidingly, and said, "You know Sun Bear, you got a lot of good footage today, almost as much as Ward Bond did. You might be discovered."

"That's nice, Charley," I told him, "but I'll tell you, I don't want to be discovered as much as I want to be paid."

Later that season I worked with him again. We were doing another segment of "Wagon Train". Sure enough, when it was over, Charley came toward me again.

"You know Sun Bear..." he said, and by the time he got that far I'd clamped *my* arm around *his* shoulder. I knew I had the advantage, if I could be patronizing first.

"Charley," I told him, "You know, it's getting awfully close to Christmas, and my landlord is putting the squeeze on. I sure need extra money, right about now."

I managed to squeeze what I felt I deserved out of him.

I enjoyed working in movies better than in TV, because I liked being out on the larger sets, and the pay was so much better. I also loved riding horses, and I'd get a lot of money for just being on one. If I rode bareback, I really raked in the cash, but sometimes it got to be pretty difficult work.

I did a picture called "Comanche Station" starring Randolph Scott, at a place near Lone Pine, California, called the "Alabama Rocks". There are tremendous rock formations there, huge outcroppings, shelves, and pinnacles; nearby, there are some very holy Native American places.

We shot a scene where we'd charge a ranch house, and we made charges on horseback all day long, starting at 6:30 a.m., and continuing until dark. The horses got so worn out that they'd drop their heads, and you couldn't get them to run anymore; I was wearing out at least three horses a day. I was always riding bareback, wearing nothing but a breech cloth, so, of course, I was wearing myself out in some very important places. The horses sweated, and so did I; my legs were so sore from the sweat that they would bleed.

The first day we tried to shoot that scene, two stunt men fell off of their horses and were busted against the rocks; they had to be sent off to the hospital. The rest of us decided that, no matter what, we were staying on our mounts; we hung on so hard during the charges that some of the poor horses were losing patches of their manes.

We worked on Saturday, which was unusual, and my Saturday check was the highest I'd ever been paid for a single day: $750. That was a good chunk of money, especially in those days. I really deserved it for that work.

I did another movie, "Tarus Bulba", starring Tony Curtis and Yul Brynner, and I made $350 a day on that one. Of course, I earned every penny of it; Curtis and Brenner played Cossack chiefs. In the movie, we were fighting the Polish army and each time one of us got killed, we took a fall over a twenty-foot cliff.

You know, it's true; the danger, the excitement, folks see on the movie screen is often more real than they imagine. I remember working in the epic "Spartacus", where I played a variety of roles. I was a Jew with a long beard; I played slaves; I played warriors. We did some really good and powerful scenes. In one, we were fighting over flaming logs; there were several stuntmen in the midst of the flames, wearing asbestos suits. They were supposed to be knocked flat by the impact of the logs; then the logs would roll over them. They had on woolen masks, under the asbestos ones, supposedly to protect them. Unfortunately, the woolen masks ignited, and many of the stuntmen were seriously burned during the shooting of that scene. I think eighteen people were sent to the hospital. My medicine protected me, and I escaped unharmed.

We had some extras in "Spartacus" who were college boys from The University of California at Los Angeles (UCLA); we needed more bodies than the casting agencies could supply. These guys needed some extra beer-money, but they didn't know what they were doing, which made them dangerous.

In one scene, there were three hundred of us fighting when the director commanded: "Now, make this one *look* real!" We were fighting with band-steel swords that don't bend easily, and with spears, and this one UCLA guy kept saying, "*We got to make it look real!*" He kept ramming his sword into the belly of a Hawaiian extra.

The swords have dull points, but still, by the time the next shooting came around the Hawaiian was really hurting. When he saw the UCLA enthusiast he ran up to him. "Okay!" he shouted. "*We'll make it look real!*" and he bashed the kid over the head with his spear. The impact broke the handle, and the extra from UCLA looked convincingly unconscious.

After watching how these guys fought, I decided that, for me, there was only one sensible course of action. When the director said "Roll em!" I stretched out on the ground, put my shield carefully over my head, and played dead. I'd had enough abuse from the novices, and

I decided, better a dead Indian than a hurt one.

In still another scene, we were supposed to gallop wide-open down the side of an enormous hill. Wide-open, of course, means as fast as your horse will go. The UCLA boys — some of them big athletic types — got to the top of the hill, looked down the less than gentle slope, and decided that the scene was not for them. Ever so slowly they walked their horses down the off-camera side of the hill.

During the same day, there was a real brush fire off in the distance. The director paced; he waited until the smoke and flames crested a nearby hill. At just the right moment, he shouted, "Roll the cameras! That's Rome burning!" And we filmed it.

"Spartacus" was just one of the exciting films that I worked on. Believe me, you can get more adrenalin pumping when you make a movie than when you watch one. In "The Story of Ruth", I led two burros and rode a horse, and found that burros have a mind of their own, especially when it comes to crossing water.

I was leading the two burros at a run, and was supposed to gallop across a small stream; when we got to the water the burros slammed on the brakes. I barely missed having my arm torn out of its socket. To get those burros across the stream, we had to put wires and ropes on them. In addition, a prop man had to crouch in back of them, prodding their behinds with a stick.

Burros are stubborn alright, but they're not as bad as camels. In a television show called "Desert Rats", filmed near Tucson, Arizona, I played an Arab camel herder. The television series was about General Rommel, the German Commander of the Panzer Tank Division during World War II.

Camels are powerful animals; on top of that, they're almost impossible to control. When camels and horses get together, it's pandemonium; the horses are so freaked-out by the camels that they go crazy. We had some very funny situations, looking back on them.

There was a wrangler, I remember, who worked with the camels and had an excellent way of dealing with them. Whenever he worked with a new kind of animal, he always observed it first and tried to figure out how its mind worked. He psyched out the camels; he discovered that they would spit in your face if they felt rambunctious. Since he was a veteran tobacco chewer, controlling them came easy to him. He'd watch for a mischievous look in a camel's eye; then he'd beat it to the punch: he'd spit tobacco juice squarely in that camel's eye.

The camels respected the wrangler; I guess they figured he was just a strange little camel. They worked for him.

I worked with some other ornery critters, but often, it was just a matter of figuring out their personalities, like the camel wrangler had. While shooting a segment of "Hawaiian Eye", the director asked me if I could work with oxen. "Sure", I said, because if you weren't agreeable, you rarely got a job. I'd led cows home from pasture, so I figured that oxen would be the same. I figured wrong.

Oxen aren't stubborn, but they're really dumb. I think what happens with them is they forget what you want them to do. In order to lead them, I discovered after awhile, you have to tap them on the head occasionally; I guess it reminds them to keep walking. So I kept tapping, and they kept walking.

I've had my share of near-injuries, while working as an actor. On one episode of "Rawhide", I was galloping over the terrain. Another Indian rider had lost his horse, and he was lying on the ground. When I saw him I had to pull up fast on my horse, in order to avoid trampling the guy. I jerked the reins up hard, and the horse did a back-flip right on top of me. I stayed down during the filming of the scene, and the director thought I'd snapped my backbone. Thanks to the Great Spirit, though, that wasn't the case. I'd shocked my system, that's for sure, and sometimes, even now, my backbone throbs from it. My back and legs were so sore from the fall that, for the next three days, I had to be helped into the saddle.

Another time, I was almost drowned during the filming of a segment of "Adventures in Paradise". They took me out in a boat to do a scene, and the director said, "Well Sun Bear, you get to play a diver in this scene. Think you can handle it?"

"No problem," I told him, always cooperative, and also mentally counting the extra pay it would mean.

A few minutes later I was sinking in beautiful green water. There were seventy pounds of weights on me to keep me down, and I wore, on my back, a defective oxygen tank. I discovered I was drowning.

I threw off the weights and thrashed back to the surface.

"I think you'd better get a Hawaiian to do this scene," I sputtered at the director. "This Indian likes it better on top of the water!"

I worked in a Blake Edwards movie called "What Did You Do During the War, Daddy?". It was full of fight scenes, and in one scene in particular, the script called for surrender of one side, then the resumption of fighting because of a dispute over some women. There was so much fighting in that scene, in fact, that we all felt we ought to get extra whammys for it.

The assistant director disagreed, so none of us really put our hearts into it. We fought, but it was more like complaining to each other. We were doing everything in slow motion. Blake Edwards was up above us in a helicopter, trying to get some good footage.

"Hey!" he called down, "What's the matter with you guys?"

"They want more money to fight better!" the assistant director called back up to him.

Blake Edwards yelled back down, from the helicopter, "It's costing us a fortune to film this scene! Give 'em what they want!"

Okay; we were ready. He upped our salary $25 per person per day, and we fought like hell.

That was a good, practical lesson on fight scenes. Ward Bond taught me another fight scene lesson. We were doing an episode of

"Wagon Train", and in one scene, another Indian and I had taken him prisoner. I was supposed to take him to the chief and flip him down on the ground, to show that we were giving him a rough time, that he was in terrible danger. Well, he was the head honcho in the show and I didn't want to hurt him, so I let him down easy.

That upset both Bond and the director. "Un-uh, Sun Bear," Bond told me, "Here's the way you do it."

He tripped me and flipped me down, and I came up spitting dirt. In the next take, I did the same to Bond, and the director was happy. I don't know about Bond, though he seemed to take it in stride.

At about this same time, Bond was having a dispute with the studio over prestige. It seemed that the studio had just bought a one-bedroom dressing room for Ray Milland. Bond, in retaliation, had demanded a two-bedroom dressing room, since he brought in more money than Milland. He threatened to go on strike if he didn't get what he wanted, so he got it.

I worked with a lot of stars in movies and on television shows, and I really enjoyed the chance to get to know them as they really were. I worked with Michael Ansara in "Broken Arrow", with Glenn Ford, John Lupton, Will Rogers, Jr. Like all human beings, some celebrities were good people, others were petty and unfriendly.

I worked with Barbara Stanwyck, and found her to be an outstanding person, one with whom it was a pleasure to work. She was honest and straightforward, and so unaffected by her stardom that she even did her own stunts. I spent an entire afternoon discussing Indian affairs with her, while we were filming a Western, and she seemed to really care about people.

I enjoyed working with Debbie Reynolds, on a "Wagon Train" episode. She played a young Mexican outlaw girl, and I was one of her *banditos*. After some fancy gun-maneuvering, I jumped onto the stagecoach in which she was riding. She took one look at me, then a second look, and said, "You're cute".

Unfortunately, I was too young and green at the time to do more than say "Thanks", and bashfully back away.

I worked with Lucille Ball, who was a really caring person, and a lot of fun. I think many of her off camera, spontaneous remarks were funnier than her on camera ones.

One of my favorite people to work with was Clint Walker, on the "Cheyenne" series. At the time, I was drafting an early version of my first book, AT HOME IN THE WILDERNESS, and Clint and I would share our outdoor knowledge. He had a remodelled ice-cream truck he used as a camper, to take him and his motorcycle to remote parts of the desert. He loved to ride or hike alone out there.

His stand-in, Clyde Howdy, was another wilderness enthusiast, and he'd accompany Clint into the desert sometimes. I still have a pair of beaded moccasins that Clyde gave to me, after I admired them on the set. Giving them to me in that way was a very Indian thing to do, and every time I look at those moccasins it makes me feel good inside.

I worked with Chuck Connors on "The Rifleman", and he spent practically an entire afternoon picking my brain about Geronimo. He was about to make a film about the great Apache leader, and since his questions seemed sincere, I told him all that I knew.

I was a technical director for the first "Bonanza" segment. It was about the Paiute Indian war, and it went off very well. Eight or nine months before the "Bonanza" series began, I'd gone to Wally Bosco, my director friend on the "Brave Eagle" series, and told him I had a new idea. It was for a show very similar to Lorne Greene's.

"Sun Bear," Wally had said to me, "the market is saturated with Westerns right now; I think another one would flop".

Eight months later David Dortort came out with "Bonanza", and it was a record-breaking money maker.

So it goes.

Not all work in the movies was dangerous or exciting. There were some quiet moments, too, and I welcomed them. They helped me to feel my spirit. I remember filming "The Greatest Story Ever Told", at night. It was very cold on the set, so people had little fires going. I wandered back and forth between the fires, and in the dark places I would pass other people, but couldn't really see who they were; I kept thinking about the phrase "Passing like ships in the night".

I'd visit the different campfires and listen to bits of conversation, just to see what folks were thinking or talking about. Often in life, I've liked to just drift in and out like that, through crowds of people, listening, watching, feeling like a chronicler of the times. It's a way in which I've improved my medicine; it's a traditional Native way. My uncles taught me this.

During one evening, we were shooting the crucifixion scene; we were supposed to be up on the walls, hollering "Crucify him! Crucify him!"

It made me feel strange, acting out that role; we Native Americans always honored our prophets, never killed them.

I've always felt that the Carpenter from Nazareth got a bad deal, being born in the wrong time and place. If he had touched down on Turtle Island, North America, I'll tell you, he would have been one powerful medicine man. His gentleness, his love for all of creation, would have made him feel right at home with our medicine people.

There were many funny moments during my time in Hollywood. Once, a friend of mine — a cowboy named Carol Henry — and I were on horseback, during filming of the "Daniel Boone" show. We were galloping wide-open toward the same spot between two trees, neither of us realizing there was room for only one horse there. I beat Carol to the spot by a split second, and he ended up going halfway up a prop tree. He suffered some scratches and bruises, but nothing serious.

A cartoonist friend named Walt LaRue laughed his head off when he heard about the incident; he immortalized it later by doing a cartoon showing Carol halfway up a tree. He titled it "The Time Sun Bear Treed a Cowboy".

Carol never lived that one down. Whenever we filmed together on horseback afterwards, he caught it from the rest of the crew. I loved the jokes about it.

I don't think white folks realize how important humor is to Native Americans. They all seem to think we're stoic, without emotion. Maybe that comes from the days when we had to act that way, or get the tar beat out of us, I don't know. Maybe it's from false notions about rituals like the Sun Dance, where white folks think we become immune to pain. Whatever the reason, we Native Americans are not wooden Indians in front of some cigar store; we like to laugh. Whenever I had to play a "stoic Indian" type who had no feelings, I always felt constipated.

I was in a "Maverick" segment one time, for Warner Brothers. One of the men in a cavalry fighting scene was a fellow who had won a contest; part of the prize was a chance to be in the movies. So they dressed up this poor guy as a blue-coat lieutenant. He was supposed to shoot at the Indians and then get shot in the chest with an arrow. The man was so nervous, we couldn't resist spoofing him a little.

We talked about an alleged time when a prop man fired an arrow too hard: it went clean through the board protecting the actor's chest, we told this guy.

He was getting really anxious; when the scene began, he emptied his pistol so fast he ran out of ammunition before they had a chance to shoot him with an arrow. He stood there, in waves of bravery and cowardice, puffing his chest out when he felt brave, sucking it back in when he got nervous. I know it's not really funny to see someone suffer like that, but at the time it was really funny to watch, in a perverse way. He looked like he was doing some sort of jig.

The prop man had to keep reloading this fellow's gun, and they had to reshoot the scene, over and over. Finally, they beat him to the draw; they got the arrow into his chest board and he did his great dying scene. He went home happy, I suppose, to wherever he had come from.

He probably talked about shooting that scene for years afterwards; how he'd suffered the slings and arrows of a bunch of wild Indians.

Another time, I got to spoof a couple of Native friends who were giving me a hard time. I was technical director for an episode of "Cheyenne", and I cast those two to be dead Indians lying on the ground. Just before filming, we had the prop man cover them with chocolate syrup to represent blood. What I knew, but they didn't, was that the particular area we were working in was crawling with ants. We started filming.

It wasn't long before the ants found the goodies; those two dead Indians came to life really quick, I'll tell you. That scene should have broken the myth about stoic Indians.

★ ★ ★

Working in pictures was good for me; that time of life was very fulfilling. I had a chance to see how an important part of the White World worked, the world of white fantasy. I gained a lot of insight.

Motion Pictures and television, I learned, do so much to form people's ideas of how life's supposed to be. The movies' emphasis on "the good life", based on competition, material wealth, and romantic love, contrasted sharply with my own vision of people caring deeply for the Earth Mother. Sometimes, the caricature of happiness made me laugh, but mostly, it made me feel terribly sad.

Everytime I saw a prop, a fake tree or a fake cloud bank on canvas, I thought about the real thing, and I understood a little better why Western man felt he had to exploit everything in nature. A real tree or cloud, you see, wasn't dependable enough for filming in a given time and place; it had to be a fake tree, an object, so that it would behave, and take cues cooperatively. In this way such things as lighting and time of day could be totally predictable.

Hopefully, some of the work I did with motion pictures — the technical directing — helped a few people to understand how the Native world really was, and how their own world could be better.

I never tried to get a "big break". I wasn't interested in being a Star. I just wanted to do enjoyable, interesting work, which would allow me to support myself, some projects that I was working on, and the family I later had. The movie industry gave me time for those other projects in Los Angeles; they were projects which played an important part in the early Native Renaissance.

I was in enough shows to make my face "look familiar" to a wide variety of people. Even today folks think they know me from somewhere, and some of the time it's from an old "Bonanza" segment.

In Hollywood, even when I wasn't filming, I'd wear western garb and my black western hat because they were comfortable. One day I was driving in downtown Los Angeles, and I got pulled over by a policeman.

"I don't have any real reason for stopping you," he told me, after he'd walked up to the car, "but you look so familiar that it's really bugging me. I don't know if there's a warrant out on you or not, but you *sure* do look familiar."

He was suspicious.

He checked me out, and I was legal; *I* knew that. We got to talking, and after awhile he said: "Hey! You don't work on 'Wagon Train' do you?"

I said, "Yes, I do."

"That's it!" he exclaimed. "Now I know why you look familiar. You killed a girl last night on 'Wagon Train'!"

Fortunately, they don't book you for movie-murder. Even as a grown-up, you can play Cowboys and Indians without being arrested.

The time will come the ancient teachings say when the sons and daughters of our oppressors will return to us and say, "Teach us so that we might survive; for we have almost ruined the Earth now."

CHAPTER EIGHT

THE NATIVE
RENAISSANCE

During the time that I was acting, I was also working very hard to help the Native people in the Los Angeles area, as well as in Reno Sparks. I did much of my work through the Los Angeles Indian Center, where I worked with Jeannie and Bob Babcock. Jeannie, who was not Native by blood, though she certainly was by her heart's direction, was the Director of the Indian Center. Later the Babcocks had a small arts and crafts shop that they called "The Old Buzzard's Roost". We stayed in the back when we visited Los Angeles. In those early days, we worked with practically nothing. Today, the Los Angeles Indian Center is one of the biggest urban Native outreach centers in the United States. In the past, it has been quite well-funded by the government.

The late 1950's and early 1960's were years of upheaval; it was the time of the early Native Renaissance. A lot of Native people were coming to urban areas, but once there, they had no support to keep a sense of their heritage. Many had come through relocation programs, and then had lost their jobs; others simply couldn't find employment, and they were literally starving. You see, this was during a time in the Eisenhower administration which history will call the "termination period" for Native Americans. There was a government push to force Indians off of the reservations, to break up the tribal system completely. A lot of us felt that the "termination program" sounded and felt a lot like the extermination programs that were applied to Natives during the 1800's. The difference was that this time they weren't trying to kill our bodies, but our hearts, and our culture.

The government would say to Native Americans: "Congratulations; you're full-fledged citizens now. Go out and pursue the American Dream". But that was just a maneuver, just one more push in the endless series of land-grab tactics.

The Eisenhower administration wanted private industry to develop reservation lands, and they wanted to terminate the Bureau of Indian Affairs. In effect, then, the government could say to Native people: "You're no longer members of a tribe, because the tribe no longer exists".

For the most part, the termination program flopped because of Native American resistance, but not before it worked effectively to disband a number of tribes. A lot of California tribes came close to disappearing, and I think maybe the biggest termination "success" was with the Klamath people in Oregon. I visited with the remaining Klamath, after a few years; I worked with others who were trying to restore some of their culture.

The mood in the country back then was to do away with tribal structures, to make the Native people just another poor, non-descript, urban minority group. It was a natural thing for a push like that to bring resistance, and I think that early resistance, as much as anything else, helped cause the Native Renaissance, and was partly responsible for early militance, and later, the occupation of such places as Alcatraz and Wounded Knee.

I guess that you could say that the Eisenhower termination period, like a lot of unjust political pushes, backfired ... but not before it managed to destroy more than a few distinct tribal societies in the name of assimilation. Many small California tribes were terminated, and so were the Oneidas in Wisconsin and the Klamaths in Oregon.

Native Americans who came to the cities to take part in the "chrome dream" were living well below poverty level. They'd come from reservations which were unbelievably poor, into a situation that was even worse. They had no place to sleep, no food; there was no government medical aid back then, no food stamp program. The Indians in Los Angeles who had a little pocket change hung out in bars — The Ritz, The Irish Pub — and their sense of balance deteriorated quickly. The way I've always felt about alcohol is that people use it as a pain killer, and those Natives who were relocated had a lot of pain to kill.

Through the Los Angeles Indian Center, we tried to raise food for them, and raise their morale. I would go out to various service organizations — the Jaycees, women's clubs — and talk to people about the Natives' problems, and I managed to raise a lot of groceries. The Indian Center made sure people had food baskets donated to them during holiday times, like Thanksgiving and Christmas. Although those are not Native holidays, it was still very depressing to be around a mass of people who were celebrating, spouting good cheer, and not be a part of the spirit of it. One Thanksgiving, I remember, out near Whittier, we took in donations of almost four tons of food through a Quaker community.

The more speaking I did to service organizations, the more politically involved I became. I saw my people being ignored, and it kindled the flames in me. I became Vice-President of the East Side Democratic Club, and joined some other organizations.

The East Side Democratic Club was a kind of melting pot; there were some Mexican-Americans, some Indians. The President at that time was a Jewish fellow. We got along well together, and he usually chose me to go to political functions. I went to a Democratic Party dinner at the Hollywood Beverly Hilton; I was on the endorsement committee for John F. Kennedy, and another endorsement committee for Pat Brown, who became governor of California.

I remember one Veteran's Day, when Governor Brown spoke at the L.A. Indian Center. People got up and made their speeches to honor the veterans of World War I and World War II. They asked me to speak, and I said I would speak last.

When the others were finished, I took the podium.

"I'm ready to speak now," I told them. "I'm glad for this holiday, for the chance you all have to honor your brave soldiers. I'd like to say a few words on behalf of mine, now, the Indian veterans of the Indian Wars ... both those who survived the old battles, and those who died fighting for their land.

"I want to express my deep hope that their efforts were not in vain, that, although they lost the big battle, their descendants today will have more chance than in the past to exercise their freedom, to raise their low standard of living."

There was a mixed reaction to my little speech. For a moment there was a hushed silence; then, there were gestures of approval.

I wrote for *La Prenta Libra* for awhile, an English/Spanish newspaper on L.A.'s east side. But it turned out not to be my trip. When I was first asked to write for it, the idea was to have Indians involved with other minority groups. The paper, though, turned out to be of a radical pro-Castro nature, and when the editor was gunned down in downtown Los Angeles, I realized I wasn't ready to die for the Cuban cause.

It came to me, one day, that the Los Angeles Indian problem was only a symptom, that the real sickness lay in conditions on the reservations. In 1958, I decided to go to Washington, D.C., to lobby for reservation housing legislation, and other Native programs.

I thumbed my way from Los Angeles to Washington. There were pictures of me in the *L.A. Mirror-News*; the *Arizona Republic* (Phoenix); and the *Washington Post* and *Times Herald*; they called me the "Indian public-relations man" just because I used a few publicity gimmicks along the way. I stood by the side of the highway wearing a feathered war-bonnet, and I carried a large poster which read "Have Blanket, Will Travel". By that time in my life I had learned that if you wanted to change anything in this society you had to let the public know what it was you were doing.

When I stopped in Phoenix, I spoke to a small Native group about my trip. They took up a collection and gave me twenty-five dollars; they said it would buy me beans and fry bread on the trail. I remember, before I left Phoenix, I put on my feathered headdress. A little Apache boy jumped up and down, poking his grandpa in the ribs.

"Look grandpa!" he squealed. "It's an Indian!"

He'd been watching too much TV, I guess; he didn't realize that he and that *all* of us were Indians.

When I got to Washington I stayed in Walter Baring's office for awhile; he was the Nevada congressman who'd pushed for my release from Lompoc Prison. I drew up a Native housing bill while I stayed with him, with the help of his secretary; then I moved to the National Indian Congress in the Dupont Circle Building.

I got some help in Washington, but not enough; the Eisenhower days, as I said, were not a good time for federal aid to Indians. The bill I drafted never made it out of committee.

I visited with Hubert Humphrey; he was always interested in what Native Americans were doing, and he knew that I was in Washington. He gave me passes both for Senate sessions, and sessions in the House of Representatives. I wanted to observe the way they worked, and I found the experience very enlightening.

Often, I remember, there'd be only one congressman in the chamber; he'd be reading out loud to a congressional recorder in an empty room. He'd be spouting off his noble aims and goals; the recorder would write it all down, and later it would go into the *Congressional Record*. That way, the congressman could point to his record in Congress when voting time came around. He could use all those documented speeches to show the great programs he'd supported while in office.

It was enlightening, too, to sit in on debates while the Alaska Statehood Bill was on the floor. The southern representatives, from Georgia, Louisiana, and so on, were against Alaska statehood, so they took turns filibustering; they stalled by making long speeches until the pro-statehood, northern representatives got restless and went out for coffee. As soon as a sizeable number of northern representatives were gone, the southerners called for a roll call vote, to kick the bill back to committee. They succeeded a number of times.

They bounced the bill back and forth, from Congress to committee, until finally the northern representatives organized; they sent out search parties to all of the local coffee shops, mobilized their forces and voted the Statehood Bill through.

Some of the congressmen were nervous about my presence; a few weeks before I got there, some Puerto Ricans had visited the session, then opened fire and wounded a couple of congressmen. That meant, I guess, that all dark-skinned people had become suspect.

They treated me well, though, and said I was the first man they knew of who had hitch-hiked to Washington and, in a sense, ended up in the House of Representatives.

Even though my housing bill flopped I enjoyed my time in Washington, and in those days I never missed a chance to take a few swipes at the white establishment. Guilt is a way of giving away your power; we Indians know that, but many people seem to thrive on feeling bad about themselves, so occasionally I twisted the old knife.

Reporters seemed to regard me as a curio; I guess I helped that image with my showmanship, my "Have Blanket, Will Travel" poster. They'd ask me to say a few words, and I'd lecture them. I remember, in one article in the *Washington Post*, I pulled an old routine against western technology; I said:

> The white men still haven't learned a lesson an old Indian tried to teach them 337 years ago. Squanto told the pilgrims, when he showed them how to plant corn, that they should also feed the ground with fish. The Indian is the supreme conservationist, who rarely wastes natural resources. But look what the white man has done. The buffalo is gone, and much of the topsoil on the plains has blown away.

Although it had been said many times before , it is still true, and even though I was in Washington on a diplomatic mission, it sure felt good to blow off a little steam.

I did it, always, with a smile on my face. I try not to get angry, because anger is another way of giving away your power. When I really want to win an argument, I try to get my opponent angry; that way, I can control the conversation.

★ ★ ★

On my hitch-hiking trip to Washington D.C., I found that I'd become pretty well-known. Wherever I stopped, people wanted to hear me speak. In a few places, I talked on local radio stations.

It was a good trip; I got good rides from interesting people. At one point I got a ride from a suntan lotion promotion man, who'd just invented the slogan "Don't be a paleface". He'd been buying feathered war bonnets to use in his latest commercial.

It was in New York City, on my return trip from Washington, that I met Betty Bernstein; she would be my lady, my companion, for the next four and one-half years.

When I got to New York, I stayed in the Bowery apartment of a friend of a friend; it was quite a twist of fate because I hadn't expected to stay there, and one morning the telephone rang. It was Betty.

She asked to speak to John, but he wasn't there. Then, she asked for Larry...no luck there, either.

"Well who are you?" she asked me. "Larry's cousin?"

"No. My name is Sun Bear."

I told her about myself, that I'd hitch-hiked from California, to try to put a bill through Congress, that I worked in motion pictures, and that I'd run an arts and crafts center for the Indians at Reno Sparks.

That seemed to form a bond between us, the arts and crafts; she was an artist, and we decided to get together. She invited me up to her apartment to see her art work.

She lived on the Avenue of the Americas at that time; there was a good view of the city, and as I looked out over the rooftops for the first time — at the clotheslines, the TV antennas, the water towers — it amazed me that so many people could live so close together. How many stories, how many lives were there to tell about? The water towers were wooden and conical, and I remember that, in groupings, they reminded me in an abstract way of the huts in an African village. There were pigeons flying everywhere.

I liked Betty at once; she had black hair and deep blue eyes, and her bearing told me she was a strong person.

She is an excellent artist, and her paintings are very well-known today. She painted a lot of abstracts; they were definitely political, in favor of third-world nations, and of women. I've always liked abstracts in art; unlike most of Western culture, which is cut-and-dried, the abstract is open to interpretation; it can speak to the spirit.

Betty and I talked a lot together, about life, about ideas that were important to both of us. We used to walk the New York streets watching the busy people. It was interesting to see life in the big city. I remember a man who sold plastic raincoats on a street corner. When the rain came down heavy he charged two dollars apiece for them. When the rain began to pass and the sun threatened to come out, the price dropped to 75¢.

City life fascinated me. One morning, I remember, I heard the clattering of horses' hooves out on the pavement. I couldn't believe it. I jumped out of bed, ran to the window, and, sure enough, there were a bunch of horses going by. They were ridden by a group of mounted police. The policemen themselves looked like they were ready for battle, and I guess they had to be; they were all decked out in leathers, with visors on their helmets.

I felt sorry for the horses, their feet clacking on the pavement, their muscles all taut and their nostrils flaring. I found out later that they have to take a lot of mental punishment. They're so high-strung and take so much car and street noise that by the time they've been there for three or four years, they have to be put out to pasture.

Betty and I stayed together in New York for a month; then, we went to Bass Lake Farm in the Catskill Mountains, in upstate New York. We were summer counsellors at a camp there; I taught nature lore and Betty taught arts and crafts.

We enjoyed that summer; all the kids at the camp were from New York City. They hadn't been exposed to much country life; a lot of them were afraid of the natural world because they'd been shut off from it. They were frightened by thunder and lightning, by trees swaying in the wind; they didn't even want to sit on the ground because they were afraid the bugs would bite them.

I did what I could to remedy that situation, to let them know that the earth was their closest friend. While we were there I caught a woodchuck. We had another counsellor named Michael; he was a medical student. With his help, we dissected the woodchuck to show the kids what was inside of it. As we labeled each organ for them, we pointed out that they had the same things inside of their own bodies. They were all very curious about the woodchuck.

After the dissection, I cut up the meat into tiny pieces. We cooked it over a fire, and everybody got a piece to taste.

With summer over at Bass Lake Farm, Betty and I decided to travel to Los Angeles. First, I met her mother; she was an interesting lady. She was from a strong Jewish background, and didn't know quite what to make of me. When Betty told her she was interested in an Indian, her mother had said: "An Indian? What's an Indian? It's not a *yid*; not a *goy*...what is an Indian?"

Betty and I went off to California. We stopped in Minnesota along the way, and got into trading wild rice. My people, the Chippewa, have always grown rice in the state's lake regions. What Betty and I did was to buy the harvested rice. I would have it threshed, and then sell it to wholesalers for two dollars a pound.

We made our way across the country, picking up extra money by selling wild rice. We travelled as far south as Nebraska, then up to Sioux Falls, South Dakota, camping in an old panel truck.

I've always been a good one for eating roadkills; if you find an animal along the highway, freshly killed, it's almost a crime to let it go to waste. I've found and eaten too many kinds of animals to list, but some of the best have been deer and pheasant.

I remember, many times, pulling up beside an unfortunate roadkill. If it was a big animal, like a deer or antelope, people would be standing around, feeling sad. If the animal was in the way or something, they'd be speculating about what to do with it. I would always help them out. I would say: "I'll get rid of that for you."

Clearly, to me, such finds were feast gifts from the Great Spirit. But, if you want to eat roadkills, you'd better be sure they haven't been dead too long. If they smell bad, or they're stiff and bloated, you'd better move them out of the road and pray them on their way.

In South Dakota, Betty and I found lots of freshly-killed pheasants by the roadside. We'd take them up, clean them, pluck them, and pop them into the frying pan. Folks would come by and say, "My, that's good looking chicken you're eating".

When Betty and I first got to Los Angeles, we were living in the panel truck; it was December, and we managed a Christmas tree lot two blocks west of the MGM studios. There wasn't much doing in motion pictures right then, so selling the trees became our only source of income.

We parked the old truck on the Christmas tree lot, so we could watch the trees at night, and it was while we were sleeping in that lot, that my daughter Winona was conceived.

After the Christmas season, we began to look around for different work. Betty decided she would like to finish her college work, to get a teaching certificate, so she enrolled at L.A. State. We moved over to the east side to be close to the campus, and I landed a few jobs with the movies and TV.

I had a lot of time to think and learn while Betty was in school, while she was carrying Winona. Since I was working for the motion picture industry, the pay was good enough to give me some free time. I hung out in Griffith Park and Elysian Park, spent time there enjoying nature, making my medicine and prayers, and trying to strengthen my spiritual path, as well as my knowledge of traditional Native ways. When time allowed, I'd go down to Nevada to visit folks, or to the Lake Isabel area, north of Los Angeles. I enjoyed the time alone.

Sometimes, out near Lancaster, which is also north of L.A., there were places where I could be totally alone in the desert. I felt many good energies there.

I became involved in more Native groups at that time, too. One which was forming in the L.A. area was called the Federated Indian Tribes, and was made up of non-drinking Native people, who were trying to restore the traditional way of life. We also formed what we called the *Black Elk Kituah* society, in honor of Black Elk, the famous Sioux holy man. On weekends we'd get together at Doc Spotted Wolf's place. He was the head of the Federated Indian Tribes, a medicine man, and also a medical doctor. Both as Dr. John Jeffries, and as Doc Spotted Wolf, he shared his knowledge with us. We would all exchange cultural knowledge, and we'd do our chants and songs. Sometimes we'd fast the whole weekend.

Doc Spotted Wolf had built a sweatlodge in his back yard, in the middle of the city. He fixed it up so the neighbors couldn't see it. After our fasts, we'd go into the sweatlodge to do ceremonies, and after we had sweated and prayed, we'd wash down with a hose or in a cold tub of water. After that we'd share a potluck dinner. So you see, if you really want to pray and do ceremonies, you can do them anywhere. This doesn't mean that you should be indiscreet in your ceremonies and expose them to curiosity-seekers who lack knowledge of their sacredness. It means that you can do ceremonies properly even in the middle of the city, if you use proper care in planning for them.

Doc Spotted Wolf was a really good and generous man, who taught me many things about ways in which the Native culture could flourish within this society. He was both a brother and a spiritual father to me, and I was, and am, very grateful for the friendship, and the teaching that he shared with me.

We had a place nearby which we called Buffalo Wallow. We'd do our pow wow dancing and ceremonies there.

In the early 60's, as a result of our push for recognition, the Native people began to get some good attention. There were some anti-poverty programs on the horizon, but nothing was being done yet on a governmental level. So we pushed a little more. We started a lot of Saturday night pow wows, which were, at first, just social events. There were many Native clubs forming: the Drum and Feather Club; Many Trails; the American Indian Dancers. The Navajo had a club, as well as the Hopi. Any Native person was welcome at any of the club meetings. I was glad to see the pride in Native heritage and ways growing stronger. We'd bring in people from different tribes and let them share their knowledge with each other. They taught each other about their dances, their drumming and their songs. It was all part of our effort to rekindle pride.

I like to believe that those small grassroots efforts set the stage, later, for bigger Native crusades, and for the government aid programs which eventually came into being.

Gradually, more Indian clubs formed in the Los Angeles area; the people would put on their dances, and do their beadwork, but soon they began to look for something deeper. They returned to the pipe and the drum, and traditional prayers, and it was good; it was the early Native Renaissance.

In 1961, in Los Angeles, I started publishing *Many Smokes*. At that time it was aimed mainly at Native Americans; it came out as a monthly mimeographed sheet, for fifteen cents a copy. I guess its conception and publication were inspired by that early political climate; my feeling in starting a national Indian magazine was that if people from different tribes could get together, they might retribalize. I hoped that they could set up a whole new tribal structure, something universal, to fill in the cultural void that was killing their spirits.

I chose "Many Smokes" as the name of the magazine, because I wanted to call to mind the smoke signals, the communication of many tribes joined together, as well as make reference to smoking the medicine pipe.

Many Smokes came out originally through the Los Angeles Indian Center, but it wasn't affiliated with it, or any group in particular; I wanted to keep it free so it wouldn't develop a prejudice toward any one tribe or region. In the early issues, I listed pow wow meetings, weddings, births, and other Indian events. It was a small thing, but it was a start; it made my people feel good, a little closer to each other.

As the magazine grew in scope, it got to be known as a writer's publication. Well-known columnists such as Matt Weinstock from the *L.A. Times*, and Paul Coates, would quote from my little *Many Smokes*. One of my editorials was reprinted in *America the Beautiful*, and another one really made the rounds. The editorial was called *Love or Perish*, and was reprinted in both *Playboy* and *The Catholic Register*. That was quite a combination.

I had begun, gradually, to cover larger, more political Native issues, news events of national scope, and as my vision has grown, the magazine has become an earth awareness journal aimed at self-reliance, living in harmony on the Earth Mother, and the general unification of all the world's people. Today, *Wildfire* is circulated worldwide; it goes to Germany, England, New Zealand, and many other areas, as well as the U.S. and Canada.

After I left L.A. there was a lull of two and one-half years in the publishing of *Many Smokes*, while I sorted out some financial and personal matters; then I resumed its publication, still independently, in 1966.

*****

I went up to Death Valley one time during this period, with a few friends, to take a look at the Shoshone Reservation. When we got there, we discovered there was hardly anybody living there, but the countryside was beautiful. The few brothers and sisters we did meet there were camping out; they told us that someone was supposed to bring in food supplies, but hadn't done it. They were hungry, so I walked with them, and showed them some food that was growing right in front of them.

"If your groceries don't come in," I told them, "you can eat some of these mesquite beans. Over there," I pointed out, "there are wild figs, and here are some other edible plants."

I found out later that their supplies never got there; they told me they were thankful for what I'd shown them, that it helped them to make it.

While I was at the Shoshone Reservation, my friends and I decided to make a medicine run. That's one way we strengthen our medicine and power, like the old Bear Medicine Men of the Pomos did.

It was a moonlit night, and I could feel power rise up from the Mother Earth. All the natural forces of the Creator were feeding my body. I felt like I had become a deer. I ran under the moon for maybe twenty miles; it didn't even tire me. I ran half the night, and when I got back to where I started from, I only slept a few hours and felt refreshed. It reminded me of the time with the peyote brothers, when I became an eagle.

It was really a powerful experience, that run; it was as if the area's good energy became a part of me.

When Winona was born, in August, I spent a lot more time at home. Betty was busy with her studies, so someone had to help out with the housework, and that was me. I had a good time with my baby daughter then, bathing her and feeding her, doing the laundry, the diapers, and all of the things that a man usually doesn't do. Winona was a bright one, and the smarter they are when they're babies, the more work I think they are.

I took her on interviews; she came with me when I worked on movie sets, and one time when I was being interviewed for a movie role, she sat patiently waiting on Tony Curtis's lap. I took her to Indian Center meetings and pow wow dances. She really enjoyed watching the dances. That was a good time in my life.

When Betty finished her degree work at L.A. State, she got a job teaching art at an east side high school, and continued further with her studies. She had bought an etching press, and was learning a lot more about her work. She was busy most of the time.

It was, I think, when she'd finished with her college work that we realized how far apart we'd grown. After four and a half years together, we thought about separating. We were two different people, after all, and we each believed strongly in our own life paths, and what we needed to accomplish.

Betty wanted to move up to Oregon, where she had been offered a teaching job at Southern Oregon State College in Ashland, and I had other plans. I'd met some Quaker people about that time who had a house up in Altadena, California. They had let me stay there during my travels, and the seed of a big idea had come to me.

I wanted to set up a community of Native people in Altadena, a place where Indian people could live and work and share together. Catherine Howell, the owner of the house, gave me free use of it, so my idea was slowly taking shape. It was part of my unfolding dream and vision.

Betty and I decided to split the blanket, to separate. Winona was four then, and we decided that a little girl needs her mother, so she went with Betty to Oregon.

I remember when I helped Betty move, we had a bowl with two goldfish in it. I took the bowl to the park near Third Street, and I let the goldfish go in a big pond. It made me think of Betty and myself, in the world-pond, travelling our separate ways.

I felt very sad, but I also felt very good inside. The goldfish helped; they went on their separate paths, but they were free. I would miss Betty and Winona, but I would get to see them...and I knew that a part of my medicine was growth, that everything that I was learning in life, everything I was doing, was vital to that growth.

Betty is a very well-known artist today, a professor of art, and a world-travelling lecturer. I wish her the best of everything; I remember her, and our years together, as a happy time, as a time of very good feelings.

Winona is now a Harvard graduate, a successful lady who works for Native rights, and the anti-nuclear movement. She's involved with the Indian Treaty Council, and Women of All Red Nations, and she travels all over the world to promote what she believes in. She has also been Principal of the Circle of Life School, an alternative high school for my people on the White Earth Reservation.

I'm very proud of Winona. It seems that our heart paths stayed close together, even though we were physically separate. We meet now, when she visits Vision Mountain, or when we share a stage, or find ourselves working in the same location.

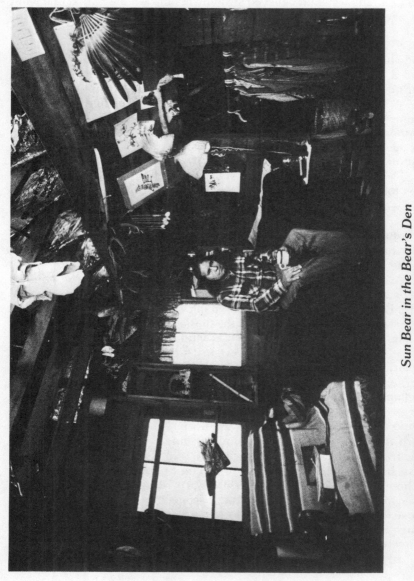

Sun Bear in the Bear's Den
Being in balance means being at home wherever you are on the Earth Mother.

CHAPTER NINE
TRAILERS AND INTERTRIBAL COUNCILS

I went up to Altadena after Betty left, and started a little community which turned out to be a halfway house for Native people. It was a good thing to do, and part of my medicine.

Those who wanted to help themselves at Altadena did very well, but there were a few there who didn't make it easy for us. Originally, the place was started as just a guest house for Native people who wanted to live and work together. I was trying to create an inner-city Indian center, but I'd made it clear from the beginning that there would be no drinking allowed. I told all of the brothers and sisters who were there that if they really wanted the thing to work, we'd have to be very strict about that; I would boot out anyone who was caught with liquor.

One night, I went up there with a friend of mine, Michael Wayne, who is a California Mission Indian. I sensed that there was going to be some trouble, and I was right. There were five guys up there who had been drinking, and they planned to beat me up and cut my hair as a gesture of contempt. I knew that Mike wasn't much into fighting, and I sensed the trouble as soon as we walked in the door, so I told Mike to just get the light switch, and back off. These fellows were armed with knives, but my medicine was stronger. I managed to disarm them. After a good scuffle, I sent them on down the trail.

Later, people would ask Mike what happened in the big fight, and Mike would just smile and tell them, "Well, Sun Bear just surrounded them."

I got some other people to move in at Altadena, who were more centered into self-improvement. Oliver Frank, a Nez Perce Indian who is an authority on the history and legends of his people, moved in, as well as some older folks who were much easier to get along with.

I was still acting to support myself, and at the same time, running the halfway house; still, I took on a third job. I took over a gas station on West Third Street in Los Angeles, near the Silver Lake District. I hired an Indian friend to run the station while I was not there, and hoped for the best, but things didn't go too well.

I had spread myself thin; I wasn't around the service station enough, really, to keep things running smoothly. One of my employees spent most of his time sleeping on the job. Bob Babcock, from the Indian Center, went by the place one day and found the attendant snoozing in a chair, with a sandwich dangling from his hand. Bob told me the guy looked very comfortable.

I lost about $1,500 in the service station venture, but I gained a lot of laughs. People, it seemed, wanted every kind of service from us except the ones we were there to give. I had a guy call up one day to tell me he needed a battery charged.

"Sure," I told him, "Come on over."

When he got there he wanted to buy a battery on credit. He said I had told him that I would charge it. He was a real smartass.

One of my strangest customers brought his dog into the station.

"Would you put a collar on my dog?" he asked me.

"Why don't you put it on yourself?"

"Because he bites. You think I'm crazy?" the fellow replied.

"I'm pretty sane myself," I told him. "And that's not really one of our services here. Why don't you take him across the street, to the Standard Oil station. The manager over there is really good with animals."

The halfway house at Altadena had run its course. It taught me more than I knew before about community life, and thus prepared me for being able, at a later time, to fulfill more of my vision. My gas station went downhill. In 1964, I decided I'd had enough of California for awhile, and I headed back to Reno. Good sage brush country, Nevada; I decided it was time to open up more to life, to learn more about my medicine, and to keep myself free to grow.

In Reno I worked for Bill Darling; he owned the Pizza Oven Delicatessen and the Pizza Oven Restaurant. I managed both places for awhile, when he went up to Canada to transact some business.

The pizza business was not too inspiring; I had problems with some of my staff. Alcohol, again, interfered. There was a cook at the restaurant who was always sneaking in the booze; when I told him he couldn't drink on the job, he'd always find a way. One time, I remember, he asked me for a quart of wine for some special dishes. I got him the wine and I don't have to tell you where it went.

The cook's name was Barney; the more he drank, the more belligerent he would get. He really tried my patience; he had a habit, when juiced up, of lecturing the waitresses, shaking his finger at them. One day he started finger-shaking right in my face. I never had a business management course in school, so I go with my instincts. When Barney stuck that finger in my face I grabbed his hand; I chomped down on the finger as hard as I could. I think that cured him.

We had another cook at the Pizza Oven who would fly into tantrums if somebody crossed him. We'd be in the middle of a dinner rush, the restaurant filled with customers and the order slips piled an inch thick, and this guy would fall down on the floor, start rolling around like a maniac, and kicking his feet like a kid. It's a good way to get rid of pain, to do that; lots of times I have my students dig a hole in the ground and shout into it to empty themselves of anger. But this cook wasn't getting rid of pain, really; he was just *being* a pain. He thought he was a tempermental artist.

When Bill came back from Canada, I was happy to retire from my management position. I hung around the delicatessen and delivered pizzas for awhile, and I worked on my gambling medicine. I'd done pretty well a few times at craps and keno; once I held the dice at Harrahs for thirty-five minutes. I was betting small that time, so I only took home about $450. The guy standing next to me, though, was a big bettor; he had confidence in me, and he took home $4,000.

I would sit in a booth at the Pizza Oven and the shills — the folks who played games for the casinos — would call me on the phone. "Hey Sun Bear," I would get a message, "There's a big game over at the Cal Neva," or "Good craps being shot at the Palace Club." I'd go down there, whenever they thought I ought to try my luck; if I did real well I'd tip the shill who called me. One time I sat down to play bingo, to take a break from the crap game I was in, and hit a lucky coverall immediately. It netted me $500.

I took a job driving a cab in Reno, while I kept on working at my gambling medicine. I didn't have gambling fever, like so many people get; I could take the dice or leave them. It just felt really good, bringing in big chunks of green energy, one after another. Medicine power is good for all things, you see; if the Great Spirit wants me to win at craps or keno, I figure who am I to turn down the opportunity? At the Bear Tribe today, we make medicine for spiritual things, of course; we also make medicine, though, for new tires or refrigerators. We believe that everything we *need* to keep us on the good road is part of the great vision.

Driving a taxi, I met many interesting people. I met some lucky gamblers, and got good tips. I met a few unlucky gamblers, and sometimes had a hard time collecting my fares from them.

Reno is famous for quick marriages and divorces, and I had my share of couples buying rides from me. I picked up a couple one time, who were both pretty drunk. They asked me to take them to the courthouse; they were getting married. "Okay," I remember thinking, "it should be quite a shocker when they wake up in the morning; I don't think they even know each other."

The lady told me to pull into a gas station parking lot; she had to go to the bathroom. While she was in the lady's room, her fiancee and I got to talking. One thing led to another, and he decided he wasn't really sure about the commitment he was about to make.

He asked what else there was to do.

"Well," I told him, "I could take you out to Mustang Ranch instead. You could really have some fun there."

We talked awhile longer and he decided that a night at Mustang Ranch, which was a house of ill-repute, might be better for him than marriage, in the long run.

So I took him there.

A few times, I took people to the courthouse to get married, only to have them discover they'd been stood up at the altar; it was a sad thing to watch. They'd go in all enthusiastic, and come out depressed and at a loss for what to do. Sometimes, they got back into the cab and told me to take them to the *Bridge of Sorrows*.

That was a popular trip for folks back then; the Bridge of Sorrows spanned the Truckee River. It was a traditional spot for despondent lovers and disappointed spouses to go to, to drop their tears into the water. They also dropped in their wedding and engagement rings.

Since the prices of gold and silver have gone so high, I think that tradition has pretty much died out, but back in those days there were rings flying into the water all the time. There was also a group of enterprising young men who would make a yearly dive under the bridge; they'd retrieve quite a haul of tossed-out treasure. The place might have been a bridge of sorrows for despondent lovers, but for those boys who scavenged the river, I think the bridge should have been called the "Bridge of Very Good Profit."

During this time, I had a powerful encounter with a rattlesnake. I was out near Pyramid Lake, making a run across the desert; I was enjoying myself, and really feeling exuberant. When I jumped over a clump of rocks and bushes, brother rattler was coiled in the sand. He didn't have any time to warn me, and I didn't have time to get out of his way, so he struck; he bit me in the upper calf.

After the rattler bit me, very quickly, I felt a rush of its energy and power; it coursed through me. It was like a vibrating, trembling energy, that travelled up one side of my body and down the other.

I talked to the rattlesnake for a moment; I apologized for invading his territory like that, and I asked that his power merge with mine in a good way. After that, I got up and walked back to my car, which was about a mile and a half away. Then I drove into Reno, and went to bed for a few days.

It was a funny thing; I guess word spread really quickly that I had been bitten by a rattler. The neighbors were all pretty curious; they kept on coming over to look at the snake bite, and to watch me. Finally, I had to tell them, "Look folks, I'd really like to get some rest. If you keep coming over here, I'm going to have to start charging you admission, for watching to see if I die."

I took a couple of aspirin, and I finally went to sleep. I had a pretty bad headache from the experience.

I feel, though, that it was a positive thing. I don't recommend it for other people, but it did do something for me. I feel that by taking in the rattler's poison, I was taking its power into me, and ever since that time, I've felt a very close brotherhood with every kind of snake. The rattlesnake, now, helps me to make rain — but I'll talk about that later.

I did none of the cutting, sucking and spitting that is recommended for snake bite; the wound was swollen and discolored for three or four days, and I was laid up in bed for that period of time, but then it went away. I feel, finally, that if I had panicked, instead of intensely believing in my blending energy with the Great Spirit's creations, that the situation could have been a serious one for me, but fortunately, I didn't.

I worked in Reno until May of 1965. At that time I had a dream about the keno game. I went to the Cal Neva the next day, a gambling casino, and played the numbers. I hit seven out of eight, which meant a jackpot of $1,100.

I was waiting at a keno marking table, until there was room for me to eat lunch in the restaurant. I marked the eight spot and I looked at it, and then at the keno board and I thought, *hey, I hit something*. At first, I thought I'd only hit a 6-spot, and that felt good because it would have meant $50. Then I realized I'd really hit it big. I felt rushes of good power.

I've done really well at gambling other times too. I've had dreams and four times I've won $1100; once, $535; and once, $100 on dream tickets. I figure that if you can bank on your dreams you have to believe in them. When the dreams aren't working, I can lose a good deal too, but I guess over a ten year period, I've won about $16,000.

My reputation has spread. Folks come up to me at the keno tables when I'm playing, and they ask me, "What are the lucky numbers, Sun Bear?" I tell them: "The ones that light up at the end of the game."

Keno is a very old Chinese game that used to be played by Chinese laundrymen; they called it keno races then, and there used to be eighty Chinese symbols on the board. Now there are eighty numbers.

Keno, as it's played today in Reno or Las Vegas, can mean very big money. You buy your keno cards and you mark your numbers down. The house draws twenty ping pong balls with numbers on them out of a cage, and if you win, you can make anywhere from $5 to $20,000.

After I hit the lucky keno ticket, my pocket was bulging with money. I put most of it into the bank, then decided to travel to California.

I'd heard a lot about the Berkeley Free Speech Movement,and I wanted to check it out firsthand.

There was so much publicity; it seemed like an exciting place to be, and it really was. I met a few folks when I first got there, and stayed in a house on Telegraph Avenue. The more I talked to people, the more often I heard that Charlie Brown wanted to meet me. I had no idea at the time who Charlie Brown was, but finally, I met him. He was an active participant in the Free Speech Movement.

For those of you who might have been somewhere else back then, the Free Speech Movement was a liberation movement that pre-dated so many others... women's lib, gay lib. The central issue of the Free Speech Movement was some students' belief that they should have a voice in the policies of the University of California at Berkeley. A side issue was students' right to use profanity. It was this side issue that was getting all of the attention in the press. I knew I was in favor of people having a voice in issues that affected them but I didn't know how I stood on the profanity issue. Most Native American language groups don't even *include* what you would call curse words — but the idea that the students were fighting for a cause seemed interesting to me.

Clark Kerr, the President of U.C. Berkeley at that time, was not too agreeable with the student demands; I think several students had been booted out of school for using profanity, and that kicked off some trouble. During the protest rallies, I remember seeing students who wore badges or carried banners which read, "Freedom Under Clark Kerr". The first letter of each word had been capitalized, so nobody would miss the protesters' message.

Berkeley was intense back then. Sometimes, things got out of control. There were, however, a couple of places where activists could meet and talk things out; one was a coffee house called "The Forum". Another was the Mediterranean. Cigarette smoke was thick and guitar music mingled with hot political discussions in these places. On Telegraph Avenue politics were mixed with marijuana — a drug surrounded by other issues of personal freedom.

I never participated in the drugs there, but I watched it all very closely. When a natural narcotic is used ceremonially for spiritual expansion, like peyote can be, then that is good. But I don't believe in using chemical additives. LSD, and other hallucinogens, I think, can be very bad, and marijuana becomes a prop.

I've seen too many lives destroyed by chemicals, and in most cases, there's no spirituality attached to their consumption, only escapism. Many folks who pop these drugs, it seems to me, don't do it to look inside themselves, to resolve their negative feelings, such as guilt or anger, but to drown themselves, to bury their heads in the sand.

Anyway, I wanted to watch it all happen during the Free Speech Movement. I wanted to learn from the joy and pain of other people. I met Charlie Brown finally, and he invited me to a Teton Tea Party. These parties were political in nature, attended by lots of practicing musicians, and had first been started in Wyoming's Grand Teton Mountains...so, coincidentally, they had a name which was related to the Native people, the Teton Sioux.

The Teton Tea Parties were really something; there were many people at them, lots of guitarists and folk musicians who later became famous for their political music, and their crusades for the environment. Wherever you looked, there were people struggling to build their values. There were lots of leeches, too, at those parties, but the lazy ones tended to fall by the wayside, after awhile.

A lot of folks at these parties were broke; that's what happens when you're struggling with your ideals. Many of the parties were held at the Forum, and most folks would just drink coffee, but some people ate, and then the rest of us would walk around looking for leftovers. Charlie Brown would walk up to a table, point at the scraps on someone's plate, and say: "Can I have that?" He'd get a slice of meat or cheese that way, I'd get us some bread, and before you knew it we had ourselves a real good meal. After the party was over, a bunch of us would go out into the countryside, where we'd scour the trees for fruit; that made a wonderful dessert.

That was the energy of Berkeley in the middle 1960's. I wanted to experience it, and I'm glad I did.

I met Annie Ross, now Nimimosha of the Bear Tribe, at one of the Teton Tea Parties. She'd hitch-hiked up from San Mateo, where she'd been living while doing some college work. I remember her walking into the place with a man hanging on each arm. She was really attractive, and we talked for a long time.

She told me that she was looking for some direction in her life, that she was in college killing time — taking some journalism courses, but majoring in nothing special. I told her about *Many Smokes*, and asked her if she would like to work with me. We left the party and went somewhere else for coffee; she noticed a Kachina doll which I had sitting in my car, and asked me about it. I told her about the Kachinas, and about a lot of other Native objects I had in the car, and she seemed very interested.

Annie is a very gentle person, very loving; in fact, her tribal name, Nimimosha, means "woman with a heart of love" or "the one who loves her relatives". She'd been coming to Berkeley because she was sort of lost herself, not knowing what to do with her life, but she told me she was frightened by the potential violence there. Also, she said, she hated the insanity of the establishment at that time. When I told her something about my philosophy, about my vision of bringing people together to live in harmony with the earth, she decided to come with me.

After we grew tired of the Berkeley scene, we went down to Reno for a visit; Charlie Brown came with us. Then we moved on to

Los Angeles, where I planned to work in motion pictures again.

Charlie wanted to stay with us, but he didn't seem quite ready for our trip, so he got off at the Self-Realization Center in L.A. and Annie and I began working together.

Annie got a job in an insurance office, and I worked in a few episodes of "Rawhide". Later, I worked in "The Greatest Story Ever Told".

While we were in Los Angeles, I drove around in a used L.A. police car, which I'd bought at a good price. It was a lot of fun; I didn't bother to repaint it, and I'd go around selling *Many Smokes* out of my squad car at the Indian taverns and at the pow wows. I remember, one time, taking a slightly drunk Native friend home from a pow wow in my police car. He wanted to stop for a six-pack, so I pulled up to a liquor store. He went in and bought his beer, and I could see the clerk inside scratching his head. He told my buddy it was the first time he'd ever seen the cops drive a drunken Indian to a liquor store.

Annie and I decided Los Angeles was not a good place to be, so after a few months, we packed up and moved back to Reno. There were two other ladies who came with us; they also wanted to work on *Many Smokes*, so we had two cars. Annie and I were in one car, and the other two women, their three dogs and a cat were in the other.

I guess you could say that this tiny caravan was the seed of the Bear Tribe Medicine Society.

My vision had been unfolding, year by year; it had begun when I was four, with the vision of the bear and the colored spheres, during my bout with diphtheria. The colored balls, now, I interpret to be the energy of the Medicine Society, that heals and teaches those who come to us to learn.

Each year, something new had come to me: a new vision, an idea, until I realized, finally, that what I wanted to do was bring a group of people together in a single place — to live, to work, and to build our own medicine power to heal ourselves, our relations and the Mother Earth.

At first, my vision included only Native Americans, but as time went by, my vision grew, and I realized that ancient prophecies not only allowed for the acceptance of all races; they actually predicted it.

The Hopi prophecies, along with many others, foretold a time of great purification, a time when the Earth Mother would shrug off the poisons of pollution, as well as the creators of these poisons. The time is very close, according to the prophecies, and many of us can see the signs. Natural disasters, such as floods, volcanic eruptions, and earthquakes were to come, and they have. Mount Saint Helens is only a beginning. The present world, it is said, will soon experience even more drastic changes.

The prophecies of the Hopi people foresaw both world wars, one to be fought against the sun sign (Japan), and one against the swastika. They foresaw the invention of the automobile, the airplane, even the atom bomb. Ancient prophecies also spoke of the time when the sons of white men would grow their hair long, wear beads, and live in communal societies. When that time came, according to the Native prophets, the cleansing would be at hand. It happened in the sixties, with flower power, the anti-Vietnam protesters, the Berkeley Free Speech Movement, and so on.

Native prophecies and visions say that those mixed-blood and white people who grew their hair long and wore beads would come to us Native healers, and ask for guidance ... that they would be incarnations of the Indians slaughtered during the conquest of the continent.

So you see, I believed, even back in the early years, that if any person came to me and asked to learn medicine ways, I should work with him or her. Not necessarily because he or she might be a reincarnated Indian, but because that person wanted to learn to walk in balance on the Mother Earth.

My view was not shared by too many Native medicine people, but more are coming around to it as time goes by.

I thought of all of these things as our caravan drove toward Reno.

When we got there, we rented an apartment that was big enough for all of us, and we started up *Many Smokes* as a quarterly magazine. This was 1966.

I remember that the first issue we produced was mimeographed, with a silk screen cover; it went so well and we got such a good response from local business people who wanted to advertise in it, that I decided to make it into a glossy national magazine.

With so much encouragement, I really hustled. I got six or seven hundred dollars worth of advertising for the next issue, which paid for its printing. We printed it through a friend of mine in Sparks, named Ted Marsten, and its circulation grew with every issue. Some of those first advertisers from Reno still put ads into *Wildfire* today.

We made enough money to support ourselves for awhile, and then I was offered a job with the Intertribal Council of Nevada, as a community developer for the Reno Sparks Indian colony. That was a dream come true for me, because of all the work I'd done there, and because I had a lot of other projects in mind for the people there.

Most of the projects we initiated were clean-up operations; we'd already painted the houses, and hauled out tons of trash. There was no garbage service for the folks there, so the first thing we did was to organize a system to get rid of the trash on a regular basis. After that, we decided to clean up an area that was filled with rusty automobile carcasses. That took a lot of money, but we got donations from people in the area. With the help of a doctor friend named Fred Anderson, we managed to raise funds from local service clubs, through government matching funds, and through local construction companies, and we built a park in the area where we'd removed the old car wrecks. Today that park site has grown into a big recreational complex.

We worked towards getting natural gas hook-ups for a lot of homes in Reno Sparks; we developed a water and sewer project there, which was very therapeutic for the residents. There were many alcoholics there, as always, where Indians are forced to live with such low standards. What I did was to get the necessary equipment and have those people operate the machinery: back hoes, tractors, trucks. I remember sometimes having to haul these people out of bed in the morning, pump coffee into them, and shove them into the heavy equipment. I wasn't nervous about them hurting themselves or anybody else, because, once I had them ready to go to work, they were alert and very happy.

A lot of those people, through this governmental-incentive program, learned to be professional equipment operators and are successfully working at their trades today.

At Reno Sparks, also, we renovated two old church buildings, and transformed them into a center for Indian programs.

The Intertribal Council of Nevada was funded by the Office of Economic Opportunity, which gave us a lot of grant money to complete our projects. The Nevada Council, after awhile, was considered to be one of the most successful in the country. This was partly because we believed so strongly in what we were trying to do, and partly because, unlike the situation in many other programs, there was no graft or corruption. Every penny that the government gave me for community development at Reno Sparks went into community improvement.

We got to be such a good example of O.E.O. success at Reno Sparks that, after awhile, the folks in Washington would send the bigwigs down to look around. They'd call me or write and say, "There's a group coming down tomorrow, Sun Bear. We want them to see your program, so they'll understand how well these projects can go."

I was proud of that.

The people at the Reno Sparks Indian Colony have continued making improvements, and today it is a very fine looking community. Many of my friends are part of that improvement.

At the same time that I was working with Reno Sparks, I was doing a lot of good gambling. My medicine stood by me; I made enough at gambling to buy a little trailer, and Annie and I moved to a mobile home park in Sun Valley, north of Reno. There'd been a little friction, with the four of us in the same apartment, so it seemed like a good move.

The trailer wasn't much, but it was home. It had no running water at first, no electricity, not even any glass in the windows. The first winter there was really rough.

Annie was working in Reno. At one time she was a receptionist; another time she did keypunch; and she even worked for a time, ironically, at a parts-supply company for earth-moving equipment. It was really something to watch her in the mornings. We'd creep out of bed and light a little sagebrush fire, at the edge of the high desert; then we'd cook our breakfast on it. Afterwards, Annie would get herself all dressed up...heels, stockings, fancy dress, the works. She would go off to the business world for the day.

After awhile, we had enough money to buy a bigger trailer, and my luck ran even better. When we'd been living at Sun Valley for about six months, the owner of the trailer park asked me if I'd like to own it. He was tired of the headaches of running it.

I said "Sure".

It wasn't an outright gift, the trailer park, but it came close to that, and it felt very good.

We managed the Sun Valley trailer park for three and one-half years, and during that time we managed to make it pay. Before too long, we actually were solvent.

Managing a trailer court turned out to be quite a challenge; it wasn't the trailers or the property — it was the people. We had folks slipping out in the middle of the night, to avoid paying back rent. Some of them, to make things worse, would pack up the furniture before they left. So we had some very empty trailers.

One night I was feeling suspicious of a particular tenant. Something told me he would be leaving, so I parked my car where it would block his exit. I walked up to his trailer in the dark, and sure enough, he was packed to go. He had loaded as much of my furniture as he could carry into his car. When he saw me coming he spun his wheels and tried to make a getaway, but I had him in a box. Finally, he gave up the battle, and I got my furniture back.

Another time, two women came in and rented a trailer — just for themselves, they said. The next thing I knew, we had a motorcycle gang called the Misfits living in our little trailer court. There were six of them, but from the noise and confusion you would have thought there were sixty.

I had to have a pow wow with them, so I went down to the trailer one night.

"Look guys," I said to them, "I don't know what you do in California, but out here we like it nice and quiet. I don't want any stealing here, or any hell-raising, and then we'll all be buddies. Is that okay?"

"Sure, Sun Bear," they told me, and they kept their word. We got along fine. During their stay they kept guard on our trailer, so if Annie was alone, they were her self-appointed bodyguards. If anyone came there and stayed "too long", one of the Misfits would come up on some pretense, to be sure she was alright.

There was only one incident involving the Misfits that could have turned into real trouble. One fine afternoon while they were all out on their bikes, a delegation of Hell's Angels came riding into the trailer court. They said they were looking for the Misfits, and I knew enough about the Hell's Angels to realize that probably meant some bad business.

"Nope," I said to them, "I can't say as I've seen anyone around here called the Misfits."

They hung around for awhile, but luckily they took off before their prey returned.

Later, I found out that the Misfits had stolen a bike from the Hell's Angels, down in southern California.

"I guess we better not steal from them again," one of the Misfits remarked, when I told him they'd had visitors. I heartily agreed with him.

While I was running the trailer court, there were times when I had to take the law into my own hands. The Washoe County Sheriff's Department didn't mind; they were pretty busy, and they knew I wouldn't overstep my bounds. I dealt with what they would call the rinky-dink problems. One time a neighbor kid stole the tires off my station wagon. I went over to see him, and I told him I was pretty angry.

"Okay," he shrugged, "I'll put the tires back on for you. I didn't know you wanted them on the car."

For awhile, we had a kid from California named Teddy living with us; he was sent to us for rehabilitation, after several episodes of delinquency. While Teddy was with us, he developed a fascination for a neighbor's snow plow blade. He just had to have it, so he arranged to get help, and carried it off in his pick-up.

The man he stole the plow blade from came cruising into my trailer court one day, because he saw his blade lying on the ground. His son was a highway patrolman, it turned out, and he threatened to have Teddy thrown in jail.

"I would hate to see that happen, " I told the man, "you know, he's down here to be rehabilitated."

We managed to work things out.

Teddy stayed with us for about another month, and when he left, I wasn't quite so patient with him. He took with him a go-cart that belonged to me.

I was pretty upset about it; I called him down in California and I said, "You know Teddy, it's a funny thing, but you and my go-cart disappeared at exactly the same time."

"I don't know a thing about it," Teddy replied.

"Now, Teddy," I told him, "I know damn well you took my go-cart."

"Well, Sun Bear, you see my pick-up wasn't running so hot, and it broke down..."

"Teddy, I don't care about your pick-up; I just want my go-cart...and quick. I don't care if you have to carry it piggy-back. And I'll tell you, Teddy, if you don't get it back here, I'll have you put so far back in the jailhouse it'll take the guards a month to find you, to feed you or give you cigarettes."

Three days later, my go-cart was back where it belonged.

Another time, a drunk young lady smashed into my fence at 3 a.m. Her car was hung up in the fencing, and her tires were spinning in the mud, so she couldn't get away. She was about as drunk as anyone

I'd ever seen, and she was moaning and groaning, "Oh my God! You're gonna call the cops, and they'll take away my license, and they'll throw me into jail!"

At about that time two sheriff's deputies showed up; they asked me if I wanted to prefer charges.

"Nope," I told them, "I don't think that I really want to do that. I'll handle this myself."

"So what are you going to do with me?" the girl asked me, after they were gone.

"I don't really know yet," I told her. "I'm thinking about it. You know, I really hate it when people drive in here at three a.m., and smash up my fence and wake me up. And it makes me sad and angry to see someone your age so drunk. How old are you, anyway?"

"Twenty-three," she told me.

What I ended up doing with her, finally, was to flip her over my knee. I gave her a good paddling, and I told her I expected to see her in the morning. I wanted her to fix my fence.

The following day she came back with her brother and her boyfriend, and they fixed up the fence so that it was better than before. They even painted it.

During that time in Sun Valley, there were more and more people coming to stay with me. Some were interested in learning Native ways; others wanted to try to form a community. I gave a lot of these people reduced rent, so they could stick around while we tried to work things out. Some of them went out looking for jobs; others helped with maintenance around the trailer court. A lot of these people, I'm sorry to say, didn't work out too well. Only one girl actually got a job, with the neighborhood youth corps. The others who went into town were wasting energy; they were young people who wanted medicine without doing any work. They wanted what I call the badges of power ... the rattles, the feathers, the joy ... without the effort. They were programmed into smoking marijuana, and they got into trouble with the police in downtown Reno. They were real smartasses, some of them; they would even smoke their joints in the police station.

But while it was happening, I didn't know any of this was going on.

I found out quickly, though. The Reno police were pretty hot about the whole thing, but Sun Valley was out of their jurisdiction. So they got in touch with the Washoe County Sheriff's Department, and one night we had a raid on the trailer court. There were three carloads of deputies with the sheriff, and one of the deputies was an Osage Indian whom I'd worked with down in Reno Sparks. His name was Billy Don.

"Let me talk to Sun Bear," he told the others, "before we go in there."

Billy Don woke me up. He told me what had been going on, and that I'd better get rid of these kids.

"Billy," I told him, "don't pull off the raid. Just walk around with me and we'll pull ID's. We'll throw a good scare into them, and I'll take care of the rest tomorrow morning."

He thought that felt good, so that's what we did; we barged into the trailers of the offenders, and we really shook them up.

The following morning, I sent them on their way.

"Well, folks", I told them, "we tried to work with a good idea here, but you seem to belong on a different path, at least for now. What I'm trying to build takes a sense of responsibility and consideration for other people. Without that to begin with, we can't show love and harmony, either for ourselves or the Earth Mother."

So they were all gone. One of my maintenance men later referred to that group as my *social experiment*; I was hoping we could all come together, and work with the Earth Mother in a productive way. They simply weren't ready. Unfortunately, there are many people who sit on the fence like that; they want to be free of the prison of society, but they're not ready to give themselves fully to being responsible for themselves and the Mother Earth.

I want to say a few more words about Billy Don here; he was quite a guy. He ended up getting the job with the Sheriff's Department because he was really tough. The fellow before him, who worked with the law at Reno Sparks, had been badly beaten; despite all the self-help programs and the improvements, there were still a lot of drunks and real hard cases in the colony.

I knew the people down there, and Billy asked my advice when he first took the job.

"I'll tell you, Billy," I'd said to him, "there's one rule I think you'll need to go by. Whatever you tell those folks you're going to do, you'd better do. If you say you're going to lock somebody up, you'd better do it. If you decide to let someone go, don't change your mind. Then they'll respect you."

There were a lot of guys there who were *rabbiting*. That means they had run off from work details of the county or city jail. For the most part, the sheriff just left them alone. He knew they wouldn't come to town to make any more trouble, so that was okay. There were, though, some pretty tough customers that Billy had to deal with. One was a guy who kept beating up his wife. We were down at the colony one day when we heard a ruckus. Billy went over there, and the fellow came out of the house swinging his fists. Billy wheeled into him and hit him over the head with a billy-club.

The whole family started screaming "Police brutality!"

Another time a guy had knifed his wife, and Billy went over and quick-drew his revolver. In an instant he'd shot the knife out of the fellow's hand. After that, the hard cases treated him with respect; they called him "deadeye".

I really love my brothers down in Reno Sparks, and so did Billy, but sometimes, I guess, you would have to use what's called *tough love*, to get some good things done.

Tough justice, in those days, applied also to my responses to some white brothers. There was a tavern down in Elko that I would go into once in awhile, when I was travelling for the Intertribal Council. One day I walked in and this big guy was sitting at the bar. I ordered a coke.

"If there's anything I can't stand, it's a gut-eater!"this fellow bellowed across the room.

The term *gut-eater* is obviously derogatory; it comes from a time in the old southwest, when the Apaches had all of their game killed off. They were starving, and they'd go to ranchers, asking for the entrails of the animals the ranchers were butchering. That's all they had to eat.

I tried to ignore this big guy, but he came up to me and popped me in the mouth; he split my lip.

I knew that if I swung back I'd probably end up in jail for brawling, so I maintained my cool; I went into the men's room and washed my face, and by the time I came out the guy was gone.

I asked the tavern owner who he was, and he told me the guy's name was Kelly Parker ... that he ran the local stockyard, and that he spent a lot of time busting Indians in the mouth. He'd start up some trouble, I was told, then split before the cops could come. Nobody had ever preferred charges.

There is always a first time, and this was it. I filed charges against Kelly Parker for assault and battery. He was arrested and let out on bond...it was a first offense. I found out from the district attorney that I was going to have to come back to Elko to testify in court. Time after time, I'd call down there, but Parker's lawyer would have had the trial postponed, hoping, I was told, that I would forget about the matter. But I kept on his back like a tick on a dog. I just kept on calling.

"I know this Indian," the D.A. told Parker one day, "he won't give up."

So, finally, we had a trial, and he pleaded guilty to the charges. It cost him $500, and he got a six-month suspended jail sentence. That was pretty light but it made him think carefully, afterwards, about punching Indians in the mouth whenever he got the urge.

Annie was such a big help to me in those days, and she still is. She managed the trailer court while I was away, and, in 1968, she did the artwork for my first book, AT HOME IN THE WILDERNESS.

I paid for the first printing of the book, down in Sparks, and after it was out I sold part of the second edition to Naturegraph Publishers, in Happy Camp, California. It is a book on wilderness self-reliance, and I'd been working on it for quite a few years. I wrote in the book about my Chippewa ancestors, and the secrets of survival that they knew. I reminisced about my youth, and talked about how to build a wilderness homestead. Stalking; hunting; preparing hides; firemaking; edible wild plants; raising vegetables; making soap...in that little book, I wrote about everything I could think of, to make people feel more at home in the wilderness.

Today, AT HOME IN THE WILDERNESS has been through many printings, and is still going strong.

I really felt good about how things were blossoming for me in Reno. That first book was out, and in Nevada there were plenty of places where I could go to be alone, to work on strengthening my medicine. My job with the Intertribal Council of Nevada had expanded; I was not only working with Reno Sparks, I was travelling to other reservations, and was responsible for developing self-help programs at twenty-three reservations across the state. My official title at that time was "Supervisor of Community Developers".

I travelled a lot then, and was paid expenses for room and board. A lot of times I'd just sleep out in the open, and save the motel money; I preferred sleeping out under the stars anyway, and the money always went for worthy causes.

I got involved during this time with a lot more Native legislation, and I lobbied a bit in Nevada's state capitol, at Carson City. A group of us were instrumental in getting a bill through Congress which made the reservation industries and businesses tax-exempt. Another bill we pushed through gave us $350,000 in matching funds from the government. It was for a work incentive program, and the congressmen involved had been stalling on it. One day I cornered the Chairman of the Senate Ways and Means Committee, in the Senate Building's men's room; I figured everybody's got to go once in awhile.

While he was trying to do his business, I transacted mine.

"Are we going to get this bill through?" I asked him.

"Well Sun Bear," he said, admiring my persistence, I think, "I guess you are. We took everything away from you Indians, and now it's time to give it back, a little bit at a time."

The bill was passed.

Another bill I got involved with was a new anti-narcotics bill the State of Nevada was considering. The problem was that the bill included peyote as an illegal narcotic, and, for obvious reasons, a lot of Native people were pretty upset about that. On three reservations in particular, the use of peyote for religious purposes was very heavy. The people didn't want to get themselves into trouble, but they felt very strongly that someone from the Intertribal Council had better go fight for them up at the State Capitol.

I was asked to speak for them. There was a legislative hearing on the question at the University of Nevada, and I went to sit in on that. The representatives present spent a lot of time dickering over how the bill should be worded, and after awhile I stood up to testify; a lot of Native people had given me letters of protest to read out loud. After I read the letters, the representatives asked me what I thought, personally, about the problem.

"The bill as written," I told them, "is a real potential troublemaker. By including peyote as an illegal drug, I think it will disrupt the religious practices of my Native brothers. These practices have gone on for hundreds, maybe thousands of years; we use peyote as a holy sacrament, and it is greatly respected, much like wine is in many of your own churches. It's a form of communion for us.

"When wine is used for religious reasons, it's fine with you folks, but when it's abused, it's against the law. You know, it's the same way with peyote. I've seen a whole lot of winos on the street, including Indians, but I don't see many abusers of peyote."

One representative, a man of Italian descent, got up after I spoke and backed up what I said. He was a Catholic and my point about the sacramental wine had hit home with him.

"If peyote is a sacrament for the Native people, then it shouldn't be denied to them," he said. "I believe that they respect it, and that they don't abuse it."

After a moment, he identified himself as the Chief of Police of North Las Vegas, and he fully recommended that Native people be allowed to use peyote for religious purposes.

When the anti-narcotics bill was finally re-drafted and passed, it was written in a manner which allowed Native Americans in Nevada to use peyote for their religious ceremonies.

That was a big battle won.

My last title with the Intertribal Council of Nevada was "Economic Development Specialist", and the last job I had was to try to develop ideas for Indian industries and for programs that would create employment on reservations.

I also wrote grants and got more funds for the Native people. At that point in my life, I felt that helping my people become more self-reliant was the major part of my medicine. I did pretty well, too, although working with the Bureau of Indian Affairs often proved to be more of a hindrance than a help. At one point, I thought I had a furniture manufacturing company from Sacramento in the bag; they wanted to relocate up on the Pyramid Lake Reservation, and they would have employed about fifty Native people. I was able to get Prudential Life Insurance Company to back the move with $350,000, and the rest was to come in the form of a federal loan. The B.I.A., though, dragged its feet for so long on that one, that it fell through. On one of the other reservations, I tried to get a service station and a co-op grocery started, but they both fell through, also.

There was one more real nice success for me at that time. I'd been writing to an apostle of the Mormon Church named Spencer Kimbal, to get some financial backing. It took a long time for him to respond to my ideas, but he finally did. He sent a represenative named Edwin Baird out to meet me, and Baird was really helpful.

I took him with me to visit a couple of reservations; we talked to the southern Paiutes at the Moapa Reservation, north of Las Vegas, about a self-help program. They'd been leasing some ranch land to Anderson Dairies, and the lease was about to run out. I helped convince them not to renew the lease, to farm the land for themselves.

The B.I.A., as always, was pretty discouraging about the idea; it's attitude was impersonal, and conveyed the message that Indians couldn't run a successful business. Part of the reason for that attitude, I think, was the fact that Anderson Dairies had been leasing that land for the last twenty years, and the B.I.A. liked to maintain the status quo. There were 570 acres involved; it was all prime agricultural land, and was yielding, among other crops, up to seven harvests of alfalfa a year. The B.I.A. charged practically nothing for the land lease; I think it was $2,100 a year.

With a little effort, I managed to convince the Native people to refuse to renew the lease. When I did that, Anderson Dairies offered to double their rent; they'd been making quite a profit at Moapa, and they didn't want to let a good thing go. The Paiutes refused their offer.

Another investor offered them $15,000 a year, to lease the same property. Still, they said no.

With Spencer Kimbal's help, we managed to borrow $80,000 for the Paiutes, so they could start up their own working farm, and as a result of that help, today they have a very successful enterprise. They hired their own people; they were able to establish both tribal and individual incomes. Gradually, they doubled the amount of tillable land down there and ended up with a lot of new facilities, including a Native Community center.

The Moapa project was so successful that a television news documentary was made about it, to illustrate how Native Americans could succeed.

All the time we were fighting to start up that Native farm, the B.I.A. kept saying, "You people aren't skilled enough. You can't do that". That's the way it is in many cases where Indians try to help themselves. The government keeps patting them on the head, telling them they just can't do it. I guess that's because we're supposed to be dumb savages, or maybe it's because it's just easier to keep minorities in line that way.

It's because of that "you can't" attitude, that many of my people develop lifelong emotional handicaps; many of them buy the message; they say to themselves, "I can't", and they don't do anything. Some grow bitter, selfish, unable to open themselves to growth and learning.

Sometimes I'll have my students dig holes in the ground and lay in them all night; in that way, I feel they can open themselves up to the Earth Mother's energy. Then, all the negative "I can'ts" that society has put on them seem to disappear. They feel the good power of the Earth surge into them; it's a strong process of self-realization, and when these folks come back from their Earth spots, they often feel much stronger. Yet, many of my Native brothers and sisters have shut themselves off to such good feelings; they find it almost impossible to open up again, to heal themselves.

When it got to the point with the Intertribal Council that I was doing nothing but writing grants, and not having a chance to travel and visit with my people, I decided that the best way I could fight the war on poverty was to give my job back to the government. I resigned.

I tried my hand at mining for awhile, at a place called Quartz Mountain, out near Tonapah. The silver did not pan out, though, so I was back on the road again.

photo: David DeForrest

Walk in Balance on the Earth Mother.

CHAPTER TEN
THE VISION GROWS

I resigned my position with the Intertribal Council of Nevada in May, 1969. I didn't stay jobless very long. About a month later, Jack Forbes, from the University of California at Davis, invited me to work with him in developing a Native American Studies Program at the University's Tecumseh Center. I took the job because I thought it would be an important step toward educating both my Native brothers and the white students who wanted to learn about our way of life.

At the same time I was helping to develop that curriculum, I also began working with an experimental college for the folks at U.C. Davis, and I worked in the initial development of Deganawidah Quetzalcoatl University (D.Q.U.). Deganawidah Quetzalcoatl was conceived of by a group of Native American and Chicano students at the University, along with Jack Forbes, and that's why it was named after, respectively, great Iroquois and Toltec prophets.

The students had occupied the site of an abandoned Air Force base near Davis. That means, literally, they commandeered it, citing an old law which allowed Native Americans to reclaim any federal land not presently being used. They wanted to build a Native American University on that old base, and they have done so.

Soon after coming to Davis, I was teaching journalism and Native American philosophy on a regular basis. I remember a few of the first things I told my journalism students. One was that I refused to wash their coffee cups for them, after class — that was part of their responsibility — and if they couldn't clean up after themselves, they'd just have to flunk. The second bit of advice I gave them, obviously more to the point, was that I wanted them to forget whatever they'd been told about editorializing. "If you don't write with a biased opinion," I told them, "if you don't editorialize, then you don't have a stand to take. You've got to be intensely involved, not distant, from your writing, so don't waste my time giving me a bunch of objective observations. It won't be worth reading what you've written. If you don't have a stand to take, don't even sit down at the typewriter."

I taught at Davis for about three months, and some of the administrative personnel expressed concern over the fact that I'd only had an eighth grade education. Eventually, I was forced to give up that position. When that happened, Chuck Sweet, who was the director of the experimental college, hired me to work there.

I taught mostly self-reliance courses. There were about seventy students in my classes, both from the university and from the community. We talked a lot about how to heal the Earth Mother. We also did a lot of gardening.

★ ★ ★

In 1969, there was another takeover of land by the Native people, far more famous than the action at Deganawidah Quetzalcoatl University. It was the occupation of Alcatraz Island.

By the end of the late 1960s, there were 250,000 Natives who had relocated to big cities across the country. Many of them went to universities, got jobs, and just tried to assimilate themselves into the white mainstream. It wasn't that easy; after so much rejection, after learning about their own culture in many colleges, some became predictably enraged. They became the radicals, the militants, the ones most determined to take back their Native American identity.

The most famous slogan of that era was "Red Power". There were such urban Indian movements as the American Indian Movement (A.I.M.), led by Clyde Bellecourt and Dennis Banks in Minneapolis, and the United Native Americans, Inc., led by Lehman Brightman in San Francisco.

On November 20, 1969, seventy-eight Indians occupied Alcatraz Island, in San Francisco Bay; they called themselves the "Indians of All Tribes", and at first, their sudden action gave Indians all across the Nation a boost of powerful energy. Alcatraz Island, like everything else, was taken from the Native people and, of course, it was the site of a federal prison for many years. But by then the prison had been shut down, and the Indians who occupied the island cited the same law about federal land which allowed the takeover of the unused Air Force base in Winters for Deganawidah Quetzalcoatl University. The original seventy-eight were mostly urban Indians — college students from the San Francisco area.

In an open letter to the American people, written by the leaders of the takeover, dated December 16, 1969, the purposes and hopes of the movement were very well explained:

We must start somewhere. We feel that if we are to succeed, we must hold on to the old ways. This is the first and most important reason we went to Alcatraz Island.

We hope to reinforce the traditional Indian way of life by building a cultural center on Alcatraz Island. We hope to build a college, a religious and spiritual center, a museum, a center of ecology, and a training school.

In late '69 and early '70 the seventy-eight original people on Alcatraz grew very large in number; before the occupation ended, there were representatives there from more than fifty tribes.

Along with Annie and another friend, I visited the Island so I could cover the story for *Many Smokes*. We'd been watching developments on the TV news, and were sent an invitation by the "Indians of All Tribes". They'd been there for several months already, and some of the leaders were discouraged, because nothing much was happening. None of the plans for a cultural center had gotten off the ground, despite the fact the government had backed off and allowed the Indians to stay.

We were in Reno when we decided to go out there; we drove to San Francisco, and when we arrived at Fisherman's Wharf we discovered that only two boat trips per day were authorized to go out to Alcatraz Island. Apparently, we'd missed both.

We stood around the Wharf for awhile, wondering what to do, when a fellow offered to take us out there in his old fishing boat. Of course, we went with him, not realizing just how serious an offense it was to go at an unauthorized time. The Coast Guard had blockaded the Island, so we ended up running their blockade. As we came into the pier at Alcatraz, we noticed that the number of Coast Guard vessels in the area had increased, and that a lot of people on the Island were making a big deal about it.

Once on the Island, we walked around and talked with whoever we could get some time with. It didn't take long to assess the situation, to understand why the occupation was falling into trouble. Alcatraz Island is a rock, and that's it. There's no place for growing vegetables; there was no fresh water, no permanent electricity.

There was a tipi standing on a high-point, and one building was used as a kitchen and dining room. Most of the bleak prison buildings were standing empty, although some were used as sleeping areas for the people. The only food on the Island was sent in by outside donations.

So, upon this barren rock, the people sat and waited. There were no building materials to make a spiritual or cultural center with; there was no money.

I spoke there about spiritual direction, about a lot of practical things, too, but when I left Alcatraz Island, I knew my brothers and sisters would not be there for long.

A few months later, the Indians at Alcatraz decided to leave the Island; the occupation had run out of steam. As I see it, the problem there was the question of practical considerations. I'm sorry to say that a lot of militant movements die out that way; they begin in anger, and that gives away the people's power.

That's why I feel so good about my vision of the Bear Tribe; we formed from an entirely different direction. We try not to yield to anger, or any of the other weakening emotions; we've formed a community which is based on love and harmony, and that's why we grow so much stronger every day.

Although the stated reasons for the occupation of Alcatraz were never achieved, the occupation contributed greatly to later movements to gain back Native rights and territory.

★ ★ ★

During the winter of 1969, I made a trip to Rhode Island with Annie; it was Christmas time, and she wanted to visit with her family. That was a very interesting trip; I'd developed a case of hepatitis, which I didn't know I had until we got there. We'd flown, and I was unusually exhausted by the trip. By the time that I knew I was sick, my case turned out to be very severe. I was confined to bed.

Annie's family lived in an old farmhouse, and there was a spirit who inhabited the place. I am very sensitive to spirits anyway, and one of the symptoms of hepatitis is described as *confusion*. I was confused, all right; my mind was working on several levels at once, and there were times I wasn't sure if I was talking to a real person, or to the family entity.

He was a friendly being, this spirit; Annie later told me the story of who he was. He was a young farmhand during the early 1920's, who had lived with the family who then owned the land. When the farmer lost everything — he was arrested for rum-running — the family, and the farmhand, were forced to leave. The young man wept, the story goes, and came back later on, in spirit. I was very glad to meet him.

He was in his fifties, about 6'5" tall, and rather clumsy. He'd bump into things, leave doors open, and, Annie told me, even occasionally take food that was in the refrigerator.

As soon as I could get out of bed, we headed back to Nevada. I was really still sick, though; I felt so weak during the trip that I could barely walk. Annie had to give me a lot of support then.

It was during the period of recuperation from hepatitis, while I was bedridden for about six weeks, that I wrote my second book, BUF-FALO HEARTS. The book is an account of Native American culture, religion and history, and focuses on the lives of many great Native leaders. Chapter Sixteen is about the life of Crazy Horse, and it was the most difficult to write. That great Oglala leader went through so much pain during his lifetime; while I was writing the chapter about him I felt as if I were reliving many of his experiences. The book had been difficult to write, but once the Crazy Horse chapter was finished, the rest seemed to flow out easily. Today, BUFFALO HEARTS has been through many printings, and has also been published in German.

★ ★ ★

The students I had at U.C. Davis Experimental College were a terrific group of people. They were interested in alternative lifestyles, and more than that, in learning to live in harmony with the Earth Mother. They sincerely wanted to know about the Native ways, so I taught them all that I could. From this group came the core of the Bear Tribe Medicine Society.

We began to meet together, often at the apartment of George and Caron Klare, to discuss ways in which we could form a real community, a real tribe of people who cared about each other and the earth. We began to put out flyers to let people know that we were forming a Tribe. Many people came, and we began to open our hearts, minds and dreams to each other. I was excited to find that there were so many people who agreed with and shared my vision.

Later in the year, some people donated a piece of land near Placerville, California, for The Bear Tribe's use. I'd been thinking about buying my own land, but at that time my feelings were very strong about not trying to own the Earth Mother. It wasn't until later, after much work and a lot of forced relocation, that I realized if the Tribe didn't have any legal title to a piece of land, we could spend a lot of energy on it, and then have to move.

We called our first camp Medicine Rock, because of an experience I had there. On my first day there, I took a walk up a dirt trail after a rainstorm. As I turned a bend in the little trail, I found a very large, very pure quartz crystal sticking up out of the earth. It was right in the middle of the trail, and looked as though it had halfway risen from the ground. I made an offering, then picked up the crystal. I felt that we were meant to have it. I put the crystal in the Bear Tribe's medicine bag, where it remains to this day.

Conditions at Medicine Rock were what you might call primitive. There was one small cabin, but no bathrooms, and the spring water had a strong mineral content that gave people the runs. There were none of the conveniences that people had grown used to. That made it a good place for us to start, because it forced people to grow close to the land. Most of the people lived in tents or built their own simple shelters. We started there with about twenty people. Annie became Nimimosha. George became Grey Wolf, and Caron became Morning Star, and they were the subchiefs at Medicine Rock. My medicine helper then was Tommy Gun, a Flathead from Montana.

At earth renewal time in 1970, we had ceremonies to adopt the people at Medicine Rock as full members of the tribe. I gave these folks their names after they made their commitment to the Tribe. A name is something for a person to live up to. It might come to me in a dream, a vision, or a quiet moment, and it shows me the good inner qualities of a person, the qualities that he or she should strive to live by.

I remember how powerful the winter solstice ceremonies were for me, and for all of us that year. To Native people, the time of earth renewal is the most important ceremony of the year. It is the time when Father Sun begins to journey back from the south, to warm the Earth Mother and bless her with new life and growth. At this time we put all the fires in a camp to sleep, and then we relight them in a ritual way. We make prayer plumes for the year, the women grind corn meal in the old way, with a mortar and pestle, and the men mix our kinnik-kinnik. We give thanks to the earth and sun for the gift of life. We cleanse ourselves in the sweatlodge, and then we feast together.

I always feel good about earth renewal, but that year was very special. We fasted together, played stick games, and told stories. After trying, in one way or another, since I was fifteen, to clarify and fulfill my vision of people coming together in a proper way with respect for each other and the earth, it was actually happening! All of the people at Medicine Rock felt a strong sense of kinship, of sharing, of love for the earth. In the sweatlodge I silently cried tears of joy at the wonder of it all.

We had decided to call ourselves The Bear Tribe not only because my name is Sun Bear, but also because the bear is a powerful medicine animal for the Chippewa people. The Bear Clan is the medicine clan of the old ways. The bear is one of the few animals which heals its own wounds, and, we Chippewa believe, has the power to heal the wounds of others. That's what our group knew it had to do — heal our own wounds and the wounds of others, so we could all join together to help with the healing of the earth. We also wanted and needed the endurance and strength of the bear who can hibernate for months, eat a few herbs, and go on about his business. We were all so excited at this point, that we did not foresee that the lessons of hibernation and re-emergence would be some of the most difficult and painful lessons the people in the Tribe would have to learn.

1971 began as a magical year for the Bear Tribe. The word of our existence, and our vision, spread quickly through the California grapevine, and through talks that members arranged for me to give at schools and churches throughout the area. I was well received wherever I went, and after each talk a few more people would come to be with us. We had acquired another base called "Little Lake" in Dutch Flat, California. The subchief there was a beautiful sister of Scottish, Apache and Mohawk descent named Oh Shinnah Fastwolf. She now travels the world over as an eclectic teacher, whose teachings come from various ancient traditions. Then, as now, she dedicates her work to the healing of Mother Earth.

In February of that year we had a potlatch in Sacramento to bring the people from the two bases together, and to introduce the Sacramento community to the work that we were doing. Over 1500 people attended. Tommy Gun moderated, Oh Shinnah sang, and I spoke to the people there, breaking them down into groups of 200 to 300.

People from the Sacramento Indian Center came to support us and to sing and drum. To show gratitude for this support, we made a donation to the Center. We invited local craftspeople to show their crafts, and they did. It was a great day, with a lot of bear hugs.

Later other members arranged a benefit called "Mother Earth Rock" for the Tribe at Friends and Relations Hall, formerly the Family Dog, in San Francisco. The New Riders of the Purple Sage, featuring Jerry Garcia and other members of the Grateful Dead band; Country Joe, Stoneground and The Ace of Cups, played; and I spoke to the large crowd between their sets, telling them about the Tribe and my vision.

Other people donated land for our use and, by that summer, we had about 200 members living in seventeen different camps in California. Letters poured in from all around the country, and we were written up in many *underground* papers.

The *Berkeley Barb* did a big spread on the Tribe and illustrated it with a bear positioned like the Statue of Liberty. The caption read, "Give me your tired, your poor". We got some of them.

We had gardens at most of the camps, whether they were located in the country or in the city. Our gardens at Davis, which took up about four acres of University property, had the reputation of being the finest on the campus. We dried a lot of these crops, and successfully experimented with drying some, like tomatoes, that no one thought could be preserved in that way.

We arranged to gather fruit and nuts from abandoned or uncared for orchards. We harvested and dried the fruit, and traded our leftovers for other staples that we needed. We were constantly working toward self-reliance on the land. At one camp, we harvested a thousand pounds of cherries that first summer. We dried them all. We were doing very well.

Although, at some points, it seemed like I could recruit 10,000 members, that wasn't what I was interested in doing. My vision told me to teach people from all walks of life, to communicate to them the fact that technology's excesses were rapidly bringing on disaster. I felt the need to tell people that if they wanted to survive the coming earth cleansing, if they wanted to be part of the new earth, they would have to re-establish their very personal ties with the natural world.

As the number of people in the Tribe grew, so did our problems. Some people seemed able to pay lip-service to what the vision was, but they weren't able to put their hearts behind their lips. Some people took on a lot of responsibility, while others wanted a pre-packaged utopia where they had to do very little work.

While at that time we allowed people to use marijuana, which we called "medicine weed", we did not allow any other drugs. Now we don't allow marijuana either. Some of the people who came could not break their dependency on other psychedelics. The drug question became a major problem. When I was away from a camp, I'm told, some people wanted to fall back into old patterns. The issue became not so much a moral one, not so much a question of what was right or wrong, as a question of truth — of people saying one thing, and doing another.

Even with the problems, I felt that my vision was beginning to really blossom. I knew that my role in the Bear Tribe would have to be balanced in two directions: I would have to be there to teach my brothers and sisters to live in harmony, but I would also have to be travelling around the country, spreading the word about our vision of healing ourselves and the Earth Mother. I believed in the Tribe so much that I took all of the money I had saved and used it to support the Tribe. I even sold some of the trailers in Reno to supply more money when it was needed.

I purchased food, and sleeping bags, sometimes for people who were missing them simply because they had forgotten where they left them. I fixed cars, bought gas, paid for postage and phone calls. Some of the other people with me also put in their money to support the Tribe. Nimimosha was even willing to stay in Reno most of the time, running the trailer court, so that we could have the income from that.

There were many beautiful people who came to us during that time, and a few who were emotionally damaged to a point where it was impossible for us to heal them. But we tried, we really tried.

In the summer of 1971, I set off on a cross-country speaking tour, with Morning Star and Nimimosha. It was a very organized thing we did; we had definite letters of invitation, and speaking dates had been set. We visited with church groups, college and university classes, and lots of people who were interested in forming their own communities.

The plan was to make a circle around the nation; we took a southern route from west to east, then we travelled up the east coast. The return trip would be made across the northern states. That way we could hit most of the places where people wanted to hear what we had to say about communities.

We left from Sacramento in the early summer; it was blazing hot, and I remember the heat mirages shimmering across the highway, and the soft mess of a ball-point pen which had melted on the dashboard of our car. We took sleeping bags and camping equipment, and stopped in Reno first. We had a maintenance man named Howard, who was going to take care of the mobile home park while Nimimosha was gone. We went down through Las Vegas, then travelled through New Mexico and Arizona. We would stop at night and cook on a campfire; it was a very good time. We experienced the Earth Mother in many ways; in Texas, we were eaten alive by chiggers, which appeared to be delighted to find new homes under our skin. There were plenty of mosquitos there too, and it might have been on that trip that I developed my attitude toward killing them. I have reverence, of course, for everything that lives, but mosquitos bring out the warrior in me.

I tell the first mosquito that lands on me, "I'm a warrior. Now either go and carry that message to your sisters, or I'll evolve you." If it flies off then, I let it go. If it tries to bite me, I smack it dead. Usually, the mosquito world gets the message pretty quick.

Whenever we didn't have a set arrival time, we'd pick a remote spot out in the desert, or near a stream; we rarely stayed in regular campgrounds. We enjoyed being at one with the Earth, and self-sufficient, even though we were buying groceries at the time. We learned as much as we could about the wild herbs and plants wherever we went. We learned which were edible, which were used for healing.

In New Mexico, we stopped in Santa Fe, and then in Taos. At the Taos Pueblo reservation we were met by a tribal elder named Tellus Good Morning. He had opened himself and his medicine to anyone who wanted to come and learn, and share with him. The Taos people in general were very open to non-native individuals, and Tellus Good Morning had a large following of young people who were of mixed ethnic background.

When we arrived, he was getting ready to tie up a peyote drum, and he invited us to what the Native people call a *tea party*. That term, to my people, is not a light-hearted one; a tea party is a specific kind of peyote meeting, where they grind the peyote buttons and make tea from them. The tea is then passed around, and taken as a sacrament.

I remember that there was a black man at the tea party, a very spiritually-committed man. He tied up the drum himself; he'd been following the Native path for many years, and was looked upon as a spiritual leader.

There were lots of other people at the Taos Pueblo who had given up their life way in the main society; they didn't have any material possessions, and they were happy. They had their spiritual wealth, and their loyalty to each other.

In Gallup, New Mexico, we stopped at the Navajo reservation, and there was a lot of curiosity about me travelling with two women. Some Navajos are still polygamous, so they thought I was travelling with my two wives, and wanted to know how many children we had, and where they were. There were a lot of jokes about it, too; there were fellows who offered to trade me horses for one of my women; I just went along with the joking, but said "No sale. I need them both".

We made our way across the southern states, and in Tulsa, Oklahoma, we stayed in the home of a very famous civil rights attorney. While there, we spoke to an alternative church group, and to folks at a Jewish bakery. Our experiences were varied. Wherever we went, there were curious questions about the nature of our threesome. It made me think that more people than the Navajos practiced polygamy — or at least fantasized about doing so.

We spoke at Oklahoma University, in Norman; then we travelled on to Dallas, Texas. In both Dallas and Austin we spoke to underground groups, and to groups who were forming their own communities.

When we got to Houston, Nimimosha got a phone call from Howard, our maintenance man at Sun Valley; it seems there were a lot of problems at the trailer park he couldn't handle by himself, so Nimimosha decided that she would have to leave us at that point. She didn't want to go back to Sun Valley, and we didn't want to go on without her, but there seemed to be little choice. Morning Star and I travelled on up the east coast, stopping in Alabama and the Carolinas, and ending up, finally, in New York City.

It was in New York on that trip, that I met Wabun of the Bear Tribe. She was called Marlise James then, and she was a free-lance writer finishing up a book called THE PEOPLE'S LAWYERS, published by Holt, Rinehart & Winston. She had heard about the Bear Tribe when she was in California researching her book on lawyers, and had written to us asking if she could interview me for an article.

She was surprised when she met me, because she had thought I was an 80-year-old Hopi. Morning Star and I stayed at her place for about two weeks, and we talked a lot about the Tribe. Star and I were so high from the trip and all of the enthusiasm that had met us around the country that we were just radiating unconditional love, and Marlise picked right up on it. We used to go on the subways beaming, to see how many people we could get to smile back at us. Marlise took us around the city and arranged for some good publicity through her former classmates at the Columbia University Graduate School of Journalism.

I saw the great amount of good energy in her heart, and how New York City life was keeping it from flowing in its proper channels, so we asked her to come out and join the Tribe. She agreed to do that after she finished writing her book.

In late summer, we were finally back in California. We went to our base camp at Vacaville, and it was time for a big peach harvest. Our arrangement with the farmer who owned the land was that we would harvest, cut and dry the peaches, and keep half of them for ourselves. We were also drying figs there, and many of the tribe members were working very hard.

We also had a base camp near Elk Grove. It was about that time, at that camp, that I had my first and last experience with marijuana. I didn't believe in smoking it, as I've told you, but some of my brothers and sisters decided I should not criticize something I had not experienced.

They cooked up a batch of brownies, which contained about two lids of marijuana. I didn't know about the extra ingredient. We were sitting around munching the brownies; I'd had about four of them when I suddenly decided that they were really delicious. I remember wondering why I hadn't noticed that with the first few brownies. After a few more minutes I went out into the front yard and sat down. Suddenly, my hand began to raise all by itself. Objects began to change shape, color, pattern ... after awhile it was like looking into a kaleidoscope. The patterns were really pretty; they looked like fluid spiderwebs. It was a powerful experience, though very different from those which I had at peyote meetings. This seemed to lack spiritual depth, but it was very sensory.

My brothers and sisters were sitting around me, laughing.

"You ate a lot of brownies," one of them told me. "They had some medicine weed in them."

Well, I got up and went into the house. I was feeling very hot, and I had to take my clothes off. I was *so hot*. Two of my sisters decided they'd help me cool off; they began to minister to my needs. They sponged me down with a cool cloth and they rubbed me down. This whole episode turned out to be, for me, a very sensual experience. It seemed like the three of us were together lovingly for a very long time. Although I like feeling good, I don't think that drugs that *turn on* your senses, while *turning off* your sense of responsibility, are good.

I have to admit it was quite an experience, but it did not change my opinion about drugs. Drugs were definitely a very bad issue between me, and some members of the Tribe. They would be, finally, a major cause for the Tribe's early hibernation.

During that period of time, in 1971, I felt that if the Tribe could coordinate its energies in the right way, we could provide for ourselves and be self-sufficient, partly by growing our own food and raising our own livestock, and partly by taking in the waste of the larger society. There were a lot of abandoned orchards around our camps that we could glean from. There were wild foods available and we ate many wild greens during the summer: lambs quarter, plantain, blessed thistle, miner's lettuce, malva.

After the harvests were finished, we went into people's orchards and took out leftover walnuts, almonds, olives — even baskets of tomatoes. Most of the folks who owned the orchards were pretty generous; when we asked them if we could go in and clean out the leftovers, they told us to help ourselves.

We harvested so much fruit, both from private groves, and from our own gardens, that we had enough to fill our stomachs and still trade in town for other goods. A lot of health food stores would take our dried fruit and exchange it for other items we needed.

Things seemed to have been going along well, I thought, until I'd been back from my cross-country trip long enough to take a close look around the camps. I realized that many of them were not running right. There was structure at most of the camps; they had subchiefs appointed by me because those particular people were willing to take on the responsibility for the others living with them.. There was Little Elk at Elk grove; Sun Marker and Corn Woman at Santa Barbara; Pipe Man at North Star Camp; and Grey Wolf and Morning Star at Medicine Rock. But there were the other folks who maybe did all right when I was around, but when I was gone, fell into damaging old ways. They were the people who drifted in, then drifted back out; or simply hung around and drained everybody's energy. They got all excited about what we were trying to do, until it was time to put some back muscle into it. Some fell victim to petty jealousies, to making power plays, and, generally, to giving away their power, or trying to take ours.

There was one incident, I remember, which was both amusing and agitating. It serves to show what can happen when people aren't quite ready for discipline. This was at Medicine Rock, before I travelled cross-country. A bunch of the people there wanted to play Indian, rather than learn to live in harmony. What they did was to have a wild drum ceremony at 3 a.m. They were pounding on the drum and whooping it up, and the neighbors around there got all freaked out. They thought something weird and terrible was happening, and called in the Sheriff's Department.

"Oh my God," the sheriff told me he had said when he heard the commotion, "There must be hundreds of them up there in the bushes."

The sheriff and his deputies stalked up through the darkness, ready, I think, to shoot at anything that moved. They felt there was something really strange going on.

Finally, he met up with one of the brothers, who he happened to know from high school. Thankfully, that ended both the stalking, and the drum ceremony.

Some of my brothers and sisters up at Medicine Rock had failed to realize that living in harmony with the Earth included living in harmony with your neighbors.

At another point, a man donated a cow to the Tribe. While I was travelling and speaking, the cow died during calving because nobody took the responsibility to give her water or fodder. After that, several goats died for the same reason. Since I had been teaching people about our interconnectedness with and responsibility to all Creation, I was pretty disgusted with my people at that point. I realized that I couldn't take many of them at their word.

Things got so bad that by late 1971, I decided to step out of the picture. I told these folks they were on their own, that as far as I was concerned, the first Bear Tribe attempt needed to be abandoned. There were good people there, but too many of them could not make a full commitment. There were folks who were just plain lazy, there were folks who came in as drugheads, and left that way; they would be better off, I decided, following another path.

I felt very bad about these things that were happening, but I knew, once again, that everything I did in life was part of my growing and my learning.

When the early Bear Tribe began to separate, I went to a hilltop near Vacaville. I stripped my clothing off, since I came into the world that way, and prayed to the Creator for a vision to keep me on the right path. A part of the vision that came to me is in the beginning of this book. I saw a golden eagle. It circled around me while I lay there on the hilltop.

I made my prayers, and I asked for a sign, for a direction. The eagle came and went, and he looked into my soul; I almost wept. I was joyful to have a sign from the Great Spirit, but I didn't know what it really meant.

I stayed there; I prayed harder and harder. Suddenly, a huge white cloud came over me; it was the only cloud in a sky of perfect blue. As I prayed, the cloud came closer and closer; then a small puff of it separated off from the rest. A whirlwind came, and spun the little puff of cloud away. Part of it dissolved, but a fluff of it joined back up with the large cloud. I knew, then, what would happen with the Bear Tribe, and I felt better.

The Great Spirit had given me a sign; the people who were with me were not quite ready to help live by my vision. Some would go back to the cities. Some would grow, and eventually find their balance. And some, the vision told me, would only split off from the Bear Tribe for awhile; they were the little puff of cloud, and they would return. The large cloud, the Bear Tribe itself, would then blossom once again. I felt this in my heart.

So I went back down to the group who were getting ready to leave, and I told them about what I'd seen.

"Many of you," I told them, "are on a different life path. Some of you will go back to your cities and your psychedelics.

"I am going on too," I said. "The Bear Tribe will live and grow, from what we've started here. I'm going back up to Reno, now, and those of you who want to stay with the Bear Tribe, who *really* want to help, can join me there soon."

I still had the trailer court, and Nimimosha was still running it. She was doing other things, too, and had found another relationship, but we still shared a great deal together in our hearts. So I returned to Reno, and after a short time, a few people from California came to join me; there was North Star, Chespellum, Morning Star and a few others.

I appreciated those brothers and sisters who came to join me during this period of hibernation for the vision of the tribe. I knew I needed time to strengthen and renew myself so I would later be ready to emerge again.

In early 1972 we bought a little press, straightened out our mailing lists, and began to publish *Many Smokes* again.

★ ★ ★

Despite the dissolution of the early tribe, I knew my vision was growing stronger. I saw major changes coming, soon, on the Earth Mother: the time of the Cleansing. I saw the resources that made technology possible dwindling at a rapid pace; and the main thing I told people back then was that in order to survive, they would have to relearn what their ancestors knew long ago. They would have to learn to walk in balance on the Earth Mother, to use the earth's natural resources in a sensitive and sensible manner, without adding chemicals to everything, and pesticides, and all the other things which destroy the planet's delicate web of life.

The early Bear Tribe was the first group of people to come with me in the right direction. We had good feelings in our camps, when we began. I remember the children over at the Elk Grove camp; there were a lot of them, and they were all about the same age. We didn't even have to sort the laundry. They would all sleep together, in an old farmhouse, and the parents would sleep outside, on the ground. In the morning the adults would be awakened by the children's hugs and kisses. It didn't matter who you were; you knew that you were loved.

Whenever the early Bear Tribe came together for big gatherings, with all of the camps there, as well as with people who wanted to see what we were doing, there was great joy.

Visitors would talk about the Bear Tribe; they would say, "Oh, yes, we know those people. They hug a lot." And that is true. We did hug a lot, and we still do.

We became a legend. Being a legend did not, however, fulfill my vision. To do that, we had to become a real community of teachers, able to consistently nurture the seeds we planted — both in the ground, and in people's minds.

BOOK TWO

WALKING THE PATH OF POWER

I say Shasta is a medicine dog because of the way we found him.

CHAPTER ELEVEN
FINDING VISION MOUNTAIN

We were back at Sun Valley, and the few folks who had followed us squeezed into whatever space they could make for themselves. There were times, I guess, when we felt we were packed in like sardines, in a couple of little trailers.

We had learned a few hard lessons about organization from the early Bear Tribe attempt; so starting up again, I think we knew a little bit better how to go about things. Personal responsibility would have to be a major issue. Controls would be a whole lot tighter, and as it turned out, it's a good thing that we stuck to that philosophy. For one thing, the fellow who originally did the printing of *Many Smokes* on our press was really inventive. He had an idea that the press could be used for several different jobs simultaneously. One, of course, would be to turn out the issues of *Many Smokes*; the other, which he neglected to tell us about, was a very amateurish attempt to counterfeit twenty dollar bills.

We caught him at that, and we sent him on his way. The art work on his phony money was really a poor job; even a five year old kid, I think, could have told those bogus bills from the real McCoy.

In January of 1972, Marlise James came out to join the tribe. She'd finished writing THE PEOPLE'S LAWYERS, and we had a lot of plans for reorganization. She had come out at just the right time, I don't mind telling you; it was during that winter that I was experiencing my first and only misgivings about the fulfillment of my vision. When I thought about the Bear Tribe of my vision, and I looked at the reality of the kind of people who had come to the first base camps, my spirit seemed to dampen. That first experience had cost me a lot of energy, as well as all of my money. Thanks to Marlise, though, and to all the other good people I had around me, we kept the dream going.

The preceding fall, we had an offer for the Sun Valley Trailer park. It came through that spring. I was glad to have a chance to get rid of it. I didn't like running a business, chasing after people for rent money, keeping them from stealing my furniture. It was getting in the way of what I really wanted to do. I traded off my equity for eleven acres of land near Los Gatos, California. It seemed like a good move at the time, until we arrived at the new land and discovered that it sat on a major earthquake fault line.

I still had to spend most of my time up in Reno. We had kept a couple of trailers up there, and with Marlise, Nimimosha, and the others I mentioned, we printed *Many Smokes* at the trailer court.

After being with the Bear Tribe for a while, Marlise James was adopted as a full member in a ceremony at Pyramid Lake. Later, she would become my medicine helper with the Bear Tribe, and from this time on I'll call her Wabun. Wabun, to the Chippewa people, is the Spirit Keeper of the East. Wabun is the spirit of wisdom and illumination; the messenger of spring and awakening growth.

It became apparent, at that point, that in order to get a firm financial base for the Tribe, we would have to be on the road again, this time selling an inventory of Native craft items.

So that spring, we set out on what is called the "pow wow circuit", going around to the various Indian festivities, selling crafts, books, whatever we could get our hands on.

We didn't have much to sell in the beginning; I had about $500 worth of inventory, a few rings, and mostly bows and arrows that we'd bought awhile back from the Cherokee people. We started out with practically nothing, hitting the Indian arts and craft shows, and, of course, while we were at them, selling copies of *Many Smokes*.

On the pow wow trail, we travelled all over the country again; we camped out, always moving. Most of the money that we took in we reinvested in more and better stock items.

We tried to hit all of the annual Indian festivities ... the dances, the ceremonials which were open to the public. Most tribal groups put on a pow wow once a year, and there are hundreds of different ones to go to, both in the country, and in a lot of the big cities. At a pow wow, traditional dancers dress up in their Native costumes. They travel themselves, sometimes thousands of miles, to get to the festivities. There are drummer groups from all over the nation: and dancers compete for prizes in a lot of different categories. There is traditional dancing, which is getting more popular all the time; there is Indian fancy dancing; fast dancing; slow and fast war dance categories; women's traditional dancing; and dancing contests, even for groups of little children.

The pow wows are great things for the people. Whole families can get together and have a carefree time. It's quite a change, for a lot of my brothers and sisters, from the bleak existence they live through day-to-day on the reservations or in the cities.

Going to the pow wows also helped me get over the bleakness that I felt in my soul because of the things that had happened to the Bear Tribe in California. For three years, on and off, Wabun and I rode the pow wow circuit. I knew, at first, that this was part of my hibernation period, but I felt that at least I was able to do something constructive. We were getting financial resources that would enable the tribe to re-emerge at a later date.

I know that this travelling also helped Wabun understand many facets of the Native culture today, and prepared her to take her place as my medicine helper. When Wabun joined the Tribe she knew very little about the Native culture ... and the pow wows, the shows, and the people that we met at them gave her a crash course that no college could ever offer.

As we travelled I met many old friends that I had not seen for awhile, and their acceptance helped me to feel better about life. We also made many new friends — people like Larry and Lee Piper of Seattle, and Joyce and Richard Rainbow of Tuolumne, California — who gave me new spiritual insights and ideas.

We even helped to sponsor a couple of Indian Shows in the Sacramento area, and that experience, though we didn't know it at the time, would prepare us for other kinds of gatherings that we were to sponsor later on.

Some of the first pow wows we went to were near Los Angeles. While we were in the area we would always stay with Jeannie and Bob Babcock, who I had known from the old days of the Los Angeles Indian Center. It was real good to see them again. Bob, who we called "The Old Buzzard", has always been like an uncle to me. He's a real old-timer, with a great love for people, and for animals. They would always have dozens of cats in their home, and dozens of homeless cats that would hang around outside, eating the food that they provided. Uncle Bob has even had a couple of raccoons for pets there in the big city. Jeannie and Wabun became good friends, and Jeannie taught Wabun a lot about the hospitality that Native women always showed to guests. Native women serve their guests lavishly and unobtrusively, and I think Wabun, with her New York feminist background, would have had a hard time learning this from anyone who did not have the grace, understanding, strength and dignity that Jeannie did in her manner of living, and of service.

From the Los Angeles area we began to go to other California pow wows, then to some in Nevada, Montana, Oregon and Washington.

Since most of the pow wows were outdoors, we'd find ourselves a shady spot and spread a blanket on the ground. We'd display our merchandise on the blanket. Sometimes we'd get a spot for free, but most of the time we would have to pay a permit fee.

A lot of the pow wows had rodeos going on, and sometimes there'd be big Indian ceremonial shows to watch. At Indian arts and crafts shows in Los Angeles and other big cities there would be 100 to 150 dealers in Indian arts and crafts, and at those shows I would get myself a booth in exchange for an ad in *Many Smokes*. I'd sell the magazine to all the dealers, as well as the visitors who walked around. The magazine proved to be a boon for everyone involved; it brought in some money for me, and it listed all forthcoming pow-wows for the dealers.

We bought turquoise and silver jewelry, I remember, just before it became extremely popular; there were a few years there, when everybody wanted to buy it. So we got in on the ground floor; we had a really good supply. We managed to put away a bit of money from the sales.

One year, I remember, we spent every bit of our cash except twenty dollars on turquoise jewelry; we bought it from Native craftsmen down in Gallup, New Mexico. We set out on a selling trip, from Gallup to Washington D.C., with a credit card for gas, and that twenty dollar bill. We did so well on that trip, selling jewelry at the pow wows, that we actually came back with a nice profit.

The pow wow years were fun and exciting, even though it was hard work a lot of the time. In between shows we would stop in every book, novelty, and jewelry shop we came across, to try to wholesale some of our inventory. We almost felt like our car was home. We'd travel in it — often long distances in short periods — sleep in it and often eat in it. I was so tight with money during this time that Wabun nicknamed me *El Cheapo*. But I knew we had to build up a good reserve in order to eventually get land and allow the Bear Tribe to re-emerge.

There were many times when we were touched by the generosity of people we would meet at a pow wow who would take us into their homes and feed us, and treat us like true brothers and sisters. There were other times when the children who sold *Many Smokes* touched us deeply with their love and generosity. Wabun remembers one young man at the Oil Celebration in Poplar, Montana, who worked harder all weekend than any other kid. At the end, he used all the money he had earned to buy a gift for his mother. Wabun was so touched that she gave him a beautiful belt buckle for himself.

We met a lot of sharpies, too, who helped us develop our skills in bartering and trading. I learned in Navajo country to let Wabun do the dealing. It is the women there who make the financial decisions, and they seemed to have more respect if they were dealing with another woman trader.

Often during this time we encountered nature in all her beautiful, and powerful, aspects. We did one pow wow in Ft. Collins, Colorado, just at the foot of Pikes Peak. Every day at four in the afternoon, the thunder beings would come to visit. We were in a booth built for the occasion by the Army Corps of Engineers. At 3:30 we would begin to put all of our merchandise in boxes under the counter so it would not get wet. One day the wind was so strong it blew the whole booth over, with Wabun and the merchandise still in it. So much for Army engineering.

A couple of times, going across the Plains states, we outran tornadoes — a good thing, since we had a lot of the inventory on a rack on top of the car, with only a tarp for cover. We just missed flash floods a few times in the high desert. Our medicine was good.

Often we would just spend our drives marvelling at the beauty of the mountains, the deserts, the ocean, the clouds, the sunsets, and the sunrises. Seeing all of this beauty healed me as nothing else could.

★ ★ ★

All of the time, when travelling, we made an effort to meet my Native brothers and sisters, and to exchange our ideas. At the same time, in *Many Smokes*, we would cover local Indian stories wherever we went.

One Indian story we covered at that time was a very big one. It was the Native occupation of Wounded Knee, in 1973. The occupation took place on South Dakota's Pine Ridge Reservation, which is primarily a home for the Oglala Sioux. Although most people have heard about the takeover, not too many people really know what went on there. So, I'll tell you some of it from my viewpoint.

In 1890, the U.S. Government slaughtered close to three hundred Sioux at Wounded Knee. That was a very famous, or infamous, massacre, which took place after the Sioux nation had signed three major treaties, each time losing more of their reservation land. In 1973, about the same number of Sioux, three hundred, went back to Wounded Knee to make another stand.

The Traditional Oglala, along with members of AIM, occupied a trading post area at Wounded Knee. Many of the people there travelled hundreds of miles in order to join what would soon be called the Independent Oglala Nation. The group, once established in Wounded Knee, were quickly surrounded and besieged by U.S. Government forces. U.S. Marshals, FBI people, State police ... all came heavily armed with automatic rifles, with armored personnel carriers, even helicopters. The government decided not to make an assault on the trading post; I guess they figured another massacre at Wounded Knee might be bad press. Instead, they decided, they would try to starve the renegades out. They barricaded the area and confiscated any food, fuel, or medical supplies from people who had reason to go past their blockades. In addition, they placed U.S. marshals on a hilltop above the trading post.

In spite of all this pressure, the people who had taken over at Wounded Knee managed to hold out until they finally came out to try for peaceful negotiations. For almost two months then, in 1973, the small patch of land known as Wounded Knee was Indian Territory.

There were a lot of reasons for the Native takeover, and they were very complicated. Since 1868, the land on the Sioux Reservation had been constantly whittled away by government manipulation. By the 1970's, Pine Ridge, like so many other reservations, was a checkerboard of Indian and non-Indian land.

There are three million acres at Pine Ridge, and by the early 1970's only half of that land belonged to Native people. A half-million acres were owned by the BIA-supported Tribal Government, and a million acres were owned by white ranchers and farmers.

Employment was practically nonexistent for Oglalas, and most of them were so poor that they were forced to lease their land to the white ranchers, at prices which were set by the BIA. Poverty and Tribal Government brutality had literally begun to force the traditional Indians to their knees, when they finally fought back.

The Tribal Government, which was formed by the 1934 Reorganization Act, was controlled by a group of people who were not acting in the best interests of all of the people. Jobs on the reservation were given out to favorites only. This group was backed by a *goon squad* comprised of Indians and whites who were armed with clubs, tear gas, and guns. Whenever anybody spoke out against policies, they were badly beaten.

Conditions became so bad that, by 1972, a lot of traditional leaders were making public protest speeches and in general, bucking the established system. They paid for their efforts; many of them were badly beaten. A lot of their families were threatened, and some homes were firebombed.

In February of 1972, an Oglala from the Porcupine Community named Raymond Yellow Thunder was murdered by two white men in Gordon, Nebraska. At first badly beaten, he was stripped naked and thrown into an American Legion building during a dance. The two men then dragged him back outside, beat him some more, then stuffed him into their car trunk. His body was found two days later. The two men responsible were charged only with second degree manslaughter, and both of them were released from jail without paying any bail.

When Yellow Thunder's family protested to the BIA, they were told to keep their mouths shut. Both the BIA and the Tribal Government refused to help them find out why justice was not being done. So the family, angry and desperate, called in leaders from AIM to launch a full investigation.

From that time on the violence increased; there were more beatings, there were more murders. In January of 1973, another Oglala named Wesley Bad Heart Bull was murdered in Buffalo Gap, South Dakota. His alleged killer, Darald Schmitz, was arraigned on manslaughter rather than murder charges. When that happened, AIM led a protest demonstration in Custer, South Dakota.

Finally, in February of '73, things had reached a breaking point, with Indians being abused and nobody listening to them. The traditional Oglala leaders met at that time with leaders of AIM, in the community of Calico, and from there they moved to Wounded Knee, hoping to gain national recognition. Their major demand was that the U.S. Government honor the treaty of 1868, which they'd made with the Sioux Nation. That treaty, signed at Fort Laramie, Wyoming, had set up the Sioux Nation to include all of western South Dakota, and close to half of each of North Dakota, Montana, Wyoming, and Nebraska. Compared to that amount of acreage, the Pine Ridge reservation was like a speck of dust. In addition to that designation of territory, the 1868 treaty promised that the Sioux would be the keepers of all of the animal, mineral, water and plant kingdoms on their land, and that they would be given the opportunity, by the government, to always maintain their self-sufficiency.

Let it be known, the manifesto of the Independent Oglala Nation read, during the 1973 takeover, *that the Oglala Sioux people will revive the treaty of 1868 and that it will be the basis for all negotiations...*

We are a sovereign nation by that treaty...We intend to send a delegation to the United Nations...We want to abolish the Tribal Government...

The traditional people were already a nation before the white man ever came...all we are doing is reminding the U.S. Government of that...

I travelled down to Wounded Knee, along with a writer friend of mine, Marcus Damien, to see what was really going on. The media, at that time, was portraying the takeover as a move by a bunch of hotheaded radicals. I knew that was not true.

When we reached Hot Springs, South Dakota, outside of Rapid City, we were told there were no motel rooms available. At the Cascade Hotel, they told us there were only rooms in town for FBI and BIA personnel. So we moved on to Rapid City.

Wherever we drove down there, we were watched by whites, and by the highway patrol. Fear and hatred were running very deep. We drove on to Pine Ridge, to try to get inside. We had to stop, once on the reservation, at a building where the Federal Marshals and the FBI had set up their battle headquarters. The place was bristling with guns, and we were searched by two armed guards before we could even get in to see about getting visitor's press credentials.

I told the officials there who I was, that I was the publisher of *Many Smokes*, and that I wanted to get into Wounded Knee to talk to the Native people. The man I spoke to said it would take about two days to get me clearance; that was routine procedure.

I was pretty disappointed; I figured that the two days might stretch out indefinitely, but, as I was leaving, the official I'd talked with called me back inside.

"It's okay, Sun Bear," he told me. "You can go in. We know who you are, and we know all about *Many Smokes*."

That was great. I was real happy that I didn't have to wait, after all, but I wasn't so happy to find out that the Justice Department knew so much about me.

We met Will Baker at the Federal Headquarters. Will was a faculty member at U.C. Davis who wanted to make a documentary film about the takeover. He joined us and the three of us drove up to the trading post area that was under seige, past shacks and old abandoned cars.

About a mile from the trading post we came to the first government barricade; the U.S. marshals there searched our car thoroughly. They even looked under the hood for contraband. They didn't find any groceries, so they were ready to let us go, but first they informed us that our gas gauge had been checked, that if it dropped much before we got out of there we'd be arrested, for aiding and abetting. Then, they let us through.

After that barricade, we had to pass through a second government road block, armed more heavily than the first. At that one I heard one guard say to another, "You think we've got the redskins surrounded? What if they have us surrounded?"

He sounded pretty nervous.

Next came the road block the native people had set up; it was manned by Indians with .22 rifles and some shotguns. Their weapons were no match for the government firepower, but it was obvious that they believed in what they were doing.

Finally, we got to the trading post. When we pulled up to the area, we had to go through another interrogation; this time by the people we'd come to see.

They wanted to know who we were and what we wanted; I had a few friends in there, and they recognized me, so everything was okay.

There were a lot of important Native leaders in the occupied area, and we interviewed some of them. Wallace Black Elk was there, and Dennis Banks; Clyde Bellecourt; Russell Means, and many others.

We spent a lot of time just interviewing anybody who wanted to make a statement, and filming our documentary which we called "Spoken From My Heart".

The folks there told us very openly what was going on. They accused the BIA and the Tribal Government of trying to eradicate their cultural identity.

"We're here," one of the leaders told me, "because we tried everything else, and the government ignored us."

They were there, they said, for a lot of different reasons, ranging from anger over the old treaty violations, to rage about the recent murders of their brothers and sisters.

"Something," they told us and other journalists, "must be done to make the American people know we are human beings. The situation on the Pine Ridge Reservation is that the traditional people have been oppressed to the point of no return. The Tribal Government has forced us to form a civil rights group to fight for our own survival."

One of the older women in the occupation didn't pull any punches in talking about what was happening there:

They want the Indians in Wounded Knee to use up their shells, so they can attack them like they did in 1890. But, because these Indians are ready to die, they ain't gonna put down their guns like they did in 1890.

They tell us we're militant, and look at them out there, with their machine guns and big equipment. We don't want to see that; the only one we want to see here is President Nixon. If he has any guts, he better get his ass down here. We got a council tipi. The old time chiefs, they used to go to Washington all the time to sit around the big round tables, but it never did no good. Let Nixon come here; we got a round table we call the Mother Earth. They tell us we're militant, and look at them out there, with their machine guns and big equipment. They call this place a historical site, but they never tell you why. It's because we got two hundred or more dead up there on the hill, with bullets in their bodies, and they call this a historical site so they can make their damn money off the tourists.

I don't care. We're gonna win. I'm not scared of those government guns up there, because we have a Great Spirit who's more powerful than all of those guns. Maybe their St. Peter will let them into his heaven with those guns, but someday they'll have to lay them down in front of the Great Spirit.

I'm not scared. I'm in AIM, and I'm ready to die here.

Enraged by the strongarm tactics of the tribal chairman to get them to knuckle under, the Independent Oglala Nation was determined to fight to the finish. They weren't kidding. They knew their lives were on the line.

They'd intercepted and recorded radio transmissions between FBI agents and the Federal marshals, and they played a few of them for us. The marshals, remember, were perched on a hilltop beyond the Native barricade, with big machine guns. They were really anxious, it seemed from the taped transmissions, to wipe out the whole trading post.

The tapes were really spooky to listen to; the government officials were all so gung-ho to save the country for democracy, as long as that democracy extended only to the white majority. Like the guards we'd heard talking out by the second government road block, these guys were really jumpy. On the tape, I remember, these two agents were talking while my people had been beating a big drum inside the barricade.

"Oh, shit, they're beating that big war drum, again," one agent told the other.

"Yeah, I know," the second one responded. "Isn't that what they did just before they wiped out Custer?"

On another tape we heard these two crazed FBI agents yelling back and forth.

"...receiving fire from the farm house..!"

"...returning fire to the farm house..!"

Somebody was shooting at one of these guys, and they were pumping this farm house full of lead.

The AIM leaders who had been monitoring their conversation, we were told, had looked around at each other while the shooting was going on.

"Who the hell's in the farm house?" one of them had asked.

"Nobody that I know," another answered.

As it turned out, the folks who were shooting from the farm house were FBI agents, and the folks who were firing back at them were also FBI. That kind of confusion went on there all the time.

The FBI would send up flares at night, because they were afraid that the Indians were going to attack them. One time, the flares set grass ablaze and burned nine buildings to the ground. So the FBI, with their usual talent for avoiding blame, reported the fact for posterity that the Native people at Wounded Knee had set fire to nine houses, and destroyed them.

Even though this was serious business, there were some mildly amusing things that happened at the time. For example, the Sioux down in the Rosebud area decided, at about the same time I was in Wounded Knee, that their brothers inside the barricade ought to have some good fresh meat to eat. So the folks inside the barricade, ready to eat a steak or two, created an Indian-style diversion like in the old days. They made a lot of noise, and acted like they were going to break out of the barricade on one side. They really whooped it up, and the FBI shifted all their people over to that one area. At just the right moment, the Rosebud people drove 19 head of cattle through the government barricade. The FBI probably wouldn't have cared, if they'd discovered how they'd been fooled. All they knew was there was a bunch of wild Indians about to break out of the barricades and take their scalps. Of course, the only thing that got butchered and skinned that night were the contraband cattle.

The Wounded Knee occupation got a lot of bad press. Many folks thought the Indians who took over were all young radicals. But that really wasn't the case. There were a lot of older people in there, laying their lives on the line for what they believed in. There were women in their sixties and seventies doing the cooking for everyone, and one of them was in her nineties. She was a survivor of the original Wounded Knee battle back in 1890.

"I didn't die here the first time," she told me, "but I'll die here now, if it'll help in any way."

There were a lot of older folks who were members of AIM, and they were proud of what they were doing.

We made our documentary film at Wounded Knee; we taped our interviews with people. There was one woman, I remember, who told us about the beating of her son. He was an artist; a painter, and he'd been beaten so badly by the goon squad that he was permanently blinded and crippled. One of the men whom I interviewed was Pedro Bissonette; he was Vice President of the Oglala Sioux Civil Rights Organization. Shortly after I spoke with him, I heard that he had been shot and killed by those opposed to his helping his people.

Before too long, it was time for us to leave. The press had to be out of the area every day, by 4:30 in the afternoon. We were told by the Native people that the shooting never began until after the press was gone.

One last parting bit of information, about the kind of propaganda and crap the government put out about Wounded Knee: when we got ready to leave, we left at the same time as a group of Indians from Canada. These folks marched out, to go to their own country; there were no incidents of violence; they simply said their goodbyes and wished the people well. Later that night, I listened to the news on TV. The Justice Department had claimed that those Indians had fired a volley of shots at them as they left.

What a pack of lies.

We had to go through a kind of FBI de-briefing, also, when we came back through the barricades. The agents questioned us thoroughly. They wanted to know, for example, if "those people in there were as wild and radical as they were a few days before?" I told them I didn't know; that I hadn't been in there a few days before. They wanted us to tell them if we'd picked up any important rumors, while we were in there. Needless to say, I wasn't feeling too cooperative.

The FBI was all hepped up to believe the worst; I think they loved it. It must've been, for some of them, like living in a western movie, surrounding an Indian village and laying siege to it. The people inside the barricade helped to deceive them, too. What they would do was to fire a whole bunch of shotguns, in staggered rapid fire. It sounded exactly like a .50 caliber machine gun.

"Christ!" the FBI agents would say listening to the noise, "those redskins aren't fooling around!"

When we left Wounded Knee, I went back to Reno. When I got there, the phone was ringing off the hook. I got a call from the Associated Press, and they said, "We heard Marlon Brando is coming down your way, then going on to Wounded Knee. Can you tell us anything about that?"

"Nope," I told them. I hadn't heard anything about that.

A little while later, CBS called me up. "We've heard," the caller said, "that Marlon Brando's stopping in Reno, on his way to Wounded Knee. What can you tell us?"

"Not a thing," I replied.

By this time, the old gleam was in my eye; I was getting into the spirit of things, so I told this Sioux that was visiting me, that the next time somebody called I was going to put him on the phone. I would tell them that he was Marlon Brando.

Why not? we decided. But nobody called back. Too bad about that.

The people at Wounded Knee would never pin the government down to honor the old treaty of 1868.

"We're looking for peaceful negotiations," the Native people had said. "There are many points we can work out if the government will sit down and talk peace..."

As always, promises were made, but not kept. Treaty negotiations had begun in early April, but kept breaking down. In May, representatives of the White House told the Independent Oglala Nation and the AIM people that if they would come out from behind their barricades, the government would talk peace. The people were really tired; they were practically out of food, so they agreed to come on out.

On May 8, the people of Wounded Knee were evacuated. They were driven out by the Community Relations Service of the Justice Department, who collected whatever weapons they had and took everyone to a central location for processing.

Many of the leaders of the takeover were arrested, and hauled off to jail. Treaty negotiations dragged on for several months in Kyle, at the camp of Frank Fools Crow, until, finally, a message came from the White House which read, "The days of treaty making with the American Indian ended in 1871...only Congress (can change that)".

So, once again, the Native people had been put off. Their demands for a return to the terms of the treaty of 1868...particularly the establishment of a treaty commission representing the President and concerned Native people...were not met.

With this breakdown of the treaty process came a warning from the traditional people. They felt they would lose more of their brothers and sisters to violence. And they were right. By the end of the winter of '73, six more Oglala, or Oglala sympathizers, were found dead. By 1974, the latest murder had become a common topic of conversation.

The Tribal Government was never fully investigated, as the Justice Department had promised during negotiations. Treaty commission meetings between the Independent Oglala Nation and the government degenerated, finally, into a meaningless series of letters.

Life goes on at the Pine Ridge Reservation; it appears that little was resolved by the occupation of Wounded Knee. Many good things, however, came out of the confrontation. For one thing, I think, the traditional people had united in a common cause, and that in itself helped them to hold onto their old life ways.

I have shared all of this with you because it is history, and I was there; however, I need to add here that I don't really believe in the taking up of arms. Although I believe that justice must be done, and that my brothers and sisters at Wounded Knee fought valiantly, I also believe that any act committed out of anger becomes, finally, an exercise in futility. I know that peace, love, harmony with the Mother Earth, are the things that I believe in. They're the basis of my great vision, and of the Bear Tribe Medicine Society.

★ ★ ★

During the time that we were travelling on the pow wow circuit, one of Wabun's jobs was to get all the little kids she could find to sell copies of "*Many Smokes*". We called what she did *kidnapping*; she really enjoyed working with the children, and I used to call her operation "Wabunhood and her Merry Men". What we would do is give each kid a stack of magazines, and they would get ten cents a copy for what they sold. We charged fifty cents apiece for the magazine back then, and these kids were really happy to make a dime on each. They would go out boldly, and sell the magazine. Sometimes, they brought in our biggest profits.

The pow wow circuit included going to the Pendleton Round-Up up near Pendleton, Oregon; that was one of the biggest ones around. We also went to the Omak Stampede, where there's a lot of Indian dancing, but also what's called a "suicide race". In this race there's a group of horsemen who compete by galloping wide open down a very steep hill. At the bottom of the hill they plunge into a good-sized river, and they have to get their horses across and up the bank, in order to place for prizes. The suicide race is held once a day, while the Omak Stampede lasts, and it's quite a sight to see; a lot of people who watch it are roaring drunk. When we went to Omak the first time, we called it the Omak "Bash"; the Indians, non-Indians, the tourists, the local businessmen ... few of them could stand up after a few hours of celebration. This would be the last big celebration for most of these folks before winter set in. They figured, I guess, they'd be sitting indoors in a month or so, so they'd better let off all of their extra steam.

There were a lot of times at these pow wows when I would climb into my car or truck, and go to sleep to the beating of the hand game drums. As I mentioned before, Native people like gambling, and the hand game is one of their favorites. Hand game teams come from all over the United States, and even Canada. Like team members of the bowling craze which swept the country a few years back, but much more enduring, some of the teams even have shirts with Indian designs on them and with their team names embroidered on the backs.

Some other pow wows that we really enjoyed going to, were the Chief Seattle Days near Suquamish, Washington, and the pow wows near Neah Bay; we'd always have a great time at those, and they'd have a big salmon feast for everyone.

We would also go to the Warm Springs Celebration, put on by the Warm Springs Confederated Tribes, up in Oregon. It's a religious ceremony performed by what is known as the seven-drum religion. When the ceremony begins, there's a circle of seven drums which beat simultaneously. That is a very powerful thing to hear. While the drums are being beaten, a group of people called *jump dancers* make a circle around them, taking very long jumps; eventually they fall into ecstatic trances. When the dancing around the drums has been completed, the dancers always end up at the spot from which they started.

During the year, the Warm Springs society which sponsors the celebration has collected money from rummage sales and so on, and at the end of the ceremony there's a big give-away of blankets, scarves, and other really nice things. Afterwards, always, there's an enormous feast.

The ceremonies continue for three days, and during that time, the Warm Springs people feed everyone who shows up; they sit them all down together, in one huge grouping of tables, and then they make their prayers. That, too, is a very powerful experience.

The teachings of the Warm Springs society have come to them through resurrected beings, through those who have died, and then returned with messages from the spirit world. Before the BIA interfered, these people never embalmed their dead; now they have to. Originally, the unembalmed bodies would be left to rest. Some would resurrect themselves. The jump dance itself is a ceremony for communicating with the spirit world.

I respect the medicine of the Warm Springs people. I respect everybody else's medicine, although I may not be a part of it myself. To me, life is a classroom. As I travel down the good road, both my knowledge and medicine continue to grow.

★ ★ ★

The two trailers we had in Reno during the early 70's were on half-acre pieces of land, and the land wasn't capable of producing very much food for us. Reno is a low water area, and our place was so small we couldn't have more than two or three visitors there at a time. From travelling the pow wow trail, we had a solid enough financial base to bring the Bear Tribe to a workable size again. What we needed was more land.

The land outside of Los Gatos was not suitable, because of its vulnerability to earthquakes, so I traded it off. I saw in my visions that it was time to be looking for a better place to plant ourselves. We'd had a few more people join up with us, and they seemed to have their hearts set in the right direction.

I had a dream about a tall mountain which was covered with beautiful pine trees; we decided to go up to Oregon and see what we could find. All the time that we were travelling that way, though, my medicine told me we would not stay in that area. I went anyway, and, as it turned out, we stayed there for about a year and one-half, for a very worthy reason.

We ended up near Klamath Falls. It was there that the Klamath

Indians had lived for centuries. During the Eisenhower administration, as I mentioned earlier, the government tried to disband the Native tribes, and the Klamaths were among those who suffered the most severe loss of land and cultural identity. Their tribal structure had pretty much disappeared.

When Native land claims up there had finally been resolved, the government awarded, I believe, $49,000 to every Klamath born before 1957. That's a lot of money to inspire instant assimilation; there's no quicker way to kill the culture of a person who is close to nature, than to give him too much money in a lump sum. Most of the Klamaths had taken their cash and either bought their way into the mainstream of white society, or squandered it.

There was a Klamath Indian named Edison Chiloquin up there, though, who said "no" to that first offer of instant wealth.

"This is my sacred land," he told the U.S. Government. "It will never be for sale."

He was one of about 150 Klamaths who said "no" and became known as the Remaining Members. In the mid-1970's, the government tried to buy off these Remaining Members, upping the ante to over $100,000. Edison still said "no".

Edison really tried to preserve his family's cultural identity, and their religion.

I'd been up to Klamath Falls with Wabun a couple of times to go to pow wows, and we'd met the Chiloquins. They offered to let us live on ten acres of land they had. All we had to do was to make our own improvements on it, and in return for living there, we would help to publicize Edison's land fight. What happened was that when the Klamaths had been terminated, an old village site where Edison's grandfather was chief had been lost. It was owned by the U.S. Forest Service. Edison wanted it back. He had offered to trade some of the land he owned for it, but the U.S. was not being very cooperative. So Edison wanted to launch a full-scale campaign over the issue.

When we knew we wanted to leave Reno, Wabun and I drove up to Klamath Falls to look at the land he'd offered us. It looked pretty good, so we sent a crew up there to renovate an old building that we planned to live in. Kwasind, a new tribe member, and Mondamin did the renovations. In the spring of 1974, the rest of us joined them; there was Wabun, myself, Nimimosha, Willow, Richard, Helen, Ruth, Chibiabos, Chris, Spotted Pony, Little Wolf and Justin.

We raised chickens, and grew a good-sized garden. We built ourselves a sweatlodge, and we even built a few more cabins. I guess, in all, we spent about $5,000 on improvements while we were there.

We worked very hard, at that time, to help Edison in his fight for tribal land. Wabun used all of her journalistic and public relations experience to coordinate this effort. We set up a benefit auction to help fund the campaign; we accepted donations of cash, and Indian craft items to auction off. We wrote articles in *Many Smokes*, and Wabun wrote and distributed a booklet on the history of the land fight. We held a Unity Gathering on Edison's land. Indians and non-Indians came from a lot of different places to participate; we got Thomas Banyacya, a spokesman for the Hopi people, and Lee Piper, the Bird Clan Mother of the Eastern Band of Cherokees, to go there. It was a powerful time.

Later, we got Edison's story on radio and TV in Los Angeles, as well as nationally, and we decided to travel to Washington, D.C., to lobby for his cause. I remember that when we went to talk to a congressman, he was being so rigid and unhearing that Wabun's frustration moved her to the point of tears. Nothing else had worked, but the threat of a woman's tears apparently frightened this politician. He began to listen, and, finally, the government began negotiations with Edison over the land he wanted.

Our participation in Edison's fight, though, seemed to be something that would not bear fruit. We had a congressman ready to draft a bill; we had the Forest Service willing to cooperate. Yet, for one reason or another, we never quite succeeded in our attempts. Either the government wasn't satisfied, or Edison wasn't satisfied, or the Klamath people themselves became agitated over the situation.

We finally decided that we were putting so much of our energy into Chiloquin's fight, that we didn't have time to build the Bear Tribe. When we got back from Washington we decided it was time to look for another location. My medicine told me to move on; we also felt that the land we had been working was not a very good place for us to stay.

The gardens were not doing very well, and there was an irrigation ditch which ran through the property. Every spring, farmers poisoned the ditch with weed killers, and it not only killed the algae, it also killed the fish and frogs. That was the final straw for me; we had no way to control the contamination there.

Although we decided to leave at that point, I believe we were doing a good thing while we were there. I think it might have helped some.

While we were in Klamath Falls, a friendly lawyer, Richard Kalar, had helped the Bear Tribe to incorporate as a religious, educational, non-profit organization under the laws of the U.S. Goverment. The Bear Tribe became the first Native medicine society in U.S. history to seek recognition under the laws of the government, and we got that recognition.

It was an interesting thing to think about. For hundreds of years, Native Americans had been practicing their religions without the sanction of anyone but the Great Spirit. Now, in the twentieth century, we found it necessary to incorporate our religion. Our Articles of Incorporation have helped several other medicine societies to gain federal recognition.

While we lived in Klamath Falls, I found Shasta, my medicine dog, or rather, he found me. Wabun and I were driving back from a pow wow in Susanville, California, and we were going up a little country road near Mount Shasta. We saw this beautiful creature, which looked like a white wolf, by the side of the road. It looked very powerful; I stopped the car and called to it, and Wabun got out and left her door open. Shasta, though, came running to my side of the car; he leapt in the window, over my shoulder, and sat himself down on the inventory of craft items in the back seat. I've never seen a dog with such a big head and such large shoulders, that did not have wolf in its blood. What Shasta is, I believe, is a cross between wolf and white shepherd.

Anyway, he jumped in right over my shoulder, and we drove on down the road. It all felt so natural — good medicine; he'd been waiting there for us to come along, in the middle of the wilderness.

I say Shasta is a medicine dog because of the way we found him, and because, in the old days, the Chippewa people had special reverence for the white dog. My people had their Bear Society, which felt it gained strong medicine from the bear. But, since bears couldn't be kept in camp, for obvious reasons, the white dog became a medicine symbol, a spiritual bear.

Shasta lays with his paws crossed in front of our medicine wheel, and guards us in the sweatlodge, along with Tsacha, his partner, Wabun's labrador/shepherd mix who found us a week before Shasta did. When I get ready to go out on the lecture trail, he sits in the road with his paws crossed. He's making medicine for me.

There was one more incident up at Klamath Falls, which I really enjoy talking about; it was good medicine. While we were there, there was a scarcity of hay. We had two horses to feed, plus Edison's eleven horses, and wherever I went the farmers told me, "Sorry, we don't have any hay for sale. But maybe you ought to go see Red Ross".

Finally I decided to go see Red Ross.

When I got out to his farm he was working in his field. I went up to him and I introduced myself.

"Hi, I'm Sun Bear," I told him, "and I need to buy some hay."

"Where are you from?" he asked me.

We got to talking and it turned out that he, too, had lived on the White Earth Reservation where I was born. He left there in 1937, and he married the first teacher I'd had in school there. Her name had been Clementine O'Rourke.

"Well, ain't that something!" Red said.

So he invited me home for dinner. He told me just to walk into his house, and say, "Hello, Miss O'Rourke."

I did that, and she was really surprised when I told her who I was. We developed a very strong friendship after that, and Red sold me all the hay I wanted. He even knocked five dollars a ton off of the price, so my horses managed to eat very well after that time.

Red helped out a lot when we were building on Edison's land, even though he teased me about some things. He called our place the "Hippie Hilton", because we all wore our hair long.

When we headed out of Oregon, we were travelling in a car

and in a yellow slat-sided truck. By putting a camper on the back of the truck, we had created a mobile home. In it we had six adults, one child, a dog, and all of our *Many Smokes* equipment. Those days were really something.

From Klamath Falls we travelled to the Pendleton Round-up to put a little more money into our pockets.

From there, we went up to Seattle, Washington, where we visited with Larry and Lee Piper. We were glad to see them, and they graciously hosted us for about a month, while we wrote, edited and printed an issue of *Many Smokes* and waited for our medicine to move us further down the road.

When we left the Pipers, we went to look at land near Joseph, Oregon; and also a piece of land up in northern Idaho. None of the land we looked at seemed quite right to me. My medicine, my dream, told me it was time to find our permanent location, a place where nobody else would control the land so we could care for it properly.

The dreams had been coming stronger all the time; they showed me a place of enormous power, a place with fir and pine trees, cliffs filled with rock caves, and an overlook beyond which lay a shimmering river. I had no idea where this mountain top might be, but when we got into the Spokane area of Washington, I suddenly knew. It would be very close to there.

I made my medicine and my prayers, to find out if this was the place for the Tribe to settle down. We arrived in the late fall and rented a summer resort near Sacheen Lake. It was very beautiful, so we stayed there through the winter, looking for land, contacting potential visitors, planning seminars and working on *Many Smokes*. We looked in the paper, drove around, and finally, one day, we found our mountain top. It was advertised in a small paper called Panaroma View. As soon as I looked at the land, I knew that I had found home.

I knew it was a power spot, but I didn't know why. We discovered after we bought the land that our mountain had been used for hundreds of years as a vision quest place for the Spokane Indians — a sacred power place. At the foot of the mountain ridge there are some medicine pictographs; I've translated some of them. Some of what they say, I feel I can share with you. The rock writings tell of a sealing of the medicine caves in our mountain. When the time is right, maybe at the time of the cleansing, the caves will open up to the right people; they will yield their medicine power to those who are worthy.

The mountain, we discovered, was called *Axtú Leman Sumíx* by the Spokane Indians. That means, loosely translated, *paint mountain, power mountain*, or *vision mountain*.

From the top of Vision Mountain, you can see the Spokane River. Long Lake, formed by the dams on the river, lies below us, and it shimmers in the sunshine, set in fields of full sweet clover.

photo: The Bear Tribe

The Bear Tribe, Winter 1987

Bottom row (l to r): Yarrow Goding, Cougar, Michelle Odayinquae, Ruth Blue Camas, Mary Fallahey.

Top row (l to r): Sun Bear, Nimimosha, Raven, Marc Creller, Gaia, Beth Davis Earthseeker, Gail Morning Wind, Shawnodese, Wabun, Simon Corn Man.

CHAPTER TWELVE
THE BEAR TRIBE AND SELF RELIANCE

We bought our land on Vision Mountain with a down-payment of cash, and silver and turquoise jewelry. The land belongs, legally, to the Bear Tribe Medicine Society, and that goes along with my vision, and my beliefs. I don't feel that a single person can own the land; it belongs to the Creator. Originally, we purchased 18 ½ acres, but we've added another 40 acres, and friends of the Tribe own another 100 or so acres near us. The Rainbow Bridge (formerly Draco) Foundation, founded by Mahad-'yuni (Evelyn Eaton), has an adjacent 20-acre piece. Evelyn, who died in 1984 at the age of 80, was our tribal grandmother, and the author of over twenty books including I SEND A VOICE and THE SHAMAN AND THE MEDICINE WHEEL, and SNOWY EARTH COMES GLIDING.

When we first moved here, I was walking up in the woods one day, toward the top ridge of the mountain. It was a very dark and cloudy day, and I saw a beam of light in just one area; it came down out of the clouds and it lit up the earth. I walked to the spot where the light shone and I sat there for awhile, feeling the power and good energy coming in from the universe. There was only one way to interpret that sign, I knew; it meant our land was sacred and holy, and we belonged here. It was after that experience that we read the pictographs, and discovered the medicine history of the mountain and the Spokane Indians.

For us, too, Vision Mountain has been a place of great vision, and of power; the energy here is very strong, and nobody comes here without experiencing the good vibrations.

It was February, 1976, when we finally started to build our first little cabin. The earth was frozen, and there was ice and snow covering the ground. We had to build fires to thaw the earth, and move a very large fallen tree, in order to expand our first foundation, a root cellar left from homesteading days.

We had electric power already; we were surprised and happy to discover that. There was a tree to the west of the site where we were building, and it had an electric meter attached to it. When we first saw it we plugged in an appliance, and the meter wheel started spinning. We put our refrigerator out underneath the tree. I thought it looked really unique out there.

The first cabin was very small; it had the root cellar, half-dug into the slope of a hill. There was a main floor, and a second story that was pretty much like a little attic. Today, we use that cabin as a playhouse and school for the children, and for extra sleeping space.

The whole tribe lived in or around that little cabin during our first spring and summer on the mountain. Things were pretty cold and cramped. When somebody walked around on the second floor, it was really something; those of us who were on the first floor felt like we were inside the kettle of a big drum. But the cabin was our home; it kept the rain off of our heads, and we all felt very grateful.

We had a spring on the east side of the cabin, and although it wasn't much more than a wet spot in the ground back then, it supplied us with water. We built our first kitchen just below it, a little 8 X 8 building where we did our cooking and canning. There was a woodstove in the kitchen, and a little bit of counter space.

The man who built the kitchen was only 5'3"; that turned out to be significant because when he was finished, he was the only person in the tribe who could stand up inside of it. In order to cook in there the rest of us had to bend over, and besides that, the oven door to the woodstove kept falling open on our shins. Eventually, we had to fix that oven door, and cut the corner posts on the building to put in shims and raise the roof. In the meantime, though, we struggled along, and we did fine.

We hauled water; we made a lot of prayers; and we managed to cook enough food in our little kitchen to feed everyone. During that first winter and spring and summer, we even did some canning of vegetables in there.

By April all of us had moved out of the Sacheen Lake Resort and onto the mountain. We dug out a hole where our spring was and it filled with cool clear water. We braced the sides of the hole and lined the bottom with stones, and we had a little reservoir. It felt good to have that spring; it was one of our first requirements for survival on the land. Our water came down from the top of the mountain. That meant nobody could poison it with chemicals. There were no dams sitting above our heads, which could burst and destroy all of our hard work. A spring, most importantly, doesn't require electric pumps to keep it going; so, a part of our water supply, at least, is completely independent of the machinery of the modern world. If we treat it with proper respect, it will always supply our needs.

Back in Oregon, Nimimosha had become pregnant, and she gave birth to a baby girl the week before we moved here from Sacheen Lake. One of the first ceremonies we did on Vision Mountain was to give the baby a name. Nimimosha, Mondamin ... the father, Wabun, and I, took the infant to the mountain top. I held her above my head and I showed her to the universe. I introduced her to the Great Spirit, and to the four directions. We named her *Wabeno-wusk*, which is Ojibway for the herb we call "yarrow". The Chippewa people considered yarrow to be a very powerful medicine plant; it represents the East, the springtime, and the early morning...and it is used to heal cuts, and to make tea for colds and other ailments. Nimimosha also chose that name to honor the tie she felt between the baby and Wabun, who is named after the Spirit Keeper of the East.

When summer came we started building our longhouse. It's perched on a hillside to the north of the first cabin, and it measures 24'x 64'. The longhouse today is the hub of our tribal life. It provides a sleeping place for several of our tribal members, as well as visitors. It is heated with several woodstoves, and inside there's a kitchen; a living area; an office; a council room; and an herb room. The longhouse is a very homey place, with drying herbs hanging from the ceiling beams, and lots of Native artwork on the walls. Sometimes we do our pipe ceremonies in the living room. We all gather in a circle and make our prayers; we offer thanks to the Great Spirit.

Putting the longhouse together was hard work, but everybody helped, both Tribe members and the increasing number of visitors who came that summer. I remember Nimimosha hanging Yarroe up in a cradleboard from one of the vertical supports while she helped to put in the flooring. Yarroe would watch and listen to the hammering and sawing, and give us her newborn blessing. Kwasind did a lot of building on the longhouse, and he knew what he was doing.

We traded what we could to get wood from area lumber companies, and we also received donations of wood and other building supplies from interested local businesses. Most of the slabwood siding and the 1' x 12's that we used were factory seconds. What that means is that there was a knothole or a crack or a splinter here and there, which more perfectionist folks wouldn't like to have showing in their homes. But the wood was fine as far as we were concerned. In fact, I think that the finish on the longhouse looks really good; it looks like a part of the mountain, with its gnarls and knots.

We rarely use our own timber here, for building or burning; we would rather let our windfallen trees rot into compost for the soil. So what we do is to trade for building supplies, or we use the wood from windfalls, slashpiles and forest burns on other people's property, when they offer it to us.

We learned a lot about building and self reliance while we were putting up the longhouse. Factory seconds are invaluable. If you work real hard at it you can re-cycle, salvage, scrounge, bargain, and improvise. We've always been willing to combine manufactured goods with natural materials. Native stone and branches come in handy for a lot of things; we use them for cabinet handles, towel racks, table legs. Substandard building materials — like salvaged siding, insulation, fixtures, window and door frames — work fine, as long as you're willing to put in a little extra effort.

So, by late autumn, we had our longhouse finished and we all moved in. Our community was growing like a garden; there was the cabin, the kitchen, the longhouse, some tipis, and very soon afterwards, we built our chicken house and our barn.

During that first summer we had begun to set up what we call our Self Reliance Center on Vision Mountain. We offered a series of seminars and workshops to people who came from all over the country. They came to learn self-sufficiency skills, the spiritual teachings of the Native people, and how these teachings related to the earth today. Our new students learned how to raise their own food; how to keep beehives; how to construct buildings; how to dry fruits and vegetables; how to build temporary shelters. During the first seminar I did, part of what I taught them was the art of splitting wood. I could see those folks really needed to learn how to do that, because I lost two axe handles in the first half-hour of the first session. I guess they thought that you chopped wood with the axe handle instead of with the blade.

Our first self reliance groups helped us to get our buildings completed and our early gardens going. We planted above the longhouse, near a spot where we have a pond. We set the garden in an area that was lower than the pond, then siphoned water downhill through a garden hose. The water was stored, halfway down, in an old hot water tank, and the system worked really well during that first summer. After that, though, we discovered that the pond would temporarily dry up in late summer, so we had to figure out a more dependable way to get water to our fruits and vegetables. Digging a well, as we had known from the beginning, was the only solution for our increasing water needs.

Learning self-sufficiency, for some of the first people in our seminars, proved to be quite a challenge. They had to learn, for one thing, just how limited our water supply was, and that to be frivolous with water, which is the blood of the Earth Mother, would mean that we might lose our supply.

Our spring water, like I said, comes from the top of the mountain, and it is pure, but the volume of water which comes in from the spring is just enough to meet our practical demands.

"When we use it to water the plants, or for the animals," I told those first people, "it will keep on flowing. But when we get greedy, when we squander it, our spring will not flow for us anymore. We have to be careful here. We don't use our water for washing cars, for running a laundromat. We don't even try to get a bath a day for everyone out of it. The Spokane River is right down at the bottom of the mountain; you can go swimming there whenever you feel the need to take off any road dust. It's not necessary to take a bath here, every day, and it is very wasteful."

Most of the people listened to that advice. There was one time, though, when we ran into some trouble. A young man was here, with a self reliance group, and he had very thick, curly hair. He insisted it had to be washed every day. We told him if he really needed to groom that often he should consider going into town to find himself a shower, that our little spring would not accommodate that kind of vanity. The guy was nice and quiet; he didn't argue with us at all, but he continued to use the water to shampoo every day. Then, one day, he decided he needed to wash his car, and after he did, our spring dried up.

This was in the middle of the seminar, and we needed water for cooking, drinking, for the animals and the gardens. It was gone.

Soon, the folks in the seminar came to me and said, "Sun Bear, we need to go haul some water. We're thirsty, and we're hot."

I said, "No!".

"Now," I told them, "You'll learn some self reliance. You'll learn what it's like to live when you don't conserve your resources, when you don't show respect for the gifts of the Earth Mother. You're going to live now with the situation that you've created.

"When the spring finally starts to flow again," I told them, "the first water that comes in is going to the cows, because they need that water in order to make milk. It's not the livestock's fault that the spring has gone dry. The cows, the horses...all of them will drink before we do. We'll be last."

That's the way it was. Within the next few weeks, after the spring had rejuvenated and the seminar was over, some of those people came to me and told me what a powerful experience that had been, having to live in an uncomfortable situation that they never thought they'd find themselves in.

Our spring hasn't dried up again, since then; we know, though, that if we get greedy, next time the water will be a little bit slower coming back to us.

In the longhouse, by the kitchen sink and by the bathroom sink and tub, we have little blessings written out, which praise the water, the life-blood of the Earth; they remind whoever stays with us to be grateful when they wash, and to give their thanks to the Creator. I stay conscious of the water when I'm travelling, also. I never flush a toilet unless I really need to.

While we're on the subject of water, I'll tell you about the well we finally dug for ourselves three years after we moved in. We knew from the beginning that we would need one, so we did some dowsing to locate a good water table. We came up with several places, but a few of them wouldn't work. One was in the middle of our dirt driveway; one was down in the middle of one of the pastures, but we broke six rock bits trying to get through to it, and it was on a lower level than the longhouse, so we would have had to pump the water uphill to get it where it was needed. So, finally, we decided to drill on a spot east of the longhouse, and on a higher elevation.

In order to get the well drilled, we had to cut down a very large Ponderosa Pine; it was really interesting, because we had this well-drilling contractor come out, and he was really upset about having to cut down that tree. He didn't want to do it.

So we cut the tree down; we made our prayers, and did a ceremony to ask permission of the tree, and to let it know that it would be giving its life to provide the whole mountain top with water.

The well-driller felt much better about seeing that tree go down, both because of the ceremony we had performed, and because he didn't have to cut it down himself. There was another reason too, I remember, for his feeling better about the entire episode.

While we were doing our ceremony, a hawk flew overhead and began to circle lower and lower, and that really touched the man. We could see that.

"I think hawks are the most beautiful birds there are," he told us afterwards. "Maybe that's because my name is Hawkins."

I think Mr. Hawkins got a lot out of drilling our well for us. Finally, we had a good supply of water.

There's another story I'd like to tell you here, about a hawk. This happened in 1978, just a few years after we moved to Vision Mountain, and I feel it reaffirmed the mission of the Bear Tribe ... which is to help restore balance, harmony, and purity to the Mother Earth.

I'd been out of the area for about three months, and on my first day back I went to Spokane to do some things. I used the phone in a local bookstore; we didn't have our own phone in town yet, so the folks who owned the bookstore ... who were good friends ... let us make calls from there.

I'd finished making my third call, and I picked up the phone to make a fourth. When I put my ear to the receiver I discovered that somebody was on the other end of the line; the phone hadn't even rung before I picked it up.

I said hello, and the voice at the other end said:

"Sun Bear! An eagle fell from the sky today and I found it; it's hurt. Can I bring it to you?"

How powerful it felt to hear that message on my first day back in Spokane, after a three-month absence!

"Of course," I told the caller. "I'd love to try helping the winged-one."

He brought the bird to me, and I saw that it wasn't an eagle; it was a redtail hawk. That, like the eagle, is a very sacred bird among

Native people. I kept the hawk in my car all day, wrapped in a sweater. I offered it water, some ground meat, and made my prayers for its healing. Finally, the hawk brother drank some water.

At sunset I looked at the bird; I could tell it wanted me to remove the sweater wrapped around its wings. I did so; brother hawk opened its wings up fully, twice ... then, it died.

We'd built our Medicine Wheel on Vision Mountain by then, and we laid the hawk in the center of the Wheel for a day, to give it honor. Then we took it up on the mountain, and laid it to rest in a sacred place.

The message the Great Spirit gave to me about that hawk was clear; there were no outward signs of injury ... it simply had dropped out of the sky. The Spirit told me the hawk had died of the poisons of pollution, of toxins in the environment which were spreading through everything, every day.

★ ★ ★

Wabun and I continued to travel to pow wows during the first year on Vision Mountain; we sold jewelry, books, crafts, whatever we could pull together to bring in money for food and building materials. While we did very well at the pow wows, we were feeling that it would be better to stay at home more often. We both felt that a time was coming when we would need to find alternative ways to support the tribe; we didn't know how we were going to do that, but my medicine told me that soon there would be some very good changes. There were.

We supplemented our income by printing our first book mail-order catalog during that first summer, and our mail-order business began to blossom. It was all beginning to help us get off of the pow wow trail, to run our *buffalo hunt* from our home.

In our mail-order and travelling bookstore now, we sell books on Native American culture and religion, as well as books on nature and the environment, on survival skills, and on other related subjects. We also offer everything from tipis to hairpipes and tiny seed beads.

Our first self reliance programs were pretty small, and not well-publicized, but, from them, we saw what a crying need there was for us to share our knowledge. The Great Spirit, through my dreams, was telling me it was time to reach out further, to speak about self reliance and my dreams and visions with anyone who was open to hearing what I had to say. At first, we travelled to local places; we spoke to church groups here and there, to college groups, as I had in earlier days. I did a program with the Spokane public schools in which I would spend a week or so talking to the young folks about Native philosophy and self reliance.

Then, very suddenly, the energy of what we were doing began to pick up. The way it happened was that in the fall of our first year at Vision Mountain, some people came to visit us from Vancouver, British Columbia. There was Jerome Twin Rainbow, Sue Ellen Primost, and several others. They liked what we were doing, and they had connections with The *3HO* people who were getting ready to do the first World Symposium on the Humanities, up in Vancouver. They felt that Wabun and I should go up there and be heard, so they arranged for us to get an invitation. We went up in October, 1976, and we gave a very successful talk. The symposium proved to be a place that offered wide exposure to us; from that experience, a lot of speaking invitations began to pour in.

In the following year, 1977, our speaking calendar began to fill up; we were lecturing regularly then, to a lot of metaphysical groups, and to church and school groups. Since that time, we've been going further and further across the world, and we've been designing seminars on an ever-increasing variety of subjects.

The seminars go over very well; we've talked to thousands of people in person every year, and to many more via the media. Besides doing the seminars, we've been invited to and have spoken at such places as the Mind, Body and Spirit Festivals in both the United States and in England; we've been to the Mandala Conference in San Diego, California; to a number of conferences of the Association for Research and Enlightenment; to the Omega Institute in New York; The Sufi School of Spiritual Healing — West, in Eugene, Oregon; The World Symposium on the Humanities in both Vancouver and Toronto; the Abode of the Message in New York; the Laughing Man Institute in Marin, California; Alpha Logics in Connecticut; the Spiritual Advisory Council Festivals in both Chicago and Orlando; the Lama Foundation in New Mexico; the Ojai Foundation in California; Another Place in New Hampshire; and to many other centers, conferences, colleges and churches, both large and small. It just keeps growing all the time.

As our outside speaking invitations grew, so did our seminars at home. Our Self Reliance program was becoming more well-defined; by 1978, it was going full force. In that year we began to offer a lot of different workshops, and we called the whole program our "Circle of Life Seminars". We offered workshops on self reliance in the wilderness; on birthing; parenting; womanhood; male and female energy...there were six different seminars.

One of our most important, and most successful programs, which began to grow in 1978, is our Vision Quest program. People come to us in growing numbers all the time; they do a purification sweat, and after intensive interviews to determine their readiness, they go out on the mountain from one to four days to fast and pray for a vision, a direction that will guide their lives. Many people have made their vision quests here and had powerful experiences. They come to us afterwards, and we help to interpret their visions; in that way they can discover their personal medicine, their paths in life.

In 1978, too, we published our SELF RELIANCE BOOK. It grew from a small book we had published back in Reno, called *Walk In Balance*. It contains a lot of important information. It introduces the

Bear Tribe to the world, first of all, and tells about what we do and what we believe in. It tells about my visions, about the Hopi prophecies and the coming Purification. The SELF RELIANCE BOOK also tells about how to relate to the Earth Mother; how to come into harmony; how to perform some simple ceremonies; and it gives good advice on how to build a community. There are poems, legends and prayers in the book; but the main part of the text is devoted to practical skills; self reliance techniques as they relate to the land; to water; food preservation; wild plants and herbs; and many other things. Some of the most appealing information the book offers to some folks is in the sections on finance and cottage industries. The SELF RELIANCE BOOK has been reprinted many times by 1983.

When people really started coming to Vision Mountain in large numbers, we were still getting a lot of *flower power* types. While these people were sincere seekers in their own ways, they were also into drug mind-sets, and sometimes, into working as little as possible. Those kinds of folks couldn't stay with us, of course; we'd had enough experience with them during the Medicine Rock days, and many of them didn't understand that making medicine meant not only praying, but doing a lot of hard work, too. Whether you're cooking, working in the garden, working in the office, filling book orders, plucking chickens, doing a sweat ceremony or a pipe ceremony, or just praying very hard at your personal power spot, you'll find that it's possible to rise at six in the morning and keep yourself busy all day here. What I always like to tell folks about the Bear Tribe is that one thing we have is 100% employment. That's a whole lot better than the national employment rate.

A lot of those folks who were coming in here were pretty strung out; they wanted a place where they could park their bodies and contemplate, and that's not the way the Medicine Society functions.

The years between 1977 and the present sort of blur together; things have been happening so fast.

As my vision grows, the Tribe grows too, but we don't follow a "game plan", a projected plan of growth and development, as much as we follow our medicine. If our medicine told us, tomorrow, to pick up and leave Vision Mountain, that's what we would do.

The Bear Tribe is a teaching society, and Vision Mountain exists as a base for us to work from. When a person comes to stay with us and learn, he learns from everything that goes on here, even from the frictions that might arise. Maybe, for example, a visitor sees that somebody here is unhappy because somebody else didn't smile at him, or they spoke sharply to him. The temptation, of course, is to say, "Hey, these folks don't get along so well", when, in fact, we do, because out of that disharmony we learn a lesson; we try to develop a healthy balance. The student who comes to us watches and learns, and we learn as well, and that interplay is part of the teaching we're all about. We don't try to back off or walk softly with each other all the time; we try to communicate and work things out.

Sometimes here, too, our medicine path may be unclear for a period of time. Society's way of dealing with that, of course, would be to figure things out, to plan a course of action, but we don't always do that here. You don't force the medicine; it will come to you. You accept the knowledge that the Spirit has given you, and then know the rest is somewhere down the line. When you really need an answer to a question, the Spirit will sing into your ears and tell you what comes next.

We try to reach a general consensus on everything that we do at Vision Mountain; although, at times, I have to make final decisions for the Tribe. We have a council circle here for making decisions, and every person in the Tribe has a right to speak out and share his or her views. To make sure that everyone has a say, we pass around what is called a "talking stick". That's another Native tradition. The person holding the stick has the right to speak, and everyone else listens with full concentration. We use a beaded stick which is decorated with feathers and deer dew claws. When a person has finished talking, the stick is passed on.

If we reach an impasse in council, ultimately, the people who make final decisions are myself, Wabun or Shawnodese. Both before and beyond that we use our medicine to determine what we should do in any given situation. The main questions we always try to deal with, are how adding something new into our lives might affect our relationship with the Great Spirit, with the Earth Mother, and with each other.

I want to tell you about the people who are the Bear Clan members of the Tribe. These are people who have made a lifelong commitment towards bringing my vision into fulfillment.

Wabun, my medicine helper, has been with me since 1972. I think that you have a pretty strong feeling about who she is from all that has been shared already in this book.

Shawnodese, born Thomas More Huber, is subchief of the Tribe, and coordinator of the Apprentice Program. He is also our financial planner and designer, and coordinates the workings of our computer. He and Wabun do *Medicine Wheel Consultations* for people, and he works with counseling and healing people in many other ways. Before joining the Tribe, in 1979, he worked as a college teacher of yoga, physiology and marine biology; as an Environmental Health Specialist; as a computer programmer. He was active with many different religious and philosophical groups in the Bay Area, in the Bodega Bay area near Eureka, California, and in Boise, Idaho. He brought with him many good ideas on philosophy, health, prosperity and positive thought. He is also a good singer, pianist and guitarist.

Nimimosha, born Anne Ross, or Annie, has been working with me since 1965. She has helped to bring the Bear Tribe into existence. She is a medicine helper to me, and the secretary and assistant subchief of the Tribe. She has edited *Many Smokes* for many years, takes care of much of the Tribe's correspondence and networking and is the coordinator of our visitors' program. She established the business systems for our mail order/catalog business, and was the Tribe's bookkeeper for one and one-half years. She is an accomplished graphics designer who works on the art for *Many Smokes*, for our catalog, and for other projects. She is a co-author of THE BEAR TRIBE'S SELF RELIANCE BOOK, and she also designed the book. Prior to coming to the Tribe, she was a student, a substitute teacher, and a legal secretary.

Yarroe is Nimimosha's daughter. She was born into the Tribe in 1976. She is an extremely open, intelligent young lady who makes everyone who visits here feel loved. She has been helping Wabun with herbal remedies since she was a toddler, and she hears and sings many songs of the Earth.

Thunderbird Woman (Erika Malitzky) was born in Cologne, West Germany, and came to the Tribe in 1979. In Cologne she worked as a laboratory assistant in the field of medical research. Since coming here, she has worked on the farm, and has directed all of our mail order book business. She is now art director and advertising manager for *Many Smokes*, the coordinator of The Bear Tribe Catalog, a graphics artist, and coordinator of our European speaking tours. She is also my German translator. Many of the songs on the Bear Tribe's chant tape *The Dawning* have come through Thunderbird Woman. She also does the artwork for a calendar that has been printed annually in Germany since 1981.

Raven (Hans Wilhelm Leo) also came to us from Germany. He was born in Friesland where he acquired a deep love for Mother Earth. After working on the farm for awhile, he took over as manager of the mail order book business, and is co-director of our Spokane offices. He also works with European and other visitors, and speaks about the traditional Native European religions, and how they relate to the Native American way.

Cougar (Don Auclair) came to us in 1981, from Arkansas where he ran his own self sufficient farm for eight years. He is now our farm manager, and the carver of some very beautiful pipes. He is an excellent all around craftsperson, and an advocate for the rights of children.

Silver Otter, Don's son Simon, helps his father with much of the maintenance of the farm, and is a self-taught chemist. He is fifteen.

Tamarisk, Don's daughter Jessie, is a lovely girl fast coming into womanhood who has maintained a vitality and openness that endears her to all the people who come through here. She also hears and sings many earth songs.

I'd also like to honor the Earth Clan members who are living and working with us at this time.

Singing Pipe Woman (Donna Dupree) has been coming to study and work here since 1980. She coordinated our 1982 Texas Medicine Wheel Gathering, then came here to go through our Apprentice Screening Program and to stay on coordinating all of our Medicine Wheel Gatherings and Intensives, and our speaking. She is one of Sun Bear's apprentices; a loving and hard-working person.

Sparrow, Singing Pipe Woman's daughter Casey, is a very intelligent young woman with a deep love for the earth, and for earth ceremonies. She is learning to develop her ceremonial and ecological skills here.

Sun Eagle (Matthew Ryan) came here from the Albany, N.Y. area. Since his 1982 arrival he has managed to upgrade our car fleet so it is more ecological and economical. Sun Eagle managed our gardens and building projects in 1983, and coordinated visitors working at the farm.

Blue Camas (Ruth Stafford) first met us when we were doing seminars on the East Coast, and, later after a visit to Vision Mountain, fell in love with it and decided to live here. She is our bookkeeper, proofreader, and seamstress. She has brought calm efficiency into our tribal life.

★ ★ ★

There's been a great surge of interest in what we're doing over these past few years. I think that the spiritual movement we're involved in has become one of the fastest growing phenomena on this continent, and in the rest of the world as well. I believe we are about ten years into the Cleansing already; it's plain to see, with the volcanoes, the earthquakes, the changes in weather patterns. I think folks are really beginning to realize that the prophecies are already being fulfilled, so they are becoming more interested in the Native ways.

Even today, I go to churches to speak and the clergymen will come up to me afterwards and say, "Gee, Sun Bear, this is the first time this place has been filled since it was built". So you see, people are wanting to hear what the Native teachings are. Often, we have standing room only where we speak, and that, too, we feel, is a fulfillment of the prophecies.

The time will come, the ancient teachings say, *when both Native and non-Native people will return to the teachings of the Great Spirit, and seek them out, and at that time the sons and daughters of our oppressors will turn to us and say "Teach us, so that we might survive, for we have almost ruined the Earth now".*

That's what's happening.

We Native people were told that there would be a period of time when we would lay as if we were dead in the dust, and our very teachings would be forgotten, even by many of our own people. Then we would come alive again, we would be walking on our hind legs, our brothers and sisters would be returning to the medicine path, and we would be teaching them the love and harmony they would be needing in order to survive the Cleansing.

As I said earlier, as we've progressed in the work we're doing, we've been invited to take our teachings all over the world. We've been to Canada; to England twice; we did a self reliance seminar at Findhorn in Scotland, in 1981. We've been to Germany three times, and plan to go there again. We've also done seminars in Switzerland; in Austria; and in New Zealand.

The first time we went to Europe was in 1980. Thunderbird Woman arranged that trip. A growing number of Germans express a deep interest in the Native American life way. I'll tell you more about that later.

I was very happy to go; I feel that it's our responsibility to go anywhere on the Earth Mother where people seek knowledge and balance and harmony.

On that first trip to Germany, we were invited to speak at the *Collegium Humanum*, in Vlotho. The people in charge there figured we'd have thirty or forty students coming to hear us, but it turned out there were more than seventy. The place was filled. They asked us to do a second seminar, and we agreed, so we ended up doing the two seminars back-to-back. The second one was filled up also. The response there was so tremendous that we went back to the same place the following year, and we did five seminars back-to-back, with a half-day break between sessions. We were in Europe for six weeks that second time. First we travelled to London, and to Findhorn. We spoke in a lot of different German cities, then did the seminars at the Collegium Humanum. Afterwards we went to Vienna, Austria, then to Switzerland.

We were very well received at Findhorn; I enjoyed being there, and the people were really trying hard to become totally self-sufficient. They told me that they felt, in many ways, that the Bear Tribe was more self-sufficient than they were.

We had a real great time in Europe on that trip, and I think we did a lot for the people who came to hear us. Today, more and more Europeans, especially Germans, are travelling over here and visiting with the Bear Tribe on Vision Mountain. They come to be a part of our apprenticeship screening program, to make vision quests, and to seek help in finding their sense of balance.

Of all the places we've been to, I think maybe I've enjoyed the visits to Germany the most. The Germans have shown the most intense interest in the Native American way of life. That may seem surprising to some of you, because a lot of people try to categorize Germans as being cold and scientific. But that hasn't been my experience with them at all. I think it's because the German people have been taken away from everything that is natural, and have been so industrialized that they seem to crave intensely a return to the natural world.

That's the way it seems to be in a lot of European countries where I've been; there's so little wilderness left over there, that when these people participate in our seminars, or come to Vision Mountain to stay for awhile, most of them say the same things about the power that they feel in the wilderness. It's new to them; and most of them seem to really love it.

The German people, I think, look to Native Americans so strongly because they know we were some of the closest people to nature on the face of the Earth. I think, too, that a lot of German people still feel a sense of frustration about the whole World War II catastrophe, because so many of them had been fooled into giving away their power.

In a lot of German towns, when we arrived at the train station, there would be Native American support groups waiting for us, waving banners and cheering as we met them. In Germany, I remember, this one particular man came up to me and embraced me, and he said, "Brother, you have returned...

"We have a legend," he told me, "from our ancient people, which says that the time would come, after we lost our spiritual path, and after we had suffered greatly, when a brother would come to us from across the water. This brother would be a natural man, and he would bring back the teachings of harmony and love.

"Sun Bear," the man said to me, "I think that you're that brother." That made me feel really good.

It was fascinating for me to hear that legend, because in the Hopi prophecies the religious elders speak about the two brothers, the one who is lost and the one who comes to teach him about harmony on the Earth. The two brother idea is mentioned in many other prophecies throughout the world. In the Americas, we've waited for the true white brother to come from the east and help us...and he now manifests himself, I feel, in the non-native people who come to us and want to help and learn. The Germans, it seems, are looking for the true brother to come to them, from the west, from the Native American people, for the same reason.

It's a very powerful thing, the meshing of a prophecy that has parallels all over the world; in each place where it is repeated, the prophecy emphasizes a time of a return to nature.

All over Europe, the people seem to feel less personal power than folks in the United States. I guess that's because, as difficult as it is over here, a lot of people can take advantage of what's called the free-enterprise system. I don't know. The Europeans, in general, listen to what I have to say, and they say to me, "Sun Bear, what you're doing is great, but we can't do that over here. We can't do anything. You can get loans and buy land, and you can become self-sufficient, but it's not possible in Europe. The land is too locked up, and the money is just not there." I try to tell them that they can do what I do anyway, that they can sit in the middle of a factory yard if they learn about their power, and be spiritual, and feel the power of the Mother Earth. They can do their medicine ceremonies in their houses, and before long, people who feel the same things will be gravitating to them. They can start out anywhere, I tell them, by working and by sharing the burdens together. From that point, the Great Spirit will take over.

Then I place a buffalo skull over the center stone in the wheel to represent the Creator and the Center of life.

CHAPTER THIRTEEN
THE MEDICINE WHEEL, AND OUR GATHERINGS

In the late 1970's I had a vision of the Medicine Wheel, an ancient stone circle which has been used for thousands of years by Native people as a place for prayer, ceremony and self-understanding. At one time there were some 20,000 medicine wheels on the North American continent alone. Today the remains of a few of those old ones — in Wyoming, in Canada, in Minnesota — are studied by scientists and curiosity seekers. It sometimes makes me smile to think that there is such an air of mystery surrounding the old medicine wheels: How were they used? Why did they have a particular number of stones arranged in a certain way upon the ground? And so on. When you understand that the basis for all vision is your very personal relationship to the Creator, and that vision is a strong part of the medicine wheel, then you should understand, too, that there are probably only a few absolute rules for placing the stones into one of these sacred prayer hoops. Whatever guidance came through visions and dreams moved the builders of these circles to build them in accordance with the universal laws they represent and honor.

It's important, I think, for me to explain two things to you here. The first thing is that when I speak of the Medicine Wheel, I'm talking

THE MEDICINE WHEEL OF MY VISION

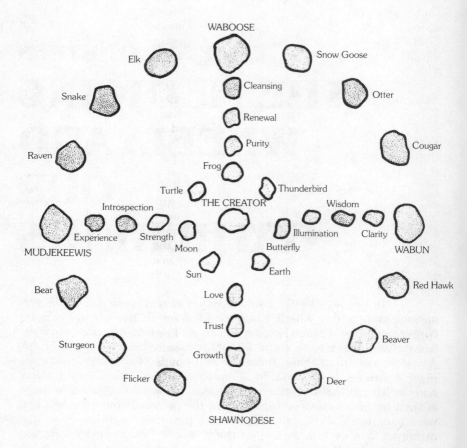

about two things simultaneously: a circle of stones placed on the ground ... and a set of symbols which have definite meaning in terms of your life. The second thing I want to make clear is that my vision of the Medicine Wheel, as I describe it to you, *is* highly personal. It came to me through the Great Spirit; through my observations (and those of other members of the Tribe) of our relationships with the human, animal, plant, and mineral kingdoms; and through some reading about the observations of other medicine people. To the best of my knowledge, my version of the Wheel and how it's used is not the same as any other. In my version, for example, some major stones are placed to honor the Four Directions, and the Center of the Universe. In one of the ancient wheels in Wyoming, the major stones seem to be placed to honor *six* directions.

This Medicine Wheel was revealed to me, to Wabun and others, as a means to help with the healing of the Earth Mother at this time. Folks who don't know much about themselves, know very little about how to help save the planet. You'll see, as I describe the Wheel to you, that it seems to be similar to an astrology system, but that's really not the case. Astrology is based, mainly, on the position of the planets and the stars. The Medicine Wheel on the other hand, is based upon a person's relationship to the earth and to all of earth's kingdoms: the animals, the plants, the minerals, and the humans. A person moves about on the Medicine Wheel in his own way, and knows his position on the wheel through intuition, or through his or her changing relationship with the members of the animal, the mineral, and the plant kingdoms. We attribute any similarities between the Medicine Wheel and astrology to the fact that all truths come from the same Source, the Creator.

In my vision I saw a hilltop bare of trees. There was a soft breeze blowing and the prairie grass was moving gently. Then I saw a circle of rocks that came out like spokes of a wheel. I knew that what I was seeing in my vision was the sacred circle of life, the sacred hoop of my people.

Inside of the center circle was the buffalo skull, and coming up through ravines, from the four directions, were what looked like animals. As they came closer, I saw that they were people wearing headdresses and animal costumes. They moved to the circle and each group entered it sunwise, making a complete circle before they settled on their place in the wheel.

First people came to the place of the North, to the winter, the time of resting for ourselves and the Earth Mother, the place that represents the time when we have the white hairs of snow upon our heads, when we prepare to change both worlds and forms. Then there were those who ended up in the East, the place of awakening, of birth and of spring, the place representing mankind's birth and beginning. Next came those who would represent the South, the time of summer, the years of fruitfulness and of rapid growth. Then there were people who came to the West, the time of fall, when we reap our harvest, when we have found the knowledge needed to center ourselves. The West is the home of the West Wind, Father of all of the Winds.

All of the people were singing the song of their season, of their minerals, of their plants, of their totem animals. And they were singing songs for the healing of the Earth Mother. A leader among them was saying, "Let the medicine of the sacred circle prevail. Let many people across the land come to the circle and make prayers for the healing of the Earth Mother. Let the circles of the Medicine Wheel come back".

In this vision were gathered people of all the clans, of all the directions, of all the totems, and in their hearts they carried peace. That was the vision I saw.

It would be pretty hard for me to sum up for you here, what all the totems, elemental clans, and directions are, or what they mean, so on page 184 I'll let you see a chart which was first published in the MEDICINE WHEEL book, which I wrote with Wabun, in 1980.

Using these you can place yourself on the wheel. Then, if you like, you can look in the MEDICINE WHEEL book at each one of the animal totems, or the mineral or plant totems relevant to you, and find out what your place on the Medicine Wheel means, according to my vision. You see, each totem at each position on the wheel possesses different powers, different weaknesses, which you can benefit from or watch out for. When you know where you are on the Wheel, or where somebody else is, you can, in a sense, understand how to relate to the Earth, or to those around you.

At the Bear Tribe, we have our Medicine Wheel set on a hilltop to the East of the longhouse. We go to it to contemplate, to feel, to smoke a pipe or to do ceremonies. The first thing we usually do when we go to be by the Wheel is to walk around it in a sunwise manner, like the people in my vision did. If we are having a ceremony, people who have places of responsibility on the Wheel stop at their spot. For instance, Wabun would stop at the eastern stone, and Shawnodese, at the southern.

The right spot will change for a person as time goes on because, even though we are born under specific totems or signs, during our lifetimes we are constantly moving around the Wheel. For example, you may have been born under the sign of the otter, but you don't stay there all of the time. You may go through a period of time when you are constantly seeing the Red Hawk, or the Raven. Then you know that your place on the Medicine Wheel has shifted. A few weeks or months or years later, when the energy is right, you may shift again, say to the position of the Brown Bear, or the Cougar. That is a good thing. It's important for a person to keep moving around the Wheel, to learn life's lessons from the various animals, plants, and minerals, so they can constantly grow. To be still on the Wheel is to grow stagnant. Even those with places of permanent, ceremonial responsibility will sometimes be drawn to other spots.

When we meditate or do our ceremonies at our wheel, we use the stones which form the spokes of the Wheel as spiritual or mental pathways, which lead us to the center-point. When we sit down and pray, we close our eyes, and we send ourselves into the center of the Wheel; it is when we are there that we may have visions, we may learn more about ourselves, or others, or the Mother Earth. There is really no limit to what the Medicine Wheel can teach us, or how that teaching may come about. Sometimes, if we want to heal a particular loved one, in our minds and hearts we carry that loved one to the center of the Wheel; then we pray to the Creator. On Vision Mountain, the center of our Medicine Wheel is a very large and beautiful quartz crystal stone. Shawnodese, Wabun and I mined that stone in Arkansas, and carried it back to Vision Mountain with us.

It is a very powerful experience simply to be near the Wheel. The energy is always very high. Although we've written out the *Medicine Wheel Reference Chart*, and the circles which show the seasons and the major animals of the Four Directions, we've mainly done that for the folks who want to read about what we do, and can't come to be with us. When you actually sit by the Medicine Wheel on Vision Mountain, you rarely need a reference chart. Once you understand the principles of the Wheel, then the animal, or mineral, or plant which you have a special relationship with at any particular time often manifests itself to you, without books or words. You may close your eyes and see that animal; it may fly overhead during a ceremony. The medicine is good, and it is always changing.

As I've already said, the Medicine Wheel has been used by most Native people, in one form or another, for thousands of years. The Medicine Wheel is a magic circle which encompasses all of our relations with the natural world. It is a sacred tool which can teach us how to eat well; how to heal ourselves and others; how to hear the songs and stories that the wind and the water bring to us. It can teach us, too, the most important lesson, which is that we are each a small, unique part of the universe, and that we are here to learn harmony with the rest of the Creation. When people feel that something is missing in their lives, they often find part of it by working with the Wheel, because it helps them to grow closer to nature, and to the elemental forces.

I'll tell you a little story, about a visitor who came to be with us recently, and about his relationship with the Medicine Wheel. It will show you, I think, just how powerful the magic circle is.

We show respect for our Medicine Wheel by never *accidently* stepping inside of it. This particular visitor was not watching where he was going, and by mistake he stepped into the Wheel in the West, at the sign of the Snake. He stepped out of the Wheel then, unconsciously,

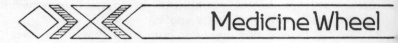 Medicine Wheel

	DATES	MOON	ANIMAL	PLANT
NORTH	Dec. 22–Jan. 19	Earth Renewal	Snow Goose	Birch Tree
	Jan. 20–Feb. 18	Rest & Cleansing	Otter	Quaking Aspen
	Feb. 19–March 20	Big Winds	Cougar	Plantain
EAST	March 21–April 19	Budding Trees	Red Hawk	Dandelion
	April 20–May 20	Frogs Return	Beaver	Blue Camas
	May 21–June 20	Cornplanting	Deer	Yarrow
SOUTH	June 21–July 22	Strong Sun	Flicker	Wild Rose
	July 23–Aug. 22	Ripe Berries	Sturgeon	Raspberry
	Aug. 23–Sept. 22	Harvest	Brown Bear	Violet
WEST	Sept. 23–Oct. 23	Ducks Fly	Raven	Mullein
	Oct. 24–Nov. 21	Freeze Up	Snake	Thistle
	Nov. 22–Dec. 21	Long Snows	Elk	Black Spruce

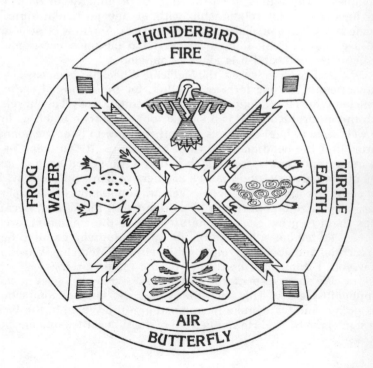

Reference Chart

MINERAL	SPIRIT KEEPER	COLOR	COMPLEMENT	
Quartz	Waboose	White	Flicker	
Silver	Waboose	Silver	Sturgeon	
Turquoise	Waboose	Blue—Green	Brown Bear	
Fire Opal	Wabun	Yellow	Raven	
Chrysocolla	Wabun	Blue	Snake	
Moss Agate	Wabun	White & Green	Elk	
Carnelian Agate	Shawnodese	Pink	Snow Goose	
Garnet & Iron	Shawnodese	Red	Otter	
Amethyst	Shawnodese	Purple	Cougar	
Jasper	Mudjekeewis	Brown	Red Hawk	
Copper & Malachite	Mudjekeewis	Orange	Beaver	
Obsidian	Mudjekeewis	Black	Deer	

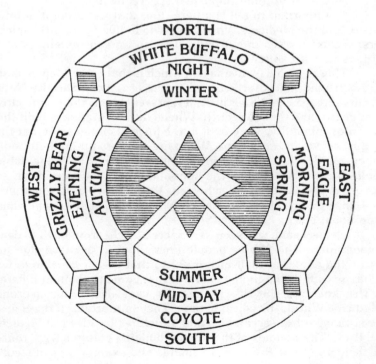

at the sign of his birth totem, the Otter, and he made his apologies and an offering to the Spirit Keepers of the directions he might have offended.

As the group this visitor was with left the Medicine Wheel, there was a gentle rattling in the bushes. A small rattlesnake had come to say hello to the group. The following morning, when our visitor stepped outside his tent there was a small, coiled rattlesnake sitting on the ground, facing him. The rattlesnake was very docile; after a few moments it stretched out and moved off a little way. We made our prayers, explained to the snake that we had a lot of visitors on Vision Mountain, and that we needed the space for ourselves; then we put him in a sack and moved him to a remote place on the Mountain.

I should explain to you here that what happened was very rare; in the past six years, we hadn't seen more than four other rattlesnakes on Vision Mountain. In addition, we look on such events as very positive things; we are not frightened by brother rattlesnake ... all wildlife is a part of us. Our visitor had simply stepped into the Medicine Wheel at the sign of the snake, and the brother, I believe, came to say hello to him. It was very powerful snake medicine, and during that summer our visitor felt very strongly — because of certain things that were going on around him — that he was very closely aligned on the Wheel with the sign of the Snake.

That kind of thing happens here frequently.

It's important to tell you here, too, that we attempt not only to understand the Medicine Wheel, but also to live by the principles it honors. We use it often in our daily lives, so we can remember all of the things that it can teach us.

There's an old Native saying which is that everything in nature tries to be round, and that is true. The circle is sacred to the Native people in every aspect of their lives; it represents to us the journey from birth to death, and then to rebirth. When Native Americans built their homes, most often they were built in the form of circles, whether they were tipis, wigwams, or hogans. When they went to purify their bodies and their minds, they did that in the circle of the sweatlodge, which symbolized both the womb of the human mother they came from and the womb of the Earth Mother herself. When they came together in council, they sat in a circle, so that everyone was included, as an equal, with an equal voice.

Life, as I said, was seen as a Sacred Circle, from birth to death to regeneration. The Native people knew how to acknowledge and celebrate the circles of their own lives, so that they were able to flow and change with the changing energies that came to them at different ages. They knew that they, like the seasons, were always moving around the Medicine Wheel, the wheel of time. They immortalized the Sacred Circle in many other ceremonies and structures besides the Medicine Wheel itself. The mounds of the mound-building cultures were round. The calendars of the Aztecs were round. The examples of this could go on and on.

In order to participate in the lessons of the Medicine Wheel, you must remember that you are always travelling around it. You enter the circle at the point of the moon, (or month), during which you were born. This entrance gives you the powers, gifts, and responsibilities of that particular moon. The different starting points are governed by different elemental clans, and these clans tell you the various elements to which you are attached.

These clans have nothing to do with the clans of kinship that exist in most tribes. Those were determined by the clans of your parents, and they, in turn, could govern the earthbound responsibilities you would have, as well as who you could marry. The elemental clans, instead, determine your relationship to the elements only, and, like all of the other points on the Medicine Wheel, they are always changing as you move through life. By learning about these clans, about all the totems and the Spirit Keepers on the Medicine Wheel, you can learn how to keep your own life in balance, how to keep the life force beating within your heart.

Most important of all is using the magic circle to remind us we're a small part of the Creator. By remembering this we are sometimes able to do away with our arrogance and pride, and it is arrogance and pride which tell us we are alone in a hostile universe. It is pride, I think, that tells us that we are the most important specks of dust in a vast universe. It is fear of that vast universe, of our *aloneness* in it, which can make us feel very much unloved.

If you open your heart to the lessons of the Medicine Wheel, then the light of the Great Spirit, of the Creator, will shine on you and brighten your existence. It will give you the gift of a happy life.

Back in 1978, the Bear Tribe published the Medicine Wheel Circle. It's a small wheel which tells about the characteristics of the various totems, as they relate to the calendar year. Wabun sent a Medicine Wheel Circle to Oscar Collier, her agent, who was then an editor at Prentice-Hall Publishers, Inc., and it arrived on his birthday. He read it and related it to his own life at that time. He felt that it could do a lot more for people than astrology could. He was so impressed that he contacted us, and, in 1980, Prentice-Hall published THE MEDICINE WHEEL. It's been very successful, and distribution grows every year. THE MEDICINE WHEEL book has also been published as DAS MEDIZINRAD by Trikont Publishers in Munich, Germany.

In 1980, we began to organize and put on Medicine Wheel Gatherings that allow hundreds, sometimes a thousand, people to come together and help to fulfill the vision I had. They help to build a Medicine Wheel, and they participate with us in ceremonies around it. From us and from other teachers they learn more about the Earth Mother, and ways to heal themselves and the earth.

We held our first Medicine Wheel Gathering in August of 1980, near Seattle, Washington. It was held in a Forest Service campground at the foot of Mount Rainier. Since then, we've had a second Medicine Wheel Gathering near Seattle, and others in the Los Angeles area, in San Francisco, San Diego, Houston, and in New York state.

Each Gathering has been wonderful in its own way. One that was a big surprise, was our first New York Gathering which took place in September 1982. We had some apprehension about biting into the *Big Apple*. New York is very far away from Spokane, and we had to make several trips back there to find a campground that could accommodate 1000 people indoors, just in case of rain. With the help of Glenn Schiffman, who coordinated our 1982 Gatherings, and Jaya Huston, who coordinated this particular one, we had just about 1000 people who attended, and really enjoyed and learned from the ceremonies. We also had two New York television stations on hand, videotaping much of what was happening during the weekend. This showed us that our teachings are of interest to people all over this country, and gave us the confidence to begin planning our first European Medicine Wheel Gathering.

What we do, basically, at these Gatherings is to re-enact my vision of the creation of a Medicine Wheel.

Gatherings usually begin on a Friday night, and end on Sunday evening.

Before the Gathering begins, Wabun and I, with the help of some other people, bless the land where we'll build the Medicine Wheel. We begin building the Wheel by placing a stone at its energy center, the vortex; that stone marks the center-point, and the place of the Creator. Next, we place seven stones around the center one. Those represent the Earth Mother, Father Sun, Grandmother Moon, and the four elemental clans. We place a rock at each of the Four Directions, to honor the spirit keepers, (Waboose, Wabun, Shawnodese, Mudjekeewis), then place the rocks which represent the twelve totems we honor in each of the kingdoms (animal, plant, mineral). After that, we place the stones which radiate out like spokes from the energy center; they are the spirit paths between each direction and the place of the Creator.

On Friday night, we welcome those who have come to be with us. We explain the meaning of the Medicine Wheel, the purposes of the Gathering itself, and the meaning of the ceremonies we're going to be performing. We ask people to be relaxed, and to enjoy the ceremonies, to remember that we are all beginners at ceremony, and that the important thing is that we do everything with as much love, respect, humor and humility as possible. Usually, too, we'll have some guest speakers there to talk to participants, and we'll share a dance or some stories with our new friends. Every Gathering is a little bit different from the others, as we grow and learn the most effective ways to teach and share our medicine.

On Saturday morning, we consecrate the Medicine Wheel. Before beginning any of our ceremonies, anywhere, we *smudge* (purify with smoke from certain sacred herbs) the folks who are going to participate, and we also smudge our medicine objects.

After everyone is smudged, we share some chants; then I place a buffalo skull over the center stone in the Wheel, to represent the Creator and the center of life. Next, people chosen ahead of time to represent the powers of the thirty-five stones in the wheel come to honor and consecrate them. Some of these folks wear animal hides; others carry feather fans, or wear masks to represent the different powers of the totems. They make their prayers and sprinkle corn meal on their individual stones; we sing songs for each of the powers that we honor. It's hard to put into words the power of a ceremony like that. There's drumming and chanting; there's dancing, and the wind and the earth sounds often come to join us. Some of the dancers don't just acknowledge a power while they're there. For a time, they *become* that power. You can see it, and you can feel it. Before the weekend begins we ask all of the participants to bring some special stones with them, rocks which they have a strong feeling about, to put into the Wheel. After the thirty-five center stones have been consecrated we ask all participants to put their stone in a protective circle about a foot back from the center circle. These rocks receive many blessings during the weekend, and, at the end of the ceremonies, we ask the participants to take them home with them, to use in their own contemplations, or in building their own medicine wheels. Thus, the circles grow.

Much of the Medicine Wheel Gathering weekend is spent performing ceremonies. Either after the consecration, or later Saturday afternoon, we have a *pipe ceremony*.

Sometimes we have as many as six different medicine people, from six different traditions, join together in a pipe ceremony. It is a very powerful and wonderful thing, to see such unity and harmony between these brothers and sisters.

Later, we talk about and demonstrate how to use the Medicine Wheel as a ceremonial center. We have a *Blessing Way* Ceremony, in which all the people at the Gathering may receive a blessing, and give their blessing to the universe; and we sometimes perform marriages for couples who have made that request of us. There are traditional sweats in sweatlodges which we've built ahead of time. I remember, at one of the early Gatherings, Nimimosha conducted twelve sweat ceremonies in two days. Wabun walked a mile in pouring rain, between ceremonies she was helping me to conduct, to tell Nimimosha how good we all felt about what she was doing for the people.

On Sunday morning Wabun invites participants to join us in a crystal healing ceremony. In this ritual, the people present use a large crystal to transmit their healing energies to the Earth, and all of their relations upon her. We aren't healing those present at the ceremony, necessarily; what we're doing is sending our joined medicine power out to others. It's a good ritual, one where a lot of folks can voice their prayers together for all of their relations in all of the kingdoms on the earth.

There are many more things that go on at a Medicine Wheel

Gathering: there is the blessing of children who attend, and a blessing by the children upon the adults; there are workshops on self reliance, the Path of Power, healing, herbs, feminine energy, prophecies, community, and many other topics.

There are many important people, both Native and non-Native, who have joined us for these Gatherings. All of them have shared so generously with all those attending the Gatherings that we would like to honor them here. Alphabetically, we list here those who have been major speakers at our Gatherings through 1983.

-Grey Antelope is a Tewa Pueblo medicine man, a healer, chanter and dancer. He has come to the Gatherings with his Humbios Clan Dancers, an inter-racial group. They have performed the sacred Buffalo, Eagle, Bow and Corn dances.

-Bear Heart is a Muskogee Indian who trained under two tribal elders and is now a tribal medicine chief. He has Sundanced with both the Northern and Southern Cheyenne people, and is a respected leader in the Native American church.

-Dr. Frans Bakker is the Director of the Radiant Life Clinic in California. He is a specialist on rejuvenation health techniques and teacher of radical spiritual healing.

-John Bradshaw of Houston is an educator, theologian and counselor.

-Dr. Paul Brenner is the author of LIFE IS A SHARED CREATION, and other books. He is the Health Director for the Center for the Healing Arts, a lecturer, holistic teacher and physician.

-Tom Brown, Jr. is author of THE TRACKER, THE SEARCH, and THE FIELD GUIDE TO WILDERNESS SURVIVAL. He is one of the foremost survival instructors and trackers in the world.

-Page Bryant, Sun Bear's first apprentice, is a psychic, radio personality, teacher and lecturer who teaches the integration of the psychic and intuitive self. She is the author of several books including THE EARTH CHANGES SURVIVAL HANDBOOK.

-Red Cloud is a Cree teacher who studied Indian medicine with his grandmother and with Nauskeechask, a noted shaman. He is the former President of the Metis Association of Alberta, Canada.

-Norma Cordell (Eagle Morning Star) is the Director of the Eugene (Oregon) Center of the Healing Arts. She is a healer and spiritualist trained by a Nez Perce shaman. She is the author of EARTH DANCE.

-Prem Das is the Director of the Mishakai Center for the Study of Shamanism, in Northern California. He has studied with the Huichol shaman Don Jose Matsuwa, and is the author of THE SINGING EARTH.

-Brooke Medicine Eagle is the great-great grandniece of Chief Joseph, the Nez Perce holy man and leader. She is trained both in the traditions of her people, and in Western psychology and body work. She lectures throughout the world.

-J.C. Eaglesmith is a Creek/Shawnee Indian who is a pipeholder in the Straight Pipe Society. He conducts seminars about the sacred pipe and the healing sweat.

-Evelyn Eaton (Mahad'yuni), who died in 1983, was a pipe woman, healer and teacher. She was a tribal grandmother to the Bear Tribe. She was the author of I SEND A VOICE, SNOWY EARTH COMES GLIDING, THE SHAMAN AND THE MEDICINE WHEEL and twenty other books.

-Wallace Black Elk is a Lakota holy man who has been trained since childhood in the traditional and sacred knowledge of the Earth people. Black Elk has been chosen by the Spirit to be a spiritual guide for all of the people. He is the grandson of the famed Lakota holy man Black Elk, whose vision was shared with the world in BLACK ELK SPEAKS.

-Oh Shinnah Fastwolf is a Scottish, Apache and Mohawk eclectic person whose teachings come from various ancient traditions. Oh Shinnah dedicates her work to the healing of Mother Earth.

-Steven Foster and Meredith Little are the founders and former co-directors of Rites of Passage, a teaching organization which guides people along the medicine path. They are now directing the School of Lost Borders in the Owens Valley of California. They co-authored THE BOOK OF THE VISION QUEST — PERSONAL TRANSFORMATION IN THE WILDERNESS.

-Adele Getty is co-director, with Sunwater, of Medicine Ways, a teaching organization in Petaluma, California. She is a wilderness leader, and a ritual consultant who works with re-connecting people with the earth through self-generated ritual.

-Rosemary Gladstar is the founder and director of the California School of Herbal Studies. She is an herbalist, a teacher, and an organizer of holistic health seminars.

-Joan Halifax is the Director of the Ojai Foundation in Ojai, California. She is the author of SHAMAN: THE WOUNDED HEALER, and SHAMANIC VOICES.

-Hawk Little John is a teacher and healer of Cherokee descent. He lectures to many people about the traditional Native ways of healing. He is also a farmer.

-Dr. Elisabeth Kubler-Ross is the Director of Shanti Nilaya in Escondido, California, a world renowned teacher and lecturer, and a founding member of the American Holistic Medical Association. She is the author of seven books including ON DEATH AND DYING and LIVING WITH DEATH AND DYING.

-Winona LaDuke, Sun Bear's daughter, is an internationally-known anti-nuclear activist, and the former director of the Circle of Life Survival School on the White Earth Reservation in Minnesota.

-Barry McWaters, Ph.D., is the co-director of the Institute for the Study of Conscious Evolution and editor of "Humanistic Perspectives". He is also the author of several books, including CONSCIOUS EVOLUTION — PERSONAL AND PLANETARY TRANSFORMATION, and THE COUPLE'S JOURNEY (with Susan Campbell).

-Manitonquat (Medicine Story) is a Keeper of the Lore of the Wampanoag people, director of "Another Place" in New Hampshire, founder of the Mettanokit community, and author of RETURN TO CREATION.

-Frank Mola is the founder and director of Alpha Logics in Bristol, Connecticut, a psychic, teacher and healer, and a successful businessman.

-Norma Meyers is a well-known herbalist and healer of Mohawk descent. She is the Director of the Tsonqua Herbal Center in British Columbia, Canada.

-Don Perrote is an Earth Man of Pottawatomi descent who presents the sacred teachings as being alive and well and relevant to today's needs. He works with the sacred pipe and the sweatlodge.

•Lee Piper is the Bird Clan Mother of the Eastern Cherokee Overhill Band. She is the author of traditional Native children's stories, a teacher and a counselor.

-Joan Price works in media, and has presented a slide presentation she developed on Native American sacred areas, and the Hopi.

-Starhawk is a ritualist, counselor, writer and political activist. She is the author of DREAMING THE DARK: MAGIC, SEX AND POLITICS and THE SPIRAL DANCE.

-Brant Secunda has completed his apprenticeship with Don Jose Matsuwa, the Huichol Shaman. He is the ceremonial leader and director of the Dance of the Deer Foundation: Center for Shamanic Studies.

-Grandfather Sky Eagle is a Chumash teacher and elder.

-Grace Spotted Eagle is Wallace Black Elk's wife. She teaches about women and the traditional way.

-Brad Steiger is an internationally-known author and teacher. He has written MEDICINE POWER, MEDICINE TALK, STAR PEOPLE, THE CHINDI and many other books. He is teaching people how to find their multi-dimensional self.

-Hyemeyohsts Storm is the author of SEVEN ARROWS and SONG OF HEYOEHKAH. He is the founder of the National American Metis Association.

-Harley Swiftdeer is a Cherokee/Metis medicine man, founder of the Deer Tribe, and teacher of the Sun Dance way, and of White Crystal Medicine.

-Jim Swan is the former director of Life Systems Educational Foundation in Seattle. He is an environmental psychologist specializing in sacred places.

-Slow Turtle (John Peters) is a medicine man for the Wampanoag Nation, and Director of Indian Affairs for the State of Massachusetts.

-John White is a well-known teacher, lecturer and author. He has written many books and edited many anthologies. He is the author of POLE SHIFT.

-Dhyani Ywahoo is the director of the Sunray Meditation Society, in Vermont. She is the lineage holder of the medicine traditions of the Anigadoah-Catawaba People, and a Planetary teacher and guide.

-Yehwehnode (She Whose Voice Rides on the Wind) or Twylah Nitsch speaks with the voice of her ancestors on the wisdom, prophecy and philosophy of the Seneca people.

-Jack Zimmerman/Jaquelyn McCandless are the focalizers of the Heartlight Community and School outside of Los Angeles. They teach about relationships in the New Age.

All of these folks, and more, who have generously given of their time to lead workshops, have become our dear friends, and have inspired untold numbers of people through their participation in our Medicine Wheel Gatherings.

We meet at the Medicine Wheel Gatherings to understand one another, and to celebrate the Earth Mother. During Gathering weekends we make the Medicine Wheel our focal point, the center of our lives, our ceremonies, and our temporary community. The Gatherings often make lasting changes in the lives of those who attend them.

We have giveaways, too, during the gatherings. A giveaway is a traditional Native American celebration, in which one gives something of special value to another person. The giveaway has been used by the Native people for many generations, as a means of reminding them that, in reality, they own nothing. In giving away your material goods, even some medicine objects, you will sometimes feel a certain freedom, and you'll acknowledge the fact that everything in the universe belongs to the Creator, that whatever you might own is, in reality, something you were only given temporary custody of. Possession requires some heavy responsibilities.

We have a giveaway of items people have brought for that purpose. We encourage people to make their giveaway to a stranger or to someone who was a stranger when the weekend began. This giveaway, we tell them, is a way of sharing their good feelings for the events of the weekend. We also make our own giveaways to our guest speakers, and to the many volunteers who have given their time to help organize and run the Gathering. Then we have a giveaway of the stones in the Medicine Wheel. We ask folks to either take their own stone back, or let somebody else take it home with them. When these folks go back home, we hope that they use these sacred stones to build medicine wheels of their own. Many of them, we are told, do just that.

There are some people who come back to almost every Gathering we give, and sometimes these folks will bring the same stones with them, time after time, to put into the new Wheel that we're building. That's good medicine.

Great Spirit . . . Hear me. I hold my pipe and offer it to you that my people may live.

CHAPTER FOURTEEN
THE APPRENTICESHIP PROGRAM

1981: I stood on a hilltop and I was in total darkness. Everything seemed bleak and desolate until I prayed to the Creator. My hand was moved upward then; I pointed a finger out into the darkness and a brilliant light came on. I pointed my finger again, and a second light came on to illuminate the void. Again and again, as I turned in a Sacred Circle and pointed my finger, lights glimmered out at me from the darkness. They were different sizes, different shapes and colors, and these brightly colored and sparkling lights, like stars, lit up what had looked so barren and hopeless earlier. The vision reminded me of the one I had when I was four years old, and I was surrounded by colored spheres.

Only, this time, the Great Spirit told me that the lights represented the people who would come to me to learn, and who would go back out into the world to use their new medicine knowledge. Then, instead of there being a handful of us trying to communicate our message from Vision Mountain, there would be a multitude of apprentices out there to help us. The lights were of many colors, as I said, and that was an important part of my vision, because it confirmed my belief that those who would come to me to learn would be of all colors, of all races, and of many nationalities.

It was a very powerful vision that I had, and one which seemed difficult to bring to fulfillment. In many ways, the people who have lived at our Spokane base for long periods of time are serving traditional apprenticeships. But the vision I had told me that our new helpers would be people who studied, then went back into the world; in that way we could spread our teachings more quickly, to more people. The vision showed me, also, that there would be a lot of new apprentices coming to us, within a very short period of time.

I knew that our Vision Mountain accommodations, as they exist now, could not hold all the people I saw becoming lights in my vision. With other Tribe members, I began planning new ways to train these brothers and sisters. It would be difficult; everyone in the Tribe was already overloaded with work. Beginning a new program like this would put more of a strain on them. Yet, I knew that the time had come to follow this new vision.

Shawnodese agreed to direct the program — to set up schedules, handle correspondence, send out news to new apprentices. During the summer of 1982, we held our first Apprenticeship Screening Program. Twenty people came and, despite the fact that we weren't as organized as we might have been, the program was a great success. Thanks to the tenacity, the patience, of those folks, we managed to work out a lot of the problems in the Program, and in the long-distance training segments which would follow their classes on Vision Mountain.

Through the Apprenticeship Screening Program, we are able to condense many lectures and workshops into one very powerful presentation ... and during that first summer, that Program and others grew dramatically. At one point, in early August, there were more than eighty people at Vision Mountain; many of them were participating in the Screening Program. Others were there to take part in one of our Earth Awareness Seminars. We were filled to capacity.

You can see then, that the vision the Great Spirit gave me came at a good time; it helped solve a growing problem of overpopulation on the Mountain, as well as showing me a more effective way to spread my teachings.

What we do with the apprentices is tell them about our visions, about the coming Earth changes, and about what we feel they can do to help heal themselves and others, to bring people back to living in harmony with the Mother Earth. I feel this new program is one of our most important accomplishments, because it combines many of the smaller efforts we were making to communicate with people — the self reliance seminars, the medicine workshops, and all the other programs we've sponsored — into one big, organized presentation.

The folks who go through our Screening Program, who like what we have to tell them and want to participate, (and who we feel have the personal power and motivation to work with us), go back to their homes afterwards and continue their apprenticeships through correspondence, and through follow-up visits. We encourage them to spend a lot of time developing their own medicine powers, while they're actively pursuing life in whatever way is right for them.

The Screening Program which we've developed consists of ten days of very intense study. The Program has changed over time, and I'm sure there will be more changes made as we travel around the Medicine Wheel and grow with it. It consists of a healthy mix of spiritual study, personal growth, ceremony, and self reliance skills. We spend a lot of time talking with our students; we try to make sure they're in harmony with what we're doing, and we also want to answer any questions or deal with any problems which they might have.

We want folks who continue with the Program after screening to have some very real spiritual skills they can use and share. We spend a lot of time teaching them about the sacred pipe; we allow participants to share in pipe ceremonies with us. If some students feel the need to have their own pipes, they ask us about that; if we feel they are ready, we awaken pipes for them. We spend a lot of time, too, with the smudging ceremony — I'll tell you about that soon — so that students can really understand its power.

We teach folks about the sweatlodge, although we know most of them won't be ready to share this ceremony with the outside world for quite some time. We want them to know, nevertheless, the good medicine of the sweat ... so we teach them how to build one, how to properly light the sweat fire, and how to be good and knowledgeable participants during a sweat ceremony.

If the Screening is held on Vision Mountain, we take students to all of the power spots there; we teach them about the meaning of these spots, and encourage them to return to each spot alone, to experience its healing energy.

We introduce folks to the Medicine Wheel, and to many of its ceremonial uses. We encourage them to find their own power spots, to spend a lot of time at them, alone. We teach them how to dig holes in which to bury their negative emotions. Some folks even bury themselves in the Earth to feel her energy; some stay that way overnight.

We teach students ways to remember their dreams, and have dream-interpretation workshops. We have separate men's and women's circles, so that students can get in touch with their separate, yet equal, spiritual energies and responsibilities. And we even teach folks some different styles of hugging, in order to share good energy!

It's a very good and effective program that we've developed, and I'm very proud of it. There are seminars, conducted by me, Wabun, Shawnodese, and, if the Program is on Vision Mountain, by other members of the Tribe ... on dozens of subjects; herbal medicine; Native American concepts of leadership; flower remedies; creation legends; sex; heart songs; tobacco offerings; prayer plumes; Earth energy; the animal kingdom; male energy; female energy; and Moon energy.

There are talks and workshops on the proper way to pick, prepare, and use herbs, especially sage and the herbs we use in making our kinnik-kinnik. There are workshops on chanting, drumming and dancing. We demonstrate the use of crystals for centering, and for healing. We teach folks how to make their own medicine pouches.

Although we touch on so many subjects that could be called "making medicine", it's important to realize that these are not how-to sessions — medicine knowledge is never that cut-and-dried. A student, once exposed to some of this knowledge, is free to relate his or her own needs and goals to the Native American way of life. Medicine power is something that one needs to nourish continually, or it will not grow.

The Screening Program contains many aspects of self reliance, along with the more spiritual aspects of making medicine. We teach students how to raise a garden with proper ceremony; how to hunt; how to take the life of an animal with proper respect; how to preserve food; and we give them some insights into my view of economics and the principles of barter.

There are general knowledge seminars, too, on such subjects as Native American history and culture; Native prophecies; and the ways of Native people all over the world. Usually, I end a program with a talk on the Path of Power, which I'll tell you about in the next chapter of this book.

Students are really energized by the power they feel during the Program; sometimes, that power, as well as the intense schedule we have to follow, can exhaust them. We plan it that way; there's a lot of pressure in the world today and if people have difficulty dealing with it, we want to know about that before they become medicine apprentices. In that way, we can deal with their problems more effectively. The Program becomes, for folks, almost a rebirthing process; so many things are happening to them on physical, spiritual, mental, and emotional levels, that a strain is inevitably there. Folks often feel both joy and sadness, anger and acceptance, as well as many other emotions during their stay here. They often feel joy at discovering a new life way, at shedding unneeded negativity and limitations. They feel sadness for past mistakes or insensitivity to the Earth Mother, and for a lot of other people who are not learning as they are. Sorrow, too, is part of it all, just because it's an inseparable part of the intensity of what's going on. When you come to Vision Mountain or to one of the Apprenticeship Screenings somewhere else, you will undergo an emotional/spiritual cleansing, and that is not very comfortable.

After they've gone home, our apprentices often write to tell us they've developed a kind of immunity to the trials of the world, the rat race. The things that used to bother them . . . the electric bills, the nine-to-five syndrome ... seem to be much easier to cope with. Medicine power has a way of doing that for you. When you begin to feel the messages of the Earth and of the Great Spirit, a lot of the things which have been tugging you out of balance seem to fade in importance. You stop giving away your power. If you smoke the pipe, if you really believe in the energies around you, and in the Creator, then you don't lose the strength, the confidence, that you gain while you're studying the Native life way. It becomes a part of you, sometimes as natural as breathing.

Folks come to study with us from all over the world; we've had people in our Screening Programs, and in later programs, from England, from Germany, and many other countries ... as well as from all parts of the United States and Canada. Invariably, when they've written to us afterwards, they've told us they no longer feel uncomfortable with their love for the Mother Earth, with their abilities to hear Earth messages and respond to them.

In 1983, a woman who is a writer came to visit with us. She had lived for a period of time at *Mahatma* Gandhi's ashram in India. She said she felt my Apprenticeship Program was the only program she'd seen which was comparable to Gandhi's; that great spiritual leader would also bring people to his ashram for awhile, train them, and then send them back to their own villages or cities. I've always admired Gandhi's nonviolent way of dealing with human problems, so what that woman told me made me feel very good.

★ ★ ★

Apprenticeship in the old times was a total commitment to learning the sacred ways of helping people, through long and rigorous training with a medicine person. When folks wanted to apprentice they approached a medicine person first with gifts — horses, blankets, furs, tobacco, food — and then with their requests to learn medicine ways. During the first year and, often, for a longer period of time, an apprentice served the medicine person by taking care of his or her physical needs ... gathering firewood, carrying water, tending horses, cooking meals. By doing these tasks with a sacred attitude, the apprentice would demonstrate the attitude with which he or she intended to serve "the people" after gaining medicine knowledge and power. During the first year, there was no guarantee that he or she would be found worthy of, or ready for, apprenticeship in a fuller sense.

Our Apprenticeship Program, obviously, is one for more contemporary times, and for the challenges of today. While we don't follow many of the old traditions, we do believe in a trial period of about a year for those students who have gone through our first Screening Program.

We're not teaching abstract theory on Vision Mountain, or elsewhere; we're not out in space here. What we teach people is real, and they need to use it in a proper manner ... all of it ... to fulfill their paths and to help others learn and grow.

That's why Wabun, Shawnodese, and I are very careful about what we teach, and to whom. We feel very good about most of the people who come to work with us, but, occasionally, we have to tell a student that we feel they are not quite ready for what we're trying to offer, that we feel they are looking, maybe, for just one part of it. With good feelings between us in those cases, we hope, we separate our paths and life goes on.

In 1983, we had the first Apprenticeship One Program, for some of the folks who went through the first screening process, and continued working throughout that year on their own. The Apprentice One Program was a more in-depth, more intensive program on medicine knowledge and power than the Screening Program itself is. Recently, we've established several clans within the Bear Tribe: the Bear Clan; the Earth Clan; the Spirit Clan; and the Rainbow Clan. Our apprentices who went through the Apprenticeship One Program became members of the Rainbow Clan; they are, in effect, nonresident members of the Tribe. They take an oath of membership, and they have some very specific responsibilities out there in the world, which are different from the responsibilities of lifetime members who live on Vision Mountain. Their medicine is good.

Some of our apprentices may eventually go out on speaking tours, or arrange speaking spots for us, and we for them. They may write articles for local or national publications, or have groups formed around them wherever they live. Hopefully, these folks will meet with us at our Medicine Wheel Gatherings, and will return to Vision Mountain many times.

I feel really good to see my vision becoming a reality, to see so many beautiful people letting the sacred energy pour through them, to bring light to the Earth, and all of her other children.

When you get past the rinky-dink world, and you grow into the medicine I'm telling you about, then you will learn you have the power to make anything happen in your life that you want to happen.

CHAPTER FIFTEEN
THE PATH
OF POWER

The vision I had about the Apprenticeship Program was important to me because it told me something essential about my medicine. I saw the lights in the darkness, like many medicine people do in the sweatlodge or when they go out on a vision quest. One of the traditional ways of defining a medicine person is as one "who sees light in the darkness" — we are always looking for that light, for that *enlightenment*, which is sent to us in visions from the Great Spirit.

There are a number of ways in which a person can attain medicine power; *see the light.* You can study with another medicine person; then, when that person dies, if he wants to, he can give you his power to use. I have studied with other medicine people, and I feel the energy of what I've learned from them very strongly. You can also come to power through a vision, or a series of visions, as many of the great medicine people of old did. That has been my way.

The path of power is different for every individual; it represents the course one should follow through life in order to fulfill his or her purpose on the Earth Mother. It is why you are here. When I speak of power I mean a way of working and using all of your energy — including your spiritual energy — in a direction that allows you to become a whole person, capable of fulfilling whatever visions the Creator gives to you.

My path of power begins when I wake up each morning. I get up and look out of the window and say, "Thank you, Creator, thank you for my life. Thank you for the Earth Mother, and all the beauty that I see in the things around me". Then I'm ready for that day, ready to move forward, and my vision has a power that pulls me forward each day to accomplish the goals of my life on Earth. If I'm looking for something, if I need something to help me along the path, I sit down with my pipe or, sometimes, without it, to make my prayers to the Creator, and I always receive an answer. I may hear a voice, or see a figure, or have a powerful dream afterwards, and then I know how to solve what had seemed to be a big problem. I continue along my path, and my medicine grows stronger every day.

Finding your path of power is not always easy. For me to do it, I had to tear up both the white man's and the Indian's scripts for life. If you wish to walk the path of power, you must do the same. After that, you must be willing to work on yourself, to empty out as much as possible of the emotional sickness you carry within you — the anger, the fear, the jealousy. I tell my students about several ways the Native people used to accomplish this through ceremonies and dances, and then I give them an exercise that they can use themselves.

In this exercise you first go to a secluded spot in nature where you make prayers and an offering over the piece of land that you will be using. You pray that the Earth Mother will transform your emotional sicknesses into good compost that will allow positive things to grow both in the earth, and in you. Then you dig a hole with your hands. If the ground is very hard you can use a stick or rock to help you. This hole can be as big as you feel it needs to be.

When it is dug, lie on your stomach with your head over the hole and begin to talk out your pain. If you need to, cry, scream, spit or vomit into the hole. If you want to pound your fists on the earth, be sure that you pick a soft spot to do that. Get out all of the pain that you can at that time, then cover over the hole and leave your pain there. When you have finished, make another prayer and an offering to the earth. Thank her for her ability to transform your negativity. Some people plant seeds in the hole that they dig, and then watch something beautiful come from their released pain.

I ask anyone who is going to work with me on medicine ways to first do this exercise, at least once. Afterwards, a person has a better chance of finding his or her path of power.

A good way to begin finding your path of power is to go out on a vision quest. During this time, people come closest to the spirit realm, because they're out there on the Earth, with neither food nor water, and the spirit realm is on the same level; it needs neither food nor water.

We call this process *crying for a vision*. We go out and we cry, asking the Creator to send us a sign, to give us something that will direct us and tell us our purpose in life. If a vision comes to a person and he moves forward with that vision, then that becomes his medicine, his path of power.

Of course, that's a very quick and easy summary; there's a lot more to it than that. There are different kinds of visions; there are different kinds of power, there are medicine objects, which I'll talk about later, and medicine attitudes to help you along the way.

When you study medicine power, and you're working with a medicine person, what you learn does not become part of your personal power until you can actually use it; in fact, being on the path of power doesn't automatically mean you'll become a medicine man or woman. That depends upon the will of the Great Spirit, and on your ability and determination to work with the knowledge that you gain, and make it grow. Being on the path of power does mean, though, that you'll be on the road to becoming a total human being.

All that I'm sharing with you right now is words; when you can do the things that I'm telling you about, then they will belong to you. That's why I don't feel badly about giving all of this information; and that's why I say this is not a how-to kind of thing. It takes a lot more than the intellectual knowledge of medicine power to become a medicine person, and much of what it takes, as I said before, is the ability to feel things, rather than just think them. For example, when a person comes to you for healing, you should be able to look at him and sense whether or not you can heal him, or if you should even try to. I tell my apprentices that the only thing I can do with some people is put spiritual band-aids on them, not heal their wounds, because their problems are not in the realm of my medicine. Sometimes I'll make a prayer over a person; I'll put a blessing on him, or draw some of the negative energies out of him with smudging, or with the sweatlodge, and so on, but that doesn't mean that I'm going to do a healing on that person. When a person comes to you, you look at him, and you know; you say to yourself, "Yes, I believe I can do something for this brother", or, "No, that's not my medicine". I usually tell a person how I feel and why.

When the medicine is ready to work for you, you know it in your heart, and nobody can rush the process; you can't "force the medicine". When it does come to you, when you can make rain, or heal another person, or reach out to the spirit forces and feel them come to you, then you're a medicine person, and not before. What I most like to say about it is that when people can walk on the fire, that's when they become medicine people.

A lot of the power to call in your medicine comes from you and your will to believe in it. If you're going to become a medicine person, you must not only feel things very strongly; you need to have the guts to act on your feelings. Sometimes you have to be willing to tell others about what you know, without worrying that they'll think you're crazy. As a small example of what I'm talking about there have been times around here when my people have received traffic tickets, after somebody had a dream or just a feeling about it beforehand. He didn't speak out, and it cost some energy and money. If you learn to believe in your feelings, and speak out about them, you may save yourself or another from some kind of trouble; you may even save a life, if you follow your feelings.

You also need to know when not to share your medicine with

other people, and that might be a little more difficult for people of this talkative society to learn. Some things which come to us from the spirit realm are very sacred, very personal, and are not meant to be talked about. You have to know what those things are; you have to be sure you're not sharing the wrong things just to build up your ego by saying, "Look what I know". Many times, we say, you can talk your power away; you can lose it by sharing what should be kept inside. Sometimes — as with medicine objects which can scatter your energy — when you talk about the wrong things you can get a very strong negative physical reaction.

When your medicine grows, you get to a point when you know you're into a different realm of energy and power. Life seems as though it is always flowing smoothly, like you are always going downhill rather than having to constantly fight an uphill battle. Then, all of these other things which you go through every day seem like little games. When you reach that point, you're dealing with a force that involves the entire universe, and you know that you have to work on that level. The power company, the car payments, and all of the other little hassles in your life diminish in importance very quickly.

There's no way to go back to the one-dimensional life that you lived before, and many times folks are frustrated because they want to *tell* others about what they've discovered. That's a hard thing to deal with, I think, to make all these wonderful discoveries, then go back to work in an office, if that's what you do, and finally realize that unless your friends and relatives have experienced what you have, there's no way to share your new reality with them. You *can* tell them, of course, but they probably won't understand you. So you learn to be silent until people are ready to learn and in the meantime, you continue on your own path, sometimes giving others a glimpse of what you know so that they will have more to live for.

You begin your path of power, as I said earlier, when you wake up in the morning and you thank the Creator for being alive. Then you look outside your window and see the whole world around you, and you thank the Creator for that. When you're ready to move further along the path, you can reach out with your heart and mind, and say, "Creator, I want everything that is out there, that I am entitled to at this time. I want to learn to see, to feel, to understand."

Each day when you make that prayer, when you reach out for your medicine, it will grow. It's as though you reach out with your eyes a little further each day. Try literally doing that when you get up in the morning; try throwing your eyes and your heart out into the universe. "I want to see further today," say, "I want to feel more of the universe". It will happen; you will see further each day. It's a very good spiritual exercise, and it is important for everyone on the path of power to remember to flex their spiritual muscles. We make our prayers that way here, and each time that somebody puts something before me, whatever it might be — their problems, their joy, or it can be anything else —

I see just a little further into the nature of those things.

I often tell my brothers and sisters, my students, that they need to grow to a point where they can find out what all the other dimensions in the universe are, besides the dimension that we live in. When we lock ourselves into this one dimension we become those one-dimensional people who have nothing to pull them forward; we sit in our apartments; we go down to the grocery store, and out to the corner bar, and then back to our television sets. A lot of people simply like to live that way because they don't know any better, or because they're just not ready to get anything else out of life.

When my apprentices or other students go up on the Mountain to cry for a vision, they're really beginning on their path of power. They go up to their power spot and they fast, and pray to the Creator. They don't ask for wealth, or to become great chiefs, but they do pray to be shown how they can be of the best service to their people, and to Mother Earth. What comes back to these folks, if a vision comes, is an individual experience; with one person the answer might come in the form of a rattlesnake; with another person it might come with a deer, or an owl, or a hawk, or it might come in the form of an old man or woman standing there as a teacher. However the message comes, it comes in that manner because the Creator has decided that's the best way to communicate with that person.

Everyone's power is very different; those of you who are creative, who can write or paint or make music, might find that your path of power involves using the arts to communicate the healing of Mother Earth. Some of you have other gifts; you might be skilled as a carpenter, a mechanic, an electrician. All of those technical skills are very valuable, and the Great Spirit will tell you how to use them.

As you move along your medicine path you learn to find your medicine tools: the pouches, the crystals, the feathers, and the pipe. The pipe is a tool for many of us; as you learn to work with it and pray with it, you learn that what it does, is to create a field of energy, so that you can communicate with the Creator through your pipe. If you are open and honest, and learn to work with your pipe in a proper and sacred manner, you may contact all the forces that have been on this continent for thousands of years. You can call the spirit forces; you can raise the wind or make rain. You can call out to the Thunder Beings and the other powers that bring the things we need in life. You can call out and bring the Spirit Keepers of the four directions to be with you.

When you find your power spot, your place on the earth where those beings will come to you and respond to your prayers, you will feel it very strongly. You'll be sitting there, when there will be a sudden spark of light, or a glistening energy field, or a change of temperature. My brother the wind may come and speak with you.

I call the wind *my brother* because we all are brothers and sisters to all creation, all living things. They're a part of us, and when we acknowledge them, we become a part of *them*. It's very easy for me to move my fingers, to make my bones move because they're a part of me. In the same way, when you accept the fact that all creation is a part of you, you can move it, you can get it to respond to you. That's why some of us can speak with the animals and have them come to us when we call them. We can talk to the trees, to the Earth, to the Creator, and ask for what we need at a particular time. We've been doing it for thousands of years. *It's not supernatural. It's perfectly natural.*

All of those spirit forces have been waiting for us to speak to them again like we used to hundreds of years ago; they've never left us, and now they are coming more fully to life. We're preparing for the Cleansing, and all of my brothers and sisters are a part of that preparation. I feel that my students, and all of the people who have come to me in recent years, want to learn because the Creator has said to them all, in one way or another, "Now is the time for you to come alive again." We *are* alive again, because we've been called back to our medicine.

"Why be in the world the way it is," I ask my students? "Why be in there pecking at each others' backs like a bunch of poor old chickens, when the entire universe can be yours, when the Creator wants you to dance and to sing again?"

We speak with the forces on Vision Mountain all the time. The first time the Little Sister, Mt. Saint Helens, erupted, back in May of 1980, we got almost an inch of ashfall on our land. When we prayed to the Great Spirit, that ashfall turned out to be a blessing because it enriched the earth so much that our gardens became jungles filled with enormous vegetables. It wasn't a blessing in all ways, though; for awhile we had to stay indoors and keep the animals penned up in the barn. Then, when the volcano erupted for a second time, we prayed to the Creator asking that the ashfall would give its blessing to another part of the earth. The sky had darkened early on a sunny afternoon, and an enormous, dense black cloud mass was moving rapidly toward us. You could see it coming from miles away. Wabun, Shawnodese and I were travelling so a few of the sisters here went up on top of the Mountain and offered a pipe; they prayed that the cloud of ash would not come over us. About three or four miles from our land, without any apparent wind, the cloud shifted to the North. What had been a huge mass of ash turned into long, grey streamers — and they went away.

Toward the middle of August, 1982, we had a dry spell on Vision Mountain, and one night there was a very powerful thunderstorm. Lightning struck a pine tree on our land, starting a small fire. A few members of the Tribe went down to the spot and thought they put the fire out, but it must have smoldered underground from the pitch in the roots, because the next afternoon the fire broke out again.

At first, there were just four or five folks down there fighting the new fire; they tried digging a ditch to surround it but the wind was too high for that to stop it. The fire began to spread and, as it did, the wind picked up even more. Each time the group rushed to stem its spread in one direction, the wind would shift and push the flames another way.

Soon, there was a ring of fire radiating out from the spot where the whole thing started; it was evident that the few people down there could not fight the fire by themselves. The brothers and sisters who were there made some prayers, and before long there were forty more folks there digging ditches. It was very powerful; there was a ring of people around the ring of fire. There were more Tribe members; there were visitors; students; and some of our neighbors. They beat at the flames with shovels and wet blankets.

But it was still too much for them to fight; sometimes the smoke was so thick that they had to run away to breathe. As they managed to beat down the flames in one area, the wind would shift and rush flames off in another direction.

Wabun had called the local fire department when the fire started, so the group knew that help was on the way. There were only a few trucks available, however, and it was obvious that if the wind kept blowing in every direction, by the time the fire department trucks got there it might be too late to control the blaze.

Wabun, still in the nearby farmhouse, got her pipe and held it, praying. Shawnodese, near the fire, also began to pray. They both prayed for the wind to shift the fire back into itself, and that's exactly what happened. The wind shifted, then died down completely. By the time the fire department arrived, a good deal of the fire had been extinguished.

While the trucks circled the blackened stand of pine trees, soaking them and the Earth, the folks who had fought the fire made a circle and held hands. They gave thanks to the Creator for answering their prayers. After making a few more prayers, and offering some chants, they asked that a protective shield be placed on that section of land. Today, the blackened Earth in that area carries new green life; the Earth Mother is healing herself. It is in that area where we want to build the Vision Mountain Center. We feel the Thunderers pointed it out to us.

I want my students to be able to hear the Earth when she speaks, and feel her, so that if an earthquake is coming or a volcano is about to erupt, or a fire is burning somewhere, they'll be ready for it. That's all part of how to survive the Cleansing, and a lot more people will survive if they learn to live in harmony.

The Earth speaks to us all of the time; unfortunately, most folks are simply deaf to what she's saying. People are often amazed when I predict the weather for them, yet that's a very simple thing to do. They say, "Sun Bear, how do you know what kind of winter it's going to be?" and I tell them that I read the book of the Earth. I knew a few years ago that we'd have some mild winters, and then we would have a severe one, and we did. You can expect more strange weather in the coming years — all over the world.

The Earth is now at a stage in the Cleansing when she's withholding her increase, and you have to be aware of that, and of why, so that you can move, if necessary, and be able to protect yourself and your families. You need to learn that there are songs that can connect you with the Earth; there are dances that you can dance.

When you go to a place on the Earth, if the land calls out to you and says dance, then you should come alive and do a dance for the power in that spot. You should let a song come up out of you for the Earth, and the words don't really matter; it's the feeling. Pretty soon, as you open up to that kind of energy, you're no longer simply *you*; you've become an Earth Spirit, just feeling and hearing everything. That's what we do at many of our ceremonies; we *transform*. We become the power that we celebrate, and that's what I'm trying to bring to people during our Medicine Wheel Gatherings.

I am waiting for the time when we can all come together to do our ceremonies, so we can actually create an energy field that will saturate the rest of the people on Earth. Then we will *be* the powers of the Earth Mother. When the Hopi medicine people put on their sacred masks and make their prayers, they become the different powers of the Kachinas. When our people put on the masks and feathers of the animal totems around the Medicine Wheel, the same thing happens. The power that comes through us is an energy, a living force, and that's why we can speak to Grandmother Moon, to Father Sun.

When you get past the rinky-dink world, and grow into the medicine I'm telling you about, then you will learn you have the power to make anything happen in your life that you want to happen. You'll learn that you can will things into existence; you can change the course of your own history. You know, when the ancient Roman generals used to go into battle, they would hurl their standards out into the ranks of their enemies so that their soldiers would have to go in there and recover them. That's where that old saying comes from: "You have to hurl your standard before you," and then you must go after it. It's really true.

At Vision Mountain we make our prayers for the things we need, and they often come to us. When you want to pray for something you go to your power spot and you talk to the Creator. I have two spots that I use on Vision Mountain; I have one that I use for particular ceremonies, and not even my own people know where it is, because it's a very special spot for me. It's a place where I talk to two different spirits; they represent the male and female powers on this mountain.

Each of our people has his power spot on the Mountain, where he can go to call the forces to him. First, you sit on the ground, and you place your hands flat on the Earth. You feel the energy of the Earth Mother surge up through you, through your male and female energy centers. You feel yourself coming alive to her, and you realize, at some time or other, that the spirit forces which are speaking to you are not necessarily speaking to you in English. That's when you're really beginning to feel the energy.

Each time you make your medicine it becomes more natural, easier, until, literally, most of the things you need for your medicine path will come to you. Even material objects, if they help us on our paths, are good things to ask for. We're not the kind of folks who cry about doomsday and say that money or goods are evil. They aren't, in themselves; it's what's in your heart, and the way that you use them that counts. Once, we needed some later model vehicles, so we could travel to do our seminars. We prayed for them, and we got them. We needed building materials to add more space to our longhouse—we got them, and built a meeting room. Awhile back, we decided we needed a house in Spokane, to use as office space; we made our prayers and now we have several houses in the city. Through our medicine, fourteen additional acres of farmland at the bottom of the Mountain have come to us. One of the wildest dreams we had was to own a computer, so that we could print out *Many Smokes*, straighten out our mailing lists, do bookkeeping and write books on it. Now, we have several computers.

All of these things, you see, have come to us through our medicine. Most of the time we had very little money to buy them, but we needed them in order to reach out and communicate with people. The Spirit heard our prayers.

We're a small group, and we're simple people, but we're doing what the Spirit wants us to do, and we're doing it all in a very powerful manner, on a constant, continuing basis. We've found our power, and we use it in a positive, and strong, and very real way, every day.

What you have to do with your own path of power is exercise it all the time. It's your spiritual muscles, your muscles of communication, and they have to be kept in good condition. Maybe you begin by sprinkling corn meal when you pray; maybe it's tobacco that you use as your sacrament to the forces of the universe. Maybe you smudge the way we do; sometimes we use different methods for opening up our channels to the Creator.

There will be times when it will feel easy to sit back and moan and say, "I wonder if my medicine has deserted me?" Sometimes you can really feel that way. You know, you get to a point where you just don't know how things are going to work out for you; everything seems to be a mess. You pray, though, and you wait, and then it's just like some heavy artillery has blasted a path ahead of you, and everything falls back into place. You've listened to your heart, and you've done what it told you to do, and the medicine has come through for you. It's beautiful, and you look up at the sky or down at the Earth and you say to the Spirit and to yourself, "Hey! Wasn't that simple?" Then you feel really strong again, because your medicine has reversed the trend of things.

Sometimes you can do that with relationships too, where you see that somebody is needlessly travelling away from you in one way or another, and then, all of a sudden, he does a complete turnaround, and comes right back to you. My medicine has done that with people, sometimes in some very literal and practical situations. I like to tell a story about the time when I had a booth at the State Fair in Sacramento. I was pretty hungry and there was a young Japanese man walking by my booth carrying a handful of delicious-looking grapes. I didn't know the guy, but I thought to myself, "Gee, I sure would like to have a taste of those grapes". The man had already passed me by, but at the exact instant of my thought he did an about-face, looked at me, then walked up to me and said, "Here, why don't you take these grapes to eat?", and he handed me the whole bunch. They really tasted good.

I am very careful, as you should be, not to ever draw someone back into a relationship if that would be a bad thing for the person. When you are walking the path of power you need to learn to discriminate, and not to put your own desires above whatever will bring the most good to all of the beings involved in any situation. You must always remember that the source of all power is the Creator.

There are many things beyond those that I've talked about, but these are good for a beginning. After you've learned to take your first step, then you can walk a little further. In that way, like a novice learning a new skill, a person can take one small step, then bigger ones; each thing you do takes you further along the path of power. Some nights I dream about an opening into great realms of power. I believe that this opening is there for those who are willing to seek it.

Survival is not glamorous but takes planning, hard work, and many prayers.

CHAPTER SIXTEEN
GIVING AWAY YOUR POWER

Beginning the path of power won't do you any good unless you do so with the proper respect and with attitudes that will allow you to use your power only to make good medicine.

The misuse of power is something which has weakened a lot of Native cultures and people. There were medicine people in the past, and there are some today, who let their egos interfere with the making of good medicine. Some of them like to play games. They like to use their power to try to hurt other people, or make problems for them, and this is a very bad sickness. There are some reservations today where there are no more medicine people, partly because they were so arrogant in their power that they used it to kill each other off. A lot of folks have the idea that all Indians are noble savages, but that's not true. I think the Great Spirit distributed an equal amount of good people among the races, and an equal amount of ding-a-lings. Maybe this belief is what makes me happy to think of myself as a human being, and not just as an Indian, or as a man. I don't like to separate myself off into one box of humanity.

I treat my apprentices like brothers and sisters, whether they're white, red, black or yellow. There are other medicine people who wouldn't do that; they would be sitting around and pretending that their medicine was a great mystery. They would hold back just for the sake of being difficult, of intimidating those who had come to them to learn.

Folks tell me all the time, "Sun Bear, you shouldn't give away your medicine power to other people like you do. You should keep it for yourself". I try to tell those people what the truth is: that the Great

Spirit is standing right behind me when I teach my brothers and sisters, that as fast as I can give away medicine knowledge the Spirit is pouring me full of new power, new medicine. That's because I'm doing what the Creator has told me I should do.

One of the few pieces of knowledge that I don't share with people at this time is the knowledge that is recorded in the Midewiwin Scrolls. I have the responsibility to use the knowledge from those scrolls to help my brothers and sisters, to heal them, but I don't translate the symbols for anyone. I show folks the pictographs on the rocks at the foot of Vision Mountain, and I translate some of those because I am allowed to. I go and I translate some of the petroglyphs on the rocks down in Lagomacino Canyon, in Nevada, where there's a half-mile of different symbols, and that's okay, because it is my medicine to do that. There are many of those petroglyphs that I understand, but don't talk about. My medicine, as always, tells me how to use the power that I have in a proper manner.

Some medicine people boast about their power; they say, by their words or manner, "Look at me. I'm wonderful!" I hope I never give you the impression that I'm trying to do that. What I share with you is meant to be taken as knowledge; I have medicine because the Creator has chosen to use me as a channel. But some medicine people, from a variety of cultures, can be very boastful; they set themselves apart from the rest of the human race, and they can lose their power in that way. Others try to send out negative energies, like I said, to cause harm. Doing this is, I feel, a prime misuse of power. When they do that, you can sometimes feel it coming; you smudge yourself and ask for a protective shield. You pray and ask the Creator to send the energy back to its source, or to let it be transformed into good energy. Then you'll be okay. When you're centered in your energy and power, it's very difficult for anybody else to hurt you.

I never raise my hand against another person, yet some very powerful things have happened to people who have tried to do me harm. The shield that I carry with me is a barrier of energy and power, and when somebody throws something up against it, it just bounces back at them. I can't even stop it. I've had people come after me with knives or guns and try to hurt me, and all I can do is say, "I just wish you wouldn't do that, my brother or my sister, because it's not good".

"I'm not angry with you," I tell them, "But there are others that will be angry." If people don't then leave me alone, they can end up getting hurt. There are forces that work with me, and with my vision, and they protect me from any unnecessary harm.

I feel that the display of unnecessary anger, on any level, is a grave misuse of power, and weakening to the person putting on the display. I tell my people on Vision Mountain, for example, when someone tends to get a little bit loud or angry with the other brothers and sisters: "Look, you don't have to show your power in that way". There's a poster hanging on the wall in my room, and I like to tell people about the saying at the bottom of it, which is, "In gentleness there is great strength". That is true. Power, most of the time, can be a very quiet thing.

I feel that anger is counterproductive. That's why, when some of my brothers and sisters get too heated up, say, at a council meeting, and they begin to raise their voices and poke their fingers at each other, I usually get up and walk out the door, because I know that very little is going to be accomplished. When you become strong in your medicine, you don't need to rant and rave to get things done.

★ ★ ★

Native American concepts of leadership are very different from those of the white society, and I want to talk about them because a medicine person was traditionally, and is today, above everything else, a leader of his or her people. To me, the difference between Native leadership and the white man's concept of leadership, is that when you become a leader in the Native way you're not a boss-man. The mainstream society conditions people into being boss-men or followers. The politicians are boss-men; they manipulate their underlings and set up laws and get away with a lot of selfishness and corruption. Company executives are boss-men, too, and it goes that way right on down the line, in an intricate pecking order in which you get pushed around; then, if you're lucky, you can turn to your own set of lackeys, and give them a few good shoves yourself.

When you become a leader in the Native way you don't give orders. If something needs to be done, you're the first one to do it. The Native leader was traditionally the first one to go into battle, the first one into the buffalo hunt, and the person upon whom, ultimately, the consequences of all group decisions would come to rest.

It's still that way. If there's something that needs to be done here, for example, that involves a high-risk situation where someone could be hurt or even killed, I don't tell anybody else to do it; I do it myself. I've done that many times in my life. I've had situations in years past where my people were hungry, and I've had to hunt deer out of season. One time I rustled and shot a cow, and the state I was in wasn't too friendly about that sort of thing. It's what had to be done, though; I had twenty people with empty stomachs. The man who owned the cow had a herd of better than a thousand head, and I knew that the hunger of twenty people was much more painful than the loss of that cow.

Being a leader in the Native way isn't always that exciting, either. While I make medicine and lead ceremonies, I also pitch in and pluck chickens when I can. If you're a leader, you should never set yourself up in an ivory tower.

I feel, too, that a true leader is never an arrogant person. When the Great Spirit gives you the gift of power, it's yours to use in a proper manner, but there's an old saying about the folks who grow too arrogant with their medicine, or their leadership: "If you walk around with your nose in the air, a bee is going to sting you on the lip". I see it happen all the time. The Creator has many ways of keeping you in line, or reminding you that, while you are loved, the Spirit's power is the ultimate power of the universe.

When I was at Wounded Knee, during the occupation, I watched many of the people who others were looking up to, calling them Indian leaders. One of the loudest of them turned out to be an FBI informer. The real leaders, the ones I thought of as really having power, were usually the quietest ones. They were the folks who were doing all the work, putting out good energy. They were truly concerned about the welfare of their brothers and sisters.

Wallace Black Elk was there, for example, and he wasn't shouting. He just went around seeing what his people needed; he made prayers for them, and he tended to the wounded. He made good medicine. I felt much stronger about him and his power than I did about the ones who were stalking around, making angry noises.

I do feel that what I saw at Wounded Knee is true everywhere today; people have been conditioned by society into believing that if you can pass out enough cigars, if you can shove the hardest, then you can become the big chief, or the President, and that that's the way it should be done.

The Native way is a different way of looking at the world, and it's difficult for people to grasp it all at once; that's why nobody will tell it to you all at once. You wouldn't believe them. I am the medicine chief of the Bear Tribe, but I'm not elected, nor anything along those lines. The people who are with me simply believe in my vision. I've never recruited members for the Tribe, nor beaten anyone over the head to make them come and listen to me. I don't believe in doing things that way; in fact, one law of my medicine is that I never even go somewhere to speak, unless I am formally invited to do so.

★ ★ ★

I'm going to share with you now some things which I feel are very important in terms of one's perspective on life. They affect one's medicine power very strongly.

A lot of people — and it doesn't matter what their economic situations might be — have what I call a "back-of-the-bus" mentality. Their conditioning has done that to them, and they feel that they can't do certain things, because they are women, or they're too young, or they're not smart enough, or somebody else is better at it than they are, and so on. That attitude is totally self-destructive, and the things that keep people in line in that way are the mind trips, the tapes that have been laid on them by society. People have to get rid of the garbage that clutters up their heads and blocks their emotions, because it drains them of their power. Their guilt trips, their fears, their jealousies, angers, frustrations ... all of those things take away their power, and that's just the beginning of it.

People give away their power on every level of their lives; it's so easy to do. They give away their power in relationships: maybe because they think they can't live without somebody, so they have to play the game the other person's way in order to keep the game going. Some people do that, I believe, because they're afraid to take control of their own lives, to become whole human beings.

Folks give away their power to please their parents, mommy and daddy, and that, too, keeps them from becoming total human beings.

They give away their power to the politicians ... they say, "Oh, well, they know better than we do, and so we'll let them run the country for us".

They give away their power to the medical doctors; that's a big one. People give away their power to the M.D.s because they are thought of as the gods who know what's best for everybody. Folks don't even ask what a lot of the medications prescribed are going to do for them, or to them. The doctor spends ten minutes with them, asks a few questions and then decides what's wrong with them. He writes up the prescription, and that becomes a ticket to salvation. Folks stick to their medication schedules religiously; they have unquestioning faith, at least until some harmful side-effects occur. The doctor, after all, has a piece of paper hanging up on the wall, a medical degree, and that is his license to have power over other people. Personally I have compassion for doctors and lawyers. If you look at what they have to do, you'll see that they are not *gods*. They are the real *garbage collectors* of this society.

People give away their power, too, to the churches, to the preachers; some of them stand up there at the podium and tell you that you're bad, that because of Adam and Eve you're a sinful creature, and you believe that. People go through hell on Earth for the clergyman; they go to their little churches on Sunday and the preachers have life all mapped out for them. On that one day of the week, they give folks a little dose of this or that and people say, "Oh, yes, this is what life must be all about".

It is easier to drift along that way.

Another place where people give away their power is at the supermarkets. You go in there, and they have that Muzak playing and you dance on down the aisles. It's really hard to feel close to the Earth, to perform a ceremony and ask for a good crop, when your carrots and corn are coming out of cellophane bags on the produce shelves.

So you see, folks give away their power on all levels of their lives, and all their lives they've been brainwashed into believing that they can't do any better. It's the *I can't* attitude, and sometimes, just plain laziness, that keeps them marching toe-to-heel like that.

Now the thing is that the Creator didn't make us that way; the Creator didn't make us powerless. The Great Spirit gave us a whole broad view of life, and of the world, and that view included our ability to relate to the plants and the minerals and the animals. Most of us have lost those abilities, because we have allowed our power, our *responsibilities*, to be taken away from us until, finally, we have no true sense of balance, or power, or purpose left in life. People have to learn to take back those powers, to live in harmony and walk independently on the Earth Mother.

People need to think really hard about that, because right now there's a whole universe out there and it belongs to all of us. Each person alive is here on the Earth Mother because he is supposed to be here at this time, and each one has a purpose. My students are supposed to be learning about medicine in our workshops, and that goes along with what many different Native prophecies have envisioned. When they are ready to move forward, to take their power back and find their balance, then the universe is there for those students on a total basis.

When we come out of our mother's wombs, we begin equally; what happens to us after that depends on whether or not we're willing to open up, to try to look out into the distance. If we lock ourselves up, if we put those little bars across our minds, we've created little prison cells for ourselves, and there are many people out there who are willing to help to keep us locked up. Each one of us, I believe, needs to come to a time in life when we look around us and say, "Hey, wait a minute! What am I doing locked in here? There's a whole wonderful universe waiting outside for me!".

That's what my students have done; they're on the path of power. They began that path of power in different ways, but all of them, at one point somewhere in the past, woke up one morning, got dressed, put on their shoes, wiggled their toes and said, "Hey, I'm alive!" Then each one of them said, "Hey, I'm going out there to visit with the Bear Tribe on that mountain. There has to be a reason why they're doing so well up there!" They came to unlock their prison cells, to get out into the real world.

Some people can actually get you to believe that all of those big glittery things out there in the chrome dream-world are *real*; the governments, the corporations, the things that only exist on paper. You think they're real, when all they are actually, are balloons being blown up bigger every day. They will even admit they're becoming more inflated all the time, and that's really true. Someday, because of their inflation, they will have to go *pop*, and you'll go with them if you give away your power.

You're living in a very exciting age; you're living at the time of the death of the *dinosaurs*. You know, we didn't see the last bunch of dinosaurs die, but we're going to see these die. Their names are General Motors, U.S. Steel, and all the rest of them, and they're no longer functional. They're no longer serving mankind or Mother Earth.

What you have to do is to be centered enough in your own power so that when it all comes down, when all the little people who've been serving the *dinosaurs* come to you and say, "Oh, my God, I've lost my job!", you can say to them in reply, "The price of acorns is still the same as it was a hundred years ago", and show them how to gather and leech the acorns. That's what has to happen.

Sometimes when I look at all these folks who are working for the *dinosaurs* — they have to be in a certain place at a certain time, they have to dress in a certain manner — I'm torn between laughing and crying. When I was 39, I quit my job because I didn't need one anymore; I figured that in this beautiful land, with all these beautiful resources, if I didn't have enough grey matter in my head to survive without that kind of servitude, then there probably wasn't much worth fighting for anyway. All of those little people go on and on, though. They work all year long, and, finally, the boss-man says, "Well, you've been a good boy. You can have two weeks vacation. Go out there and live it up!" Isn't that just wonderful? Two weeks. By the time you figure out all the things you've been missing all year, that you would like to do, those two weeks have slipped by. So what's the use of it? You go out for your two weeks, then you come back in, and they slap the collar around your neck and put you back on the assembly line for another year ... and that's just standard procedure. Finally, you get to where you can hardly make it to work anymore, and then they say, "Well, friend, we're sorry to let you know it, but you can't make the grade anymore ... and the social security system just dried up. Sorry about that, too, friend."

Most folks who let themselves get all wrapped up like insects in a spider's web hate it deep down inside. They know that once upon a time they were free people, that they walked upon the Earth Mother, and took their sustenance directly from her.

You can pick out ten bank presidents, five lawyers, and eight housewives; sit them down around a campfire and watch what happens to them. They grow quiet. They start watching the flames in the fire, and watching the coals turning different colors, then all of a sudden you look at their faces and they've all turned back into cave men and cave women.

They all sit there and they *ooh* and *aah* and they say, "Isn't it beautiful!" and their hearts come alive with something that reminds them that for thousands of years we lived close to the Earth and, truly, we were brothers and sisters. You see a bank president, who in the ouside world might shake hands with you very cooly, suddenly put his arm around your shoulder and lose all of his pretensions. He's actually been moved, for a moment, out of the realm of the untouchable society.

That's what has to happen.

The powers that I feel closest to in my medicine are my brothers, the Thunder Beings.

CHAPTER SEVENTEEN
MAKING RAIN

The powers that I feel closest to in my medicine are my brothers, the Thunder Beings. I feel that calling them to me, making rain, is one of the best examples of what I've been telling you about in earlier chapters; that when you're strong and centered in your medicine you can tune into the elemental forces. You can lock into their energy and have them respond to you, and the process is not the mysterious act of a magician.

Many times, wherever we go, we of the Bear Tribe bring rain with us; this is true at our Medicine Wheel Gatherings, on our lecture and seminar tours, and even when we're just going somewhere to visit. Frequently, when we are in an area that's been dry for a long time, people say to me, "Sun Bear, we need some rain very badly here. Will you bring it to us?", and I usually do. Sometimes these folks get more rain than they asked for.

I was participating in a seminar a few years back at Mount Hood, in Oregon, where it hadn't rained for a year-and-a-half. This was in the late 1970's and there were drought problems. I could feel that the land was just crying out with thirst. The people there asked me to make a prayer for rain, which I did, and by the time that I got up to make my first speech it was thundering so hard that the building we were in was shaking from the power of it, and I had to speak to my audience between the peals of thunder. There was a big storm that night ... the biggest they'd had there in many years. It blew down trees and did a lot of damage, but the Earth Mother got her badly-needed drink of water.

I was at the Ananda Ashram in Monroe, N.Y. to give a lecture a few years later. The folks there had planted their gardens, but the rain just wouldn't come. Everything was dry. They asked me to pray for rain, which I did. We all made prayers together, and sang some rain songs, and the rain poured down very shortly afterwards. It got so strong, in fact, that it kept right on raining for about three days. The storm washed out many of their new seeds and their early crops.

The same thing happened up in Boston when I was speaking at a seminar for the Interface organization there, as well as in other places. It happens, in fact, most of the time when my energy is strong and I speak to the Thunderers in the proper manner.

I've worked with my brothers, the Thunderers, for a good part of my life. When a storm is rolling in, I go out and welcome them. I offer up my pipe sometimes, and can feel their energy surging into me; at times, it can be an uncomfortable sensation, because I feel it's the ultimate in natural raw power. Thunderstorms; tornados; earthquakes; they will all talk to you if you are open to hearing them, and to feeling them. When people ask me how I make rain, I simply tell them that I don't make it. This is the truth. I ask for it. If it is meant to be, it comes. I know that it is not good to try to use the elemental forces to bolster your own sense of power. I only ask that the Thunderers work with me if it is for the good of Mother Earth, or our relations upon her.

In February, 1982, I went to New Zealand, where I was invited to participate in a Black Bear Festival. In the *Maori* Native language it is called *Mangu Pea*. While I was over there, I shared my medicine knowledge with a lot of very good people.

The Festival was to be held for three days, but I got there early. Lonnie Christie, the lady who was producing the Festival, came to me with a few of my Maori brothers, who said to me, "Sun Bear, it hasn't rained here in a very long time. Will you make a prayer for us?" I did.

New Zealand is a country which was sub-tropical rain forest at one time ... but I feel that because the people there have cut down the trees, they've changed the climate completely; so now the land is subject to periodic droughts. You could look around for vast distances there, and you would see great cracks puckering the Earth, and that everything was parched and becoming lifeless.

I made my prayers. I offered up the pipe, then passed it around the circle. I called on the power represented by my bear claw necklace, and, in a little while, a bit of a sprinkle began to filter down onto the land. The people there were very pleased with that; they were all smiling and nodding their heads, but then it started to rain in earnest.

It poured down in sheets for the next three days, and finally Lonnie came to me and said, "Sun Bear, the weather forecast calls for more rain. If it continues like this, we won't be able to hold the Festival. Will you make another prayer and try to stop it?"

"Lonnie," I told her, "I've never worked with my medicine in that way. I just asked the rain spirits to come to us. I can't do what you ask, but I'll tell you what: I'll make a prayer to my brothers, the Thunderers, and see if they will split the clouds. That way, maybe we can put some of the rain off for awhile."

I went off by myself, then, and smoked my pipe. After I was finished, I put the stem to my forehead and asked the Creator and the Thunder Spirits to split the clouds for a period of time. Then I gathered together the work crews who were setting up for the Festival ... the carpenters, the sound technicians, and so on, and along with Lonnie and some more of my Maori brothers, we all stood out in the rain in a big circle, and made a prayer. There were about thirty-five of us, and the whole group understood my medicine, I believe; they sure knew what we were praying for. The rain was running down their necks. Later that afternoon I prayed a third time, this time with Lonnie and one of the Maoris whose energy I felt really good about. We could feel the power of the Thunderers as we spoke to them.

By the following morning, the storm had broken up completely; there were just a few scattered clouds drifting in the sky. All day long it was the same way; there was a little bit of sunshine, and a few puffy clouds wandering here and there. That evening, though, when the Festival had begun and I got up to make my first speech, a black cloud, about five acres in size, hovered over us. Lightning shot out of that cloud, and the thunder rumbled, as it poured down on my audience for about five minutes — so hard that they had to run for shelter under the speaking platform. Then the rain stopped as suddenly as it had begun, and I told my audience, "That was my brothers, the Thunderers. They're reminding us of their power. They're telling us that they love us, but that they can bring their energy back whenever they want to, that we need to respect them". It was good. We didn't have any more rain then, until after the Festival was over.

★ ★ ★

My Maori brothers are a very fine people; they're sincere and very reverent toward the Earth Mother. We had a very good visit together. When I first got there, I greeted them in their traditional manner. You rub noses with the men and you kiss the women, which was just fine with me. I went around in a big circle doing that with each one of them, and the energy was very strong, and very friendly.

The whole experience in New Zealand was a happy one; I hope to work things out so that I can go back there on a regular basis, because I feel very close to the Native people and the spirit-keepers of that land.

★ ★ ★

Sometimes I feel like I'm a bird dog for the elemental forces. I go out into the world and look for spots where something is needed ... rain, sunshine, whatever, then I call upon the powers, and ask for their help at a particular time, in a particular place. The power of the pipe, if it's used for that purpose, is always very strong. It feels to me as though mankind was put on the earth to serve as keepers of the land in a visible form. The invisible powers that are the spirit-keepers come to us, and when we lock ourselves into their energy we conduct it; we are working together, like electricity when it flows through certain kinds of crystals. It's all very simple: when you're making that kind of medicine, you feel as though you're an Earth Spirit, a channel in physical form. Sometimes I feel like my feet just go down like roots into the earth, and my mind and my heart are expanding endlessly into the universe.

When I go to speak to people in other parts of the country, or of the world, what I usually tell them is that the rain spirits are alive; that they can hear people's wishes. The problem in many places, I feel, is that folks put out negative energy toward the Thunder Beings. Aside from cutting down the trees, and wreaking havoc on the geography and climate of an area, people say things like, "Well, I hope it doesn't rain today. I have a picnic to go to", or, "There's a football game". Even little children look out of the window at the rain and sing a little song that starts with, "Rain, rain, go away". That's a prevalent attitude, and all that negative energy — it's really true — gets up into the heavens, and folks actually will the rain spirits to go away. It's just like psychosomatic illnesses; you can do these things with your thoughts and your feelings. Then, when people get desperate for some rain for drinking water, or to nourish their lawns, it doesn't come and they just can't understand why it's so dry.

Members of the Bear Tribe usually bring rain with them wherever they go because they love the rain spirits. We love all of the spirit powers of the elemental forces. We respect them, and we welcome them, and they come to be with us because they're a part of our reality, a part of our prayers to the Creator every day.

We have also learned to accomodate them in our events. We have had several very wet Medicine Wheel Gatherings. Our first and second ones in Seattle came with much rain. Luckily people in the Seattle area are used to the rain spirits and so they were happy to do ceremonies, singing and dancing in the rain, realizing that it was a blessing and cleansing. We learned, after these, to hold the Gatherings in places with enough indoor space to accomodate people who might not be as used to rain as Seattlites. That lesson came in handy for our first Texas Gathering, near Houston, where it poured for most of the weekend, only slackening off for those ceremonies that needed to be held outdoors around the Medicine Wheel.

Ceremonies can be joyful releases that transmute anger into good feelings, grief into joy of living, fear into love, and loneliness into unity.

CHAPTER EIGHTEEN
CEREMONIES AND MEDICINE OBJECTS

Ceremonies and medicine objects are powerful tools that can help you to live a more balanced and harmonious life if they are used properly. Like anything with power, they also have their dangers if they are used incorrectly. By now, hopefully, you realize that the stereotype of an Indian medicine man dressed in fur and feathers, shaking a rattle while intoning a chant, and giving his patient a strange combination of herbs that will either kill or cure, is a very simplistic picture, with many incorrect assumptions. When people see a scene such as that in the movies or on television, they often think of the medicine man as a "witch doctor", who, out of his ignorance, is trying desperately, with savage tools, to bring about a cure that has little chance for success.

Every medicine object that I and other medicine people use has a very specific purpose. Each chant, each ceremony, is designed to work with subtle energies that can help people to become more nearly whole and complete. These medicine objects, chants and ceremonies have as much power today as they did hundreds or even thousands of years ago. It's all in knowing how to use them.

Many people who come to me now are enchanted with the tools of a medicine man. They like to wear beads and feathers and fur vests. They collect rattles, drums, pipes and claws, but they don't know how to use them properly once they have them. They want the badges of medicine power. without the study and knowledge that would allow them to use these objects to help the earth and all of their relations upon her. I won't help such people unless they are willing to put in the necessary work.

Some folks come to us and they ask, "Where are the eagle feathers?" or "Show me the peyote buttons", but that's not at all what we're about. We're not interested in breaking the laws of the U.S. Government, but more than that, we're not interested in giving folks the wrong tools, or the wrong ideas about power. We want people to learn because they feel that what we're doing here is very real, very important, and because they want to know everything they can about how to walk in balance on the Earth Mother.

I'm going to share some things with you here about ceremonies and medicine objects because I want you to increase your understanding, and open up to the idea that you might want to learn more about these subjects. I want you to even consider the idea that someday you might want to participate in a ceremony, with an understanding of what that ceremony is about. Thousands of people, of all backgrounds, have already joined us in our Medicine Wheel ceremonies, and gone away with a better understanding of themselves, and their relationship with everything else on the earth. That's what ceremonies are for.

However, if you don't believe in the sacred energy, the life-giving energy that you can feel, but not see, there is no way that anyone can convince you that it exists. Yet, I'd ask you to remember what you have felt looking into the face of an infant, or petting your favorite dog or cat, or looking at a breath-taking sunset, or being drawn to your favorite piece of jewelry. At moments like these, you have felt drawn in a way that you could never prove. You have seen and experienced the sacred energy.

In the old days, my people knew that they had a responsibility to the earth and to all of the other beings upon her. They knew that there was an energy that only they could give to all of these other beings, and were willing to give it. They recognized the circle of life, and were aware of the things that all of their relations gave to them. They knew that they needed the elements, the plants, and the animals for their lives to continue, and did not take the gifts of these beings for granted. When they found a rock they wanted to have because of the energy contained in it, the rock would first be asked if it wanted to be with them and, if it did, an offering would be left and a prayer made before they took it.

If they needed water from a spring, again, there would be a prayer and offering to the spirit of the spring. Before planting or harvesting gardens or gathering wild plants, they would make prayers and offerings. Before going on the hunt they would make prayers. Sometimes there would be dances to honor the spirits of their relations: like the corn, and deer dances that are still done by the Pueblo people in the Southwest. Often there would be thanksgiving ceremonies for the gifts of life that these beings gave to them.

My people had a very sophisticated knowledge of the life force, that scientists are just beginning to discover today through things like Kirlian photography. They knew that the sacred life energy was present in all of the beings upon the planet and they also knew how to honor and work with this energy. They knew that by praying — centering their thoughts in a respectful way — they gave some of their energy to the rock, the plant, the water, the animal, and that this would keep the energy circle from being depleted by whatever they needed to take in return. They knew how to look at nature in such a centered way that they could give energy just by their looking. They would become one with whatever they saw, and this oneness would create a life-giving energy exchange. Is that hard to believe? Haven't you ever really looked at another person and felt such an exchange take place? Maybe you've even experienced this with a pet or a plant that is dear to you.

My people knew that prayer was one good way of giving energy to their relations, but they also knew that there were other, more powerful ways of doing it. Chanting is one of them. Dancing and drumming and rattling are others. These all change what scientists today call your brain waves. They allow you to become more relaxed, more at one with the things around you. When you put praying, chanting, dancing, and drumming together into a ceremony, you have one of the most powerful ways of giving energy back to the earth and all of her other children. It's important to remember that: ceremony is one of the most powerful tools for keeping the life energy circulating well upon the planet.

Ceremonies, I believe, kept the Native people from needing psychiatrist's couches. Properly understood and done ceremonies not only give energy to the other kingdoms upon the earth; they also release many of the negative things that people feel. Ceremonies can be joyful releases that transmute anger into good feelings, grief into joy of living, fear into love, and loneliness into unity.

For all of these reasons, I teach people about ceremony today. One of the first ceremonies that I share with people is that of smudging. Smudging is a process of using smoke to clear away negative energies, and to attract positive energies to you. We use a big shell, or a pottery or stone bowl, and we mix sage and sweetgrass in it. If you want to smudge on your own, at home, and you can't find sage or sweetgrass, you may use a high grade of tobacco with as few additives in it as possible. Tobacco, like sage, tends to draw the negativity out of things, and the sweetgrass brings in positive energies that we benefit from. Other plants, like cedar and juniper, may also be used because of their special healing powers.

You light the mixture and let it smolder, then draw the smoke toward your heart and over your head to receive its blessings. It's good to use a fan or feather to keep your mixture smoking well. After you've smudged yourself, you offer the smoke to the four directions; then you smudge the other people who are with you. They should all be in a circle, and the smudge should go in a sunwise manner, like most things in our ceremonies.

Many people in the healing professions have found that smudging is very helpful. We have many kinds of therapists, and some doctors, who smudge their offices between patients so that the negativities of one person will not effect the next person. It's also good to smudge your home daily. Often, if you do so, people will come in and ask if you have recently painted or redecorated. They'll notice that something feels better, even if they can't quite figure out what it is.

Smudging is an essential first step for most other ceremonies. We begin the Medicine Wheel Gatherings by smudging. If people can let go of their negativities, and feel the good energy centered within them, they will get a lot more out of anything that comes later.

The pipe ceremony is a very important one that I share with people. The pipe, to my people, represents the universe. It is a very sacred altar that can be taken anywhere. In it, all of the kingdoms are united. The bowl is made of stone or clay to represent the elemental kingdom. The stem is of wood, and represents the plant kingdom, and the pipe is decorated with fur and with feathers, to represent the animal kingdom. It is used by us two-leggeds, thus bringing all of the kingdoms into our ceremonies. Often the pipe has four streamers, of red, black, white and yellow, representing the colors of the four directions, and the four races of humans.

The bowl represents the female energies, and the stem, the male. The bowl, we say, is the flesh and blood of the Native people; the stem is the bones. The symbols of the pipe are never-ending; they are like the universe itself.

If you are offering the pipe, you first smudge it, your tobacco or kinnik-kinnik and matches, and any other objects that you use with your pipe. When we do a pipe ceremony, we fill the bowl with tobacco in a ritual manner; first, we offer pinches to the Great Spirit, to the Earth Mother, and to the four directions. We may also offer pinches of tobacco to the four kingdoms, to the four elements (earth, air, fire and water), to the plant kingdom, to the four kinds of animal creatures (the winged ones, the water beings, the creepers and crawlers, and the four leggeds), to the human kingdom, to the spirit keepers, and to any special purpose for which we are offering the pipe.

When we light the pipe, too, we offer a puff of smoke to each of the four directions, to the Great Spirit, and to our Mother Earth. In filling the pipe, we have placed ourselves into the altar, the bowl, and as we light the pipe, we believe, we send out our prayers with the smoke into the universe. The smoke from the pipe is the breath of our prayers, as it drifts up from the bowl … and we believe that when we draw in through the stem, the smoke we take into our bodies is the breath of the Great Spirit. With the smoke — an ethereal substance which can penetrate between the realms of the physical and the spiritual — we send our prayers to the Creator. Those prayers, most of the time, are for unity, healing and for understanding.

The pipe is a powerful tool for healing and helping the earth, and all of her children today. Many non-Native people now seek to have pipes, and, if they want to use them in proper ways, I feel good about helping them. We tell people that the pipe is just a pretty piece of wood and stone until it is awakened and consecrated by a medicine person. Then it becomes a sacred and powerful tool that should be used and treated with respect.

After we consecrate a pipe for a person, we ask them then to give it away to the universe. To do this, you must offer it to the four directions, to the Great Spirit, to the Earth Mother, to the Grandmother and Grandfather spirits, and to the universe. In this offering you acknowledge that, while you are using this pipe, you recognize that it is not yours. It belongs, like everything else, to the Creator. It is good to give away to the universe any medicine objects that you acquire because it helps you to recognize the real source of their power.

There is another kind of giveaway ceremony that we also practice and teach. In this giveaway a person who has had something special happen to him gives gifts to others around him, so that they can share in his feelings. For instance, if someone has a child, or if two people get married, they would have a giveaway to share their joy with those around them. In old times, and sometimes today, when a person dies his relatives give his possessions away to people who knew and loved him. That way, when the recipients look at the gifts they have received they remember the good things they shared with the person who has left the earth, and they send good thoughts or prayers to him.

We have giveaways at each Medicine Wheel Gathering to thank all of the people who help to make these ceremonies possible. At Earth Renewal ceremonies we have giveaways to the people in the Tribe, and to those who choose to share these times with us. If an individual in the Tribe is feeling happy about something, he might have a giveaway to share this happiness with those around him. The giveaway is a good way of sharing your love.

Another ceremony that we feel good about sharing with people, is that of the sweatlodge. We use the sweatlodge often in our community. It is a powerful experience for us, one that helps us to cleanse, heal, open, learn and grow. The sweat lodge is a dome shaped structure made from saplings. It is shaped like a turtle, to represent this continent which we call Turtle Island, and it is covered with materials that keep in the heat, and keep out the light. In the center of the lodge is a hole where we place rocks that have been heated in a fire pit outside. The door of the lodge faces east, and a spirit path leads to an altar mound in front of the door. This mound is built from the earth removed from the lodge's center pit. After proper prayers to the fire, we enter the sweatlodge. Sometimes we wear clothing, and sometimes not. When all are seated inside the lodge, and the rocks, with the proper ceremony, have been placed in the pit, we close the lodge flap and sprinkle sage on the stones to rid the lodge, and those in it, of any negative energies. Then we place sweetgrass on the stones to bring in good energies. We pour water over the stones, and steam billows in the darkness. Sweat begins to run down our faces, over our bodies, and takes the poisons out. We invite in the Great Spirit, and the Grandmother and Grandfather Spirits. Then, one by one, we invite in the powers of the four directions: Waboose, the spirit of the North, of night, of the physical being and the white buffalo; Wabun of the East, the spirit of the dawn, the intellect, illumination, attended by the golden eagle; Shawnodese, the spirit of the South, the mid-day, the heart, attended by the coyote; and Mudjekeewis, the spirit of the West, the father of the winds who takes care of spiritual life, and comes with the grizzly bear.

We sing songs, rub sage on the sore parts of our bodies. We make our prayers, together or individually. Sometimes salty tears run from our eyes, helping with the cleansing. The sweats sometimes last for hours.

If a person has had enough heat, he says, "Thank you, all my relations", and goes outside. If he wishes to return later, he may. We take our children into the sweatlodge and let them sit behind the adults if they wish, so they get less heat. The sweat is not an endurance test. It is the womb of the Earth Mother, the place we go to cleanse and renew ourselves, and be reborn. It is also a place where we can send our prayers for healing to loved ones all over the earth, and to the Earth Mother herself.

We celebrate many other ceremonies in the Tribe: ones for planting, harvesting, gathering; for the full moon; for the changes of seasons; for the elements; and for the animals who help us to live. We feel that all life, lived well, is precious and can be a ceremony and a prayer of thanksgiving. The power of ceremonies is in the doing, not the telling. When you are ready to learn more, the teacher you need will come to you.

Power objects, or medicine objects, are tools which can help you in ceremonies, or can help you to communicate with the spirit realm. Smudging equipment and also the pipe are, of course, very important medicine objects. Some people also wear or carry medicine pouches or bags which contain personal power objects that bring them spiritual energy. I have several medicine bags that have come to me from other medicine people. One of them was carried on a whaling ship for a period of time; it was used by the Northwest Coast Indians when they went to sea to hunt whales.

These medicine pouches which have come to me from other people are sometimes called pledges, which means that the gift of them binds us together; that when one of us is in spiritual or physical trouble, the other one is pledged to make medicine, or to actually come to the side of the person who needs help. We've pledged our power to each other, and we'll use it whenever it becomes necessary.

In my own personal medicine bag I keep the pledges that have been given to me. I have four gold coins from some Bronco Apaches. They said they brought the coins to me because I was the only medicine person they knew at that time who they felt really strongly about. They said that they'd seen other medicine people, who seemed locked into their own trips so much, that they didn't believe in them. So I have those four gold coins, along with many other pledges from different medicine people of many traditions in my pouch, and I carry them with honor. There are other things, too, in my medicine pouch, that I've put in there over the years.

Our medicine pouches contain a little bit of sage, a little tobacco, a kernel of corn, a bean, and a squash seed. The last three represent the Three Sisters; they symbolize the beginning and the continuation of the life cycle, and they're very important to our life path because they've provided us with food for thousands of years. I encourage my apprentices, and anyone else who wants to prepare a medicine pouch, to include those items along with their personal power objects.

The medicine pouch is something that you carry with you and work with much of the time. As you work with it, you'll find that people will bring you gifts of power, and you'll find many of your own. You might come across a particular stone, or a shell, which feels really strong. We say, it *speaks* to you. You purify it, make prayers over it, give it away to the Universe and then place it in your pouch.

If you're going to do a ceremony, or going to a place where there is a sacred altar, you can place your pouch there if it is alright with the person running the ceremony. For example, you might place it on the altar outside of a sweatlodge. During the time of that ceremony, your pouch will absorb the energy that is coming from the ceremony, the Earth, and the spirits. This will help to make your pouch more powerful.

When you're going out to cry for a vision, you can hold your pouch and make your prayers, and it will help you to center your energy and be strong.

The medicine pouch may become part of what's known as a medicine bundle. The bundle can be wrapped in hide or cloth, and may contain, besides your pouch or pouches, your pipe if you have one and want it in there, and whatever other objects you feel are important for making good medicine. It's really a matter of personal choice; I have one pipe in my most sacred bundle, but I have other pipes which are not included in it. You might put your sage, sweetgrass and smudge bowl into your medicine bundle. You might have a little figure of a bear, or a frog, maybe a crystal ... anything which feels powerful to you, with which you make your prayers. I know of many medicine people today who use different kinds of suitcases as their medicine bundles. They have work to do in many places, and their medicine objects are safer travelling in a hard, rather than soft, pouch.

The medicine pouch is rarely opened in front of other people ... unless you feel you have a strong reason to open it and share it. You might open your bundle when you are performing ceremonies. For instance, we open the Bear Tribe bundle when new members make their oath to the Tribe. It is not good to show your bundle casually. You can give away the power of your objects if you do that.

I have an otter skin bundle now which is very respected medicine among my people. You obtain that when you have attained a certain level of power. Because this bundle is very sacred and very powerful, I will only use it when it feels right for me to do so.

The medicine bundle can be used in different ways. It can be used for healing, for crying for visions, and it can also be used as a defense. I told you, awhile back, about the man who had ridiculed the Midewiwin medicine men, and how one of them had pointed his bundle at the intruder and *shot him with the medicine*. The man was instantly paralyzed, until he had apologized. Then he was healed.

When the old Midewiwin medicine men would do their dances, they would carry their ceremonial otter bundles with them. They would dance, or pray in a circle, and, from time to time, they would point them at each other. Their power was so strong, that if a particular person's medicine was not strong enough, he would collapse right there in the circle. The medicine man who had pointed the bundle would then have to heal the person who had collapsed.

As you develop personal medicine power, it is up to you to do what feels right in your heart with your medicine objects. Sometimes pipes and pouches are passed on when a person dies; at other times they're buried with him or in a separate location. While you're practicing your medicine, you may even give away objects from your medicine pouches. I've had people open up their bags and give me things that they had carried for a long time, because they felt very strongly that they wanted to do so. These, sometimes, are the pledges I've told you about, and not all of them come to me from Native Americans. Tom Brown Jr., author of THE TRACKER, gave me a medicine object awhile back that he had carried with him since he was a young child. The gift feels very powerful.

Power objects, as I've said, have the ability to call in certain spirit forces, but you have to know how to call them in. That's why we say these objects, when they're sitting in museum cases, are asleep. The power doesn't come through them until you take power *over* them. For example, when a person comes to me for a blessing on his or her pipe, the blessing allows him to work with the power of the pipe. A pipe is a beautiful piece of artwork, but until it is awakened by a medicine person it isn't a power object. So when a person comes to me and asks me to bless his or her pipe, and I decide to do so, I'm giving that person power. Unless he or she knows how to tune into that power, it will do that person little good. Sometimes, for that reason, I'll tell a person to wait awhile longer, that I don't feel he or she is ready to have that pipe awakened.

★ ★ ★

When an object comes to you for medicine purposes, you need to take power over it; you must make certain prayers and do certain things before it is yours to use. Until you do that, it can scatter the energy you're trying to work with; it can even make you seriously ill.

I have an object that somebody gave to me recently, which I haven't taken power over yet. The person had been over to Egypt, and had chipped off a piece of one of the great pyramids. He gave that stone to me at one of my seminars, and I thanked him and put it into my shirt pocket. Immediately afterwards I started to feel very ill. I grew weak and had a headache, and felt like I was going to pass out. Everything had been fine before, so I took the stone out of my pocket and put it up in my room, and I felt fine again. Later that night, I tested the stone a second time; I put it back into my pocket, and got sick again. Since then, I have kept it up in my room; I haven't taken power over it yet, but when I do, I feel I'll be able to speak with the spirits who are the powers of the pyramid. That's how it works, and that's what I'm reaching for with that object. Use caution in accepting gifts of medicine objects. If an object feels bad to you, put it aside. Some objects have energy that can be disharmonious to particular people.

In the past, I've gone into places that were power spots, and I've felt their power in a very negative way. I've also felt negative energy from some medicine objects. They can really put some pain into you, and you have to study them very carefully to see what the problem might be. A particular object, for example, might have belonged to a medicine person whose life ended violently, and that negative energy will have to be cleared away before you can work with the object.

One of the pipes that I have, belonged to Yellow Hand, a Cheyenne medicine man. Yellow Hand was murdered by Buffalo Bill out on the plains, and when I began using that pipe, I had to make special prayers first, to acknowledge Yellow Hand's spirit passing. I had to ask for the release of the bad energy so that I could work with it.

That pipe was a gift from another medicine man. He had kept it for a long time until he met me and was told, by Spirit, that I was the person who should hold that pipe. This pipe has become a very powerful tool for me.

When I went to the second World Symposium on Humanity in Toronto, there was a Native Unity Gathering happening nearby, and I was invited to go there. I met and spoke with Wallace Black Elk, and shared the pipe with him and a number of other medicine men from many tribes. After the pipe ceremony Wallace told me that he felt the power of the pipe was very strong, and could be used especially to bring unity and to work with the elements.

His feelings proved true almost immediately. At one point during the Symposium, the people there were beginning to fight with each other. One of the leaders of the Symposium asked me to bring help to the situation. I spoke to the group for awhile, and then I offered my pipe. Immediately, the fighting ceased, and the Symposium continued in a good way.

Sometime later I was invited to a seminar on Gabriola Island, off of Vancouver. I did a pipe ceremony there and as I called in the powers of the directions, a woman standing at the east of the circle, and a man standing at the west both fell to the ground, went into an altered state, and saw the Keeper of the Direction in which they had been standing.

A similar thing happened when I offered the pipe during a ceremony I performed on Da Free John's land in Northern California. As I called in the Spirit Keepers of the four quarters, two of the men in the circle fell. One was in the north, and the other, in the south. They also saw the Spirit Keepers of those directions.

Another time I offered the pipe during one of Rosemary Gladstar's seminars at a hot springs in Northern California. As I made my prayers, a beautiful, old redwood tree that had been slowly leaning over for decades, fell to the earth and slid down the mountain above us.

In Boston, during a seminar, I offered the pipe and the Thunder Beings came crashing overhead. A little while later I was talking about cockroaches, and how they could predict earthquakes. Just as I finished discussing their talents, two of the largest ones I had ever seen came out from opposite corners of the room, and marched straight up to my feet. My friend Slow Turtle of the Wampanoag people was there, and has had a lot of fun telling people I can call not only the Thunder Beings, but also the cockroaches.

I have, also, a medicine stick that belonged to a very powerful medicine man of an Eastern Tribe. It came to me from somebody down in Florida, and when I saw it I recognized it at once; it has a wooden head carved on top, and from that head a single horn projects. The head represents the keeper spirit that this medicine man worked with, and the horn represents its power.

The stick is very strong medicine, and I had special need of it as a connection with some of the Eastern people, because some of them haven't understood my work and why I teach non-Native people. So I took power over it, and I've used it, and now I have a good relationship with most of them. There are still some who disagree with my teaching philosophy, but I accept that and let it be.

I don't know how the stick got out of the hands of its original owner; maybe when he died his family gave it away because they didn't understand its value. It ended up in an antique shop, and when the person brought it to me, I knew what it was because I've seen some like it, but only very rarely.

When I show it to my students I hold my hand over the face, because that's how I originally took power over it. In that way, I explain to them, it understands that I am going to be working with it, and it will be helping me with my medicine and my path. That's one of the ways, you see, that the Creator has given to us to work with the spirit forces.

We use a medicine stick in many ways; sometimes we just hold one to build our power. I use this particular one when I need help and I want to make a prayer; I ask that the spirit of the stick come and bring its power so that I can work with it, so that its power will act as a bridge to other dimensions.

During the summer of our first Apprenticeship Program, in 1982, I took some of my students to the top of the Mountain one night, and told them about this medicine stick, and I showed it to them, all the time keeping my hand over its face. We talked about it for a very long time. Then I made a prayer, and, as I did so, I removed my hand from the face on the stick and held it up. I said:

> *Creator, I ask that this ancient power that has been with our people for thousands of years, this one that we work with, who calls for the winds and the storms, the one that is the force that has been on our land for thousands of years ... I ask that this power that gives us the ability to reach into the dimensions of all other paths and worlds, may come. I ask that my people might hear and be expanded by the knowledge that comes to us. This is what I ask, Creator. This is what I ask. Thank you.*

When I said that, I closed my eyes and lowered my head, and there were about thirty of us sitting around in a circle on the ground. It was a still, calm night before I made my prayer; then, afterwards, the wind rose higher and higher, until it felt like it would take away the tipis which were standing very close to where we were. Then I said, "Ho! It is good", and the wind died down, and my apprentices understood what I had been telling them, much more clearly than they had when I had simply been telling them with words. For the next three or four days, the wind would come up in sudden gusts, and we had some little gifts of rain and cooler weather. That's how medicine power works.

I'm going to share with you now some things about eagle feathers, although you can't find them useful at this time, because the U.S. Government has said that it is illegal for anyone but Native American medicine men to possess them. What I tell you, therefore, is for you to know, but not for you to try to put into practice.

The eagle is the most respected bird to the Native people, because it's the eagle which has the power to see from the greatest distance. The eagle, too, flies higher than any other bird, so it's always been regarded as having the power to reach up to the spirit realm.

We use eagle wing and tail feathers in many ceremonial ways. We use a whole wing, sometimes, as a fan, and we use the feathers from the breast of the eagle on prayer plumes and other ceremonial objects. The feathers from the breast area, and up around the neck, are called breath feathers; they are fluffy and move with the slightest puff of air, so we say they represent the breath of life, the power of all things.

When we use the feathers ceremonially, we are trying to draw out the power and energy which comes from the spirit realm, and through the Mother Earth. When I use a fan, or a single feather, for something like smudging, (and, this is true of many other feathers besides those of the eagle), I'm using that object to bring good energy into a person's heart and spirit. At other times, I use a feather as a tool to draw negative energies out of somebody.

If I'm going to do a healing on someone, I may put my hand on him or her in order to do that healing. Sometimes, though, if a person is very sick, or is the host for some really bad energies, I may not want to draw those energies into myself, so I touch the person with a feather instead. The feather clears out the bad things, and, after that, I can make my prayers with the individual. The feathers also act as a transmitter which can strengthen the energy that I send into a person.

The feather is a power object after it's been blessed by a medicine person. Besides the eagle feather, the feathers of the hawk are considered to be very sacred, as the hawk, too, is a messenger to the spirit realm. Owl feathers, too, are highly respected among most Native people, although some tribal people will not use them because they feel that the owl is the messenger of death. In general, though, the feathers of all birds are considered to be worthy of high respect, possible power objects, because birds can be links between the earth and the spirit realm.

It's illegal for most folks to possess eagle feathers today, because the bald and golden eagles, as well as other types, have become endangered species. Up until 1972, when the Bald and Golden Eagle Protection Act was passed through Congress, many sheep ranchers hired bounty hunters to slaughter the eagles from airplanes, in order to protect their livestock. Between the bounty hunters and poachers, the eagles were nearly wiped out. It's a very old story; because of a lack of respect for wildlife, the balance between the species has been very badly upset. In order to get eagle feathers today, you must have an eagle feather permit from the government, and, without that, I think there is about a ten thousand dollar fine for possession, and sometimes a prison sentence. Unfortunately, this law has sometimes been used to persecute people who are sincerely trying to follow the Native way.

There are other power objects that I use. I have had a very large grizzly bear claw that I wore on a thong around my neck, and that, too, is a very strong piece of medicine. I used it in ceremonies, and I've used it, too, for what some folks might call more earthly reasons. If I needed help in gambling, for example, I reached for it, and it usually came through for me.

The necklace was given to me as a gift by a medicine friend. On one side of the claw there are four silver serpents which represent my power to make prayers to my brothers, the Thunder Beings; to call upon them to make rain when we need it. There was a turquoise stone on the other side of the claw which is carved into a rattlesnake effigy, and it represents the power of my brother, the rattlesnake, to reach out with my prayers for rain, to take those prayers to the spirit forces. We do a ceremony, sometimes, during which I thank the rattlesnake, and within four days we have the rain.

The medicine of the feathers, and of different power objects, is comprised of sacred rituals which we have worked with for thousands of years. As each person learns to work with his medicine power, to work with these ceremonies and to create new ones, he begins to feel the energy come into him. He learns to call in the forces and the spirits. He *feels*; that's something I can't repeat too many times. The process is not something you *think*; it is something that you feel. Learning how to do that is an extremely important step in one's path of power.

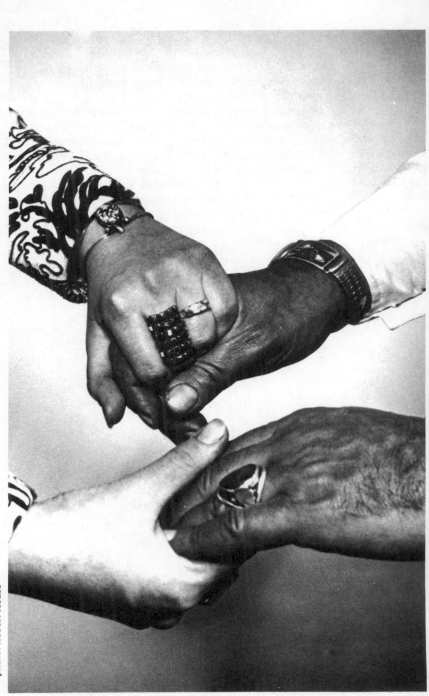

A woman's power is the reflection of the Earth and a man's power is the reflection of the Sun.

CHAPTER NINETEEN

SEX, AND NATURE'S CYCLES

The Native people have always watched nature; it is their textbook for living. Charlie Russell, the great Western artist with a tremendous love for Native people, once wrote a poem that was printed in THE CHARLES M. RUSSELL BOOK, by Harold McCracken (Doubleday, 1957). It reads:

WHEN TRACKS SPELL WAR OR MEAT

Nature taught her child
To read, to write and spell,
And with her books before him
He reads his lesson well.
Each day is but a page
His God, the sun, has turned.
Each year, a chapter nature taught
Her child has read and learned.
A broken twig, a stone is turned
Disturbed by passing feet
His savage eye has caught it all
For tracks spell war or meat.
Nature holds his Bible
With pages open wide,
He questions not her miracles

'Tis done; he's satisfied.
He loves his mother country
Where all her creatures trod,
Yet he is called a heathen
Who has always lived with God.

Native Americans have not only watched nature's cycles; they've always understood that it is the blending of male and female energies that brings forth new life. They view sex as a natural part of life. Many Native cultures, in fact, refer to making love as *sharing energy* or *merging energy*.

The primary ceremony of many tribes takes place during the winter solstice, the time of the Spirit Keeper Waboose. It's a blending of the male and female energies that we honor during this time because it's the union of the Father Sun and the Mother Earth that will take place in the spring, that will produce new life. In honoring that union of Sun and Earth the Native people are honoring the process of human sexuality, on a symbolic level.

We continually acknowledge the fact that *it takes two*, the male and the female, to re-create life on every level of existence. It's that acknowledgement, I think, that keeps us from becoming too arrogant, from thinking that we don't need anybody else in life. Independence is a good thing, but not to the point of arrogance or extinction.

Along with the honoring of Father Sun and the Mother Earth, the Native people also acknowledge the male and female rains, the heavy and the light rains. In the ceremonial paintings of the Southwest, in the Navajo *Yei* rugs, there are male and female spirits represented. Some paintings show male and female gods; the heads have different shapes to them.

The honoring of the male and female energies is a constant theme that runs through all of our ceremonies. First we have the Earth Renewal ceremony; then we have a ceremony to acknowledge the spring planting season. At that time, we honor the fertility of women, and their power to bring forth new life. When we plant our garden we build a ceremonial circle within it, and our sisters go out and make a special blessing on the land. In the old way, the women would take off their garments and walk naked around the area of the garden. They would drag their garments behind them on the ground.

I often wonder, when you hear about Lady Godiva, who made a naked ride through the streets of Coventry, in England, if she wasn't hooked in some way to some of our Native rituals.

After we've planted the garden, the next part of the ceremonial cycle comes at harvest time, and the harvest ceremonies are meant to be *thank you* rituals.

The seeds are important to us, too, at harvest time; they're the link back to another cycle of renewal. The Pueblo people, and many others, keep the *sacred seeds*. With many tribes it's the women's responsibility to care for the seeds, because that, in itself, is an acknowledgement of their connection to the Creator, as channels for creating life.

Traditionally, the men and women worked side-by-side in the gardens and orchards, because in that way they blended their energies to help the fruits and vegetables flourish.

The Native people feel that everything on Earth contains life — the plants, the trees, the animals, the insects, the minerals and the waters. We're part of that life chain, as well, and since it's a blending of the power of *all* the energies in the universal chain that keeps everything healthy and growing, we feel that we have a sacred responsibility to participate in the web of energy as naturally as we can.

We're just like the grass, when you look at the complex harmony of the cycles. Last year's grass dies and goes into the Earth, and, from its nutrients, new life comes forth. In the same way, when we pass on, our bodies go into the Earth, and from the disintegration of our flesh comes even more new life. Maybe it's a pine tree that grows, or maybe it's something else, but there's always that continuing cycle, and we acknowledge it.

Many non-Natives, in contrast, don't see that cyclical process as being very beautiful; they think of their bodies becoming part of the soil and they shudder. They spend fortunes at funeral homes for the most expensive, air-tight, water-tight containers they can buy, to keep their bodies safe from the natural elements. They deny their role in the universal scheme, but the Mother Earth, of course, will eventually take them back anyway; she needs them, you see, in order to live and grow.

The Native people feel that in the natural cycle of life, the most powerful thing we can do is to share our energies with each other. Like mature seeds, we can't sit around on our stalks and dry up; we need to get out into the world and participate in some way. The *sharing of energy* can be translated into sexual intercourse, as well as many other things. Another way to share energy is as a healer, and the power that helps us to make medicine is the same power as our sexual energy. It's a matter of channelling this power.

There's a sacred circle on our bodies; it goes around the heart and lungs, and down below the sexual reproductive areas. Most of the vital energies for humanity's survival lie within that circle. That's where your male/female energy is, within that circle, and a man or woman has both of those energies within themselves. We believe that there are male and female parts to all of us.

To work as a healer with the energy in the sacred circle, you can run your hands up over your own body, and you can feel the energy surge up inside of you. You can take the energy from your sexual areas and move it upwards, to your stomach, your chest, your throat. You let your muscles open up, and you relax. You can begin that process by placing your hands first on the Earth; then, end the process by laying your head down on the Earth. Draw that energy up from the Earth Mother, and clear your head out. You can kick out your intellectual blockages in that way, so that you will feel things from the bottom of your heart.

Once you've built up the energy inside of yourself, you can then transmit it to another person. You can use it for healing, or for making love. It makes little difference; the process is the same.

So the sexual centers can actually be used as areas in which you store up the natural life forces; then that power can be converted to be used for other things. The gypsy people, when they do a healing, make magnetic passes over their bodies, so they're doing the same thing that I'm talking about. If you watch a gypsy healer, prior to a healing ceremony, he'll rub his body all over with his hands to pick up the vital energy that he or she needs to use, and to transmit. To make the flow of energy even stronger, gypsy male healers work on female patients, and vice versa.

If your energy field is really low, you can begin the healing process by hugging a tree; I do that often. Trees are conductors of energy between the heavens and earth. When you hold and hug a tree, you feel the energy and it can be like a blood transfusion. Part of what you are feeling is from the sap, the life blood going up and down the tree. In this and other ways, you can tap into the network of life energy that's in all creation, in order to revitalize yourself. When I was over in Germany, one time, after I'd been there for two weeks, I was really feeling drained. I'd been to one city after another, and I'd met and talked with an enormous number of people. They were beautiful people, but I had grown tired. I was in Stuttgart, when I told the folks that I was with that I had to get away for a few hours. I said to them, "I want you to take me to the Black Forest. I need to go out there and revitalize my energy for awhile" and so we did that. We went up there for an afternoon, and I wandered around for awhile. I put my arms around a beautiful red fir tree and I just held it, and I felt the life force energy just rushing into me. Hugging that tree was just like having a blood transfusion.

In life, that's the energy that keeps us going. When a man and woman come together and embrace, they can feel that same force surging, an interplay between the male and female energies; then, they come alive. Sexual energy, I think, is the kind most people can relate to when I talk about the natural cycles because they've all felt it at one time or another. So it's something that is real to them, something they have less trouble understanding, when I say they need to learn to feel. When you can draw that energy into you on any level, from any of life's creations, it's like taking super vitamins; you're picked up; you feel on fire. You say, "Hey, I was so tired just a few minutes ago, and now I'm feeling so good! Isn't it wonderful?"

Sexual energy is the same power that's in every creation on Earth, but, in Western society, we put that energy into a little container; we put it in a little box like everything else we have to deal with. After all, you can't get your "job" done, you can't really function efficiently as part of the chrome dream, if you're off wandering around, feeling your vital energies all the time. So your whole life is separated off into little compartments, and you say, "This is what I do for a living; this is what I do for recreation; this is what I do on Sundays", and so on.

Sexual energy has its own little box up on the shelf in white society. It's up there in the closet of your mind and heart, but you hold it back. People say, "No. Don't think about that now. Don't do anything about it now", because they feel that they need to have society's permission to work with that kind of energy. Society only gives permission to use sexual energy to those with marriage licenses, with the hope that they only use "it" to create more children, not to have pleasure and experience life fully. Listening to and obeying this attitude is another way a lot of folks give away their power.

The Native people don't separate things off in that way; each feeling, each nuance of life, is a part of the whole, and our life force energies enter very strongly into our religion.

That's why Native people speak of the white man's religion as a "Sunday religion", because that's the only time when many white folks open up the little box that has *religion* inscribed on it — on Sunday mornings. The rest of the time, it often seems like the white man doesn't have much feeling about religion, because it isn't on the schedule, so his churches are often closed with lock and key. The Native people have all of nature as their cathedral at all times.

The view of the Native people concerning sex is obviously very different, not only on this continent, but in the rest of the world as well. In Africa, in Polynesia, all over the world, the sexual parts on the statues and other art forms of primitive people represent the energy of fertility; they are honored, very much acknowledged and accepted, and, on much of the Native statuary the sexual organs are very much enlarged, to emphasize their importance in the web of life. Awhile back, I bought a statue of a man and of a women, in Mexico. They were from the Native people, and the man was shown with a very large and erect penis. The woman's stomach was enlarged, perhaps with child, and had four circles drawn around it. These represent the strength the woman gets from the womb. We had a lot of fun displaying these statues, seeing how many ways they could fit together. Eventually we gave them away to another medicine man, who was very honored to receive such a sacred gift.

There are many stories from Native people that speak very frankly about human sexuality, and how we came to be. It is acknowledged in many Native creation stories that women were the first people created, and that they are complete people because of their ability to bring forth life. Men were created later and often in strange ways. One Canadian tribal creation story says that the first woman, Copper Woman, grew the first ancestor of man from mucus from her body which she placed in increasingly larger sea shells. The little mannikin kept growing parts of his body from organs in the sea shells. The hair on his chest and face came from a seal blanket, and his penis came from the neck of a clam. My own people have stories about the first man, who is both the creator of the world, and a fool, having a thirty foot penis which gets increasingly shorter because he doesn't know exactly what to do with it, so he keeps on doing the wrong thing and losing part of it.

In the main creation legend of my people, we tell of a sky woman who watches happenings on the earth like some people today watch television. At one point, because people aren't living by the Creator's plan, the earth is covered by water, and all that is left are some tall rocks, and some animals. Both the sky woman and the animals miss having people on the earth. The sky woman grows lonely, and asks for an end to her loneliness. A spirit man comes to her, and she becomes pregnant. She gives birth to twin boys — one all spirit, and one all matter — and, being so different, they hate each other, and fight until both are destroyed.

The spirit woman prays again, and another spirit man comes to her. When she becomes pregnant, the animals decide they will invite her to come live on the earth. They hope that if her new children have enough room to run and play, they won't destroy each other. But there is no place for them to live. A giant sea turtle comes and offers his back as their home. The sky woman comes down, sprinkles some earth on the turtle's back, and breathes into it. The earth covers the turtle's whole back, and the turtle can go back into the water. To honor his sacrifice, my people have called this continent Turtle Island. The spirit woman, eventually, has her children and they are composite beings, composed both of spirit and matter. Yet, they are different, for one is a man, and the other a woman. While they sometimes fight, they don't destroy each other, and they always yearn for union.

Native people the world over, before "progress" came to them, had much more pleasure from sex than most people have today. They thought it was natural, fun, and, sometimes, funny. There are ceremonies in some tribes in which male clowns, wearing large replicas of penises come up and grab the women. There are ceremonies in other tribes in which people slip off into the bushes, and nobody raises an eyebrow. In the old days, in some tribes, when a boy reached puberty, he would spend a period of time with an older woman who would teach him about his sexuality, and show him ways in which he could please a woman. A girl reaching puberty in these tribes would be taught by an older man.

Instead of making people promiscuous, these ceremonies and practices taught them how to be happy. They knew how to feel, merge, release, and regenerate all of their vital energy. We didn't have this dual attitude of sex as being either *holier than thou* or *dirty pictures on bathroom walls*.

Unfortunately, back in history, sexuality among the white race was very much suppressed. Back in Europe at the time when the churches took over the life and philosophy of the people, church leaders saw that a lot of folks who were living out in the country were performing their ceremonies at various times of the year the way we Native people do. They had their rituals for planting and for harvest, and they were acknowledging the same male and female energy forces.

The church took a look at that and said, "Well, if they have the power to do those ceremonies and make things grow, what are they going to need us for? We'd better put a stop to it. If those folks have their own power, they won't put money into our collection plates."

So they tried to put a stop to it. The people had their own power back in those days, and that was a very real threat to the power of the Church. I've told you about the pictographs that I read all over this continent; in Europe, you can see the same rock writings and paintings of shamen who are wearing deer skins, and other animal hides. The histories that those pictographs reveal show that for thousands of years before Christianity came along, the people of Europe were no different from any other Native culture. Some people call the changes that were made then "progress" and think that it was a wonderful thing. If it was, the Mother Earth would not be in as much need of healing as she is today. Progress has filled her, in many cases, with the open wounds and toxic substances that have been bringing her out of balance, and it has filled her human children with the same wounds and poisons.

The people who stayed out on the land in Europe became known as *pagans*, a term which actually means *country people* but which was interpreted as being somewhere between *country bumpkins* and *worshippers of the devil*. These people, the pagans, were regarded as folks who didn't know much, but who were very much a threat to "civilization". People who live in cities, of course, ever since cities have been in existence, have always been touted as being much smarter than the country folks. You can see how that attitude fits into the unnatural scheme-of-things.

So the ceremonies that we've talked about were made illegal by the church and many people who practiced them — some say as many as nine million — were killed because of their beliefs. The churches literally took the power away from the people. They no longer let them go to the mountain to make their prayers in the way which felt best to them. They no longer allowed them to make their ceremonies which exalted the life force running through all of creation.

When the Puritans came over to North America, they did the same thing to the Native people here. They got really freaked out when they saw the *Indians*; they called them wild, half-naked savages. They tried to assimilate them in a very ordered manner, or they killed them off ... whichever, at the time, seemed to be more expedient.

The Native people were only doing what came naturally to them, but when the priests came over and saw the Native women, for example, along the California coast, with their breasts hanging out to greet the sunshine, they were horrified. Those women were just wearing grass skirts, and nothing else, and the priests said, "Oh, my God, these people are terrible creatures! They're sinners!".

Where was the sin, though? It must have been in the priests' heads, because the nakedness that the Native people had lived with for thousands of years certainly wasn't offensive to their own sense of decency. I tell people that *sin* is what the priests carried in one hand when they brought the *Good Book* in the other.

Native people all over the world didn't have any sense of guilt about their bodies or other natural things. The Creator gave them their bodies, and they knew there was nothing wrong with displaying part of the beauty of the creation.

What happened in North America, eventually, was that the drive to stamp out the Native religion coincided with a lot of other practical necessities for the white settlers, making the use of the reservation system very desirable. Aside from the obvious function which reservations had of keeping the Native people from the majority of the land so that it could be *developed*, the reservations also served as little boxes in which religious assimilation could take place. When the government finally got the Native Americans onto reservations, it was much easier to control their religious practices, to dictate, finally, which branch of Christianity each tribal group would best fit into. The white folks had a mission board back in New York City, and the board divided the reservations up and they said, "This reservation will be Baptist; this one, Presbyterian; this one, Catholic; and this one will be Episcopalian." The Native people on the different reservations were assigned to be various kinds of Christians and in that way, the reasoning went, they would soon be *civilized*.

These Natives didn't believe in the right things, you see, and they didn't wear the proper clothing, and that was dangerous because it was a threat to the establishment. The Native religions, like the pagan religions in Europe, were based on personal power.

It was bad business, too, you know, to let the Native people run around half-clothed; the guy going around with just a breech cloth would be a lousy clothing customer.

It got to the point where the Native peoples' religions went totally underground. It wasn't until 1978 when the Indian Religious Freedom Act was signed into law, that the Native people of this continent, who had been here since the Creator had put them here, had the legal right to practice their own religions again, to hold the traditional ceremonies of a legitimate way of life.

The Native philosophy, or feeling, as I've said, is that all things are a part of the total being, part of the life cycles that I've been telling you about. The male/female energies that we feel within ourselves and share with others are very sacred to us. In the Southwest, in South America, *everywhere*, there is a new interest growing in the old Native medicine ways. In Mexico, the healers talk about *kipura*, and what that literally means is the life force, the power, and it's the same word that they use to say *sexual energy*.

When a person is in harmony, and understands that the Earth

is in the process of procreation all of the time, they will use the life force within themselves, or outside of themselves, harmoniously, without hesitation.

People come to a medicine man and they expect to find some kind of celibate, some kind of saint who is untouchable, and then they're disillusioned, or they grin with amusement, when they discover that we really like sex as well as the next person. They call us rogues, sometimes, or scoundrels, and we're not; we just enjoy life and the sexual energy which is a part of it.

Sometimes I like to talk about the non-Native's expression *the birds and the bees*, because the bees are a really good example of how the life force energy is transformed into sexual energy. The bees never rest; they land on one flower after another, and what they're doing is part of *procreation*. Bees must be the sexiest little buggers in nature, and I sometimes like to joke and say that maybe if I am reincarnated I'll be lucky, and come back as a bee.

I've shared my energy with a lot of women; that's the way it is supposed to be for me. I believe that the Great Spirit made men and women as they are so that they can reach out and enjoy each other. I believe, too, that what happens between two people is only between them, and is a gift to enjoy. That doesn't mean that I participate in orgies, nor that I advocate that kind of behavior for anybody else. When folks come to Vision Mountain, and they ask me about our sexual ways, I usually tell them they can do whatever they feel good about. "Just as long as you leave me, and my medicine dog, Shasta, alone", I joke with them.

If the truth were known, we'd find that most men of power — from saints to gurus — have liked to share energy fully. The only difference between them and us Native medicine men is that they don't admit to what they practice.

Someone wrote an article for "*Many Smokes*" not too long ago, and in it, he talked about the old Native way of predicting which children would grow up to be medicine people. Some Native people, in the old way, would watch the children and determine which ones would have strong medicine by their early sexual drives. Those young people who were really showing a lot of natural sex energy, it was believed, would grow up and channel that energy into medicine. This was not only true of Medicine *Men*, you understand, but of Medicine *Women* too.

With the Native people, you find some folks who are way up there in age, and they're still very sexually active. That's supposed to be abnormal by this society's standards. For us it's not abnormal, because we don't have anybody to tell us that sexual drives are supposed to die out at 50, or 60, or whenever. We don't need that kind of propaganda, because we're not hemmed in by that false sense of propriety, like many other folks are.

There are many funny stories about people going to visit the old medicine men, and being surprised to find them very much sexually alive. I heard a story not too long ago about a great Plains medicine man. He was about eighty at the time that the episode took place. I met a lady who had gone to visit with him, and I asked her how her visit went.

"Oh," she told me, "that old man chased me around the table for four days."

That doesn't surprise a Native American very much, although it sure had surprised the lady who told me about it. That holy man's energy was simply alive until his final moments. Isn't that a wonderful way to be?

There's another old man I know of, over a hundred years old, who was at a conference a few years back. He disappeared one night, and some of his people were wondering what had happened to him. Nobody knew. But the following morning he came back to the meeting with a young lady hanging on his arm. He had a big smile on his face, and everything was right for him in the world . It turned out that he had just stepped out for the night, to share some of his energy.

There's another story that I've heard told about a brother from the South who was in a ceremony where people were being asked to recount their sexual adventures. He told about being with a few ladies, and people who knew him knew that he was leaving many out. When asked, he said that if he were to tell about all the ladies he had known the sun would rise, and set and rise again before he would be done.

I was at another meeting once when a lady friend of ours went off with a grandfather to hear about his tribe's history. As she was leaving, the man's grandson said, "Watch out for Grandpa." Since the man was in his eighties, she assured the grandson that she would be careful he didn't fall on the stairs or anything. The grandson grinned.

When I next saw her she told me that grandpa was quite healthy, and that the only accident he had to watch out for was being so active he would fall out of bed.

★ ★ ★

The Bear Tribe has always been known for its bear hugs. We feel that it is good for people to make real physical contact with each other. Now even the scientists are catching onto that. There was a study a few years back that said that you need eight hugs a day in order to stay healthy. But so many people are uptight about sex that they are lucky if they get a hug a month.

Once Wabun and I spoke at a big conference in Vancouver and we finished up by inviting people to give out some bear hugs. One woman in her sixties came over to me and asked for a hug. I gladly gave one, and talked to her for a while, stroking her hair as tears streamed out of her eyes.

"Thank you, Sun Bear," she said to me, "That's the first hug that I've had in twenty years."

How many other good people, like her, I wonder, are out there, deprived of full health and happiness by a society that fears love and the natural cycle?

photo: National Geological Survey

I feel that the time for the PATH OF POWER is now. The Earth
changes which were prophesied so long ago have become realities.
Volcanic eruptions, earthquakes, floods, droughts . . . all of these
have developed more active patterns.

CHAPTER TWENTY

TODAY AND TOMORROW

I think that the reader of this book should come away from it with a very real notion of why my vision, and the Bear Tribe Medicine Society, is very real, and why I've felt a strong sense of urgency over the past few years to have my story told at this point in time.

There are many things happening today which make me feel that I have lived to see the partial fulfillment of my vision, and that makes me a very lucky person. It is one thing to know one's path of power — that in itself is a blessing — and another thing to be able to maintain the journey on the good red road. I am very grateful that the Great Spirit has allowed me to renew my vision on a continuing basis.

My vision is an unfolding one. When it first came to me it was not an entire life-plan, but it was a beginning. At various times in my life I've been able to go out on the mountain, to ask the Creator, "Where do I go from here?", and the Spirit has answered me. Even the meaning of my name *Gheezis Mokwa* (Sun Bear), is a thing which has revealed itself to me more along the miles of the journey.

First, there was the vision of the bear and the colored spheres, when I was four years old. Later, other visions, other events, filled in many blank spaces for me. Some years back I was up in Neah Bay, Washington, visiting and working with the Makah people up there. A young man that I'd worked with before asked me to come there, to speak to the people about a new alcoholism program they were starting. "When you come up here," he had told me, "bring your buffalo skull with you".

I had no idea how he even knew that I had a buffalo skull, but he knew, so I brought it with me. I ended up giving it as a present to their medicine man, and, when I did that, the tears started streaming down his cheeks, and he said, "I've prayed for four years for you to come here, and bring me the power of the buffalo". He put sweetgrass and sage in the eyesockets of the skull, and it was a very powerful experience. He said, "Now, my vision has been fulfilled. The buffalo and the whale have been brought together". His people, on the Northwest Coast, had had that vision for a very long time.

After that good energy had passed between us, he and his people shared some things with me about their Bear Medicine. One of them said to me:

I knew you would be coming here with your teaching, and I'll tell you why. I want to share with you a story of our people.

There's a meadow not too far away from here, and many years ago two children were playing in it. As they played a man came along and he was naked. After awhile he laid down and rolled on the ground, and he turned into a bear. He walked for awhile in that form, and then he laid back down and rolled again, and he turned back into a man.

The children came up to him to see what he was doing, and he said to them, "Now you know my secret. I have the power to turn into a bear, because I'm a nature man, and I come here from the sun".

They told me that story, they said, because of my name, and because of the teaching that I was doing, and because of the good medicine that we had been sharing together. Many times — like the time when I was in Germany and the man told me that he'd expected me to come there because of their ancient prophecies — that kind of thing does happen. Folks tell me their legends, and they say that they've been waiting for me to show up. They regard me as a nature spirit, as a natural man, because of the way that I work, and what I teach.

The following day, the Makah Medicine Man took me out for a walk on their reservation, and he showed me a medicine plant which was growing by a creek, and said, "When you want to work with healing, you take this plant and you eat it, and then you wash yourself in the water from the creek. Then, you'll be able to do powerful ceremonies. This is very secret medicine," he told me. "It's for Bear Medicine Men only".

I felt very honored that he shared that knowledge with me.

The Chippewa-Ojibwa people have what we call the Migration Scrolls, and these scrolls talk about the journey into the four worlds of the Chippewa ... each world has been ended, and joined to the next, by a period of Cleansing. We've already been through three of these worlds, and the last of them is coming with the present Cleansing.

The Migration Scrolls show that the bear is a sacred animal of this continent. The bear represents the Great Spirit, both in the Scrolls themselves, and in some of the ceremonies that we perform.

The Bear Spirit works for the Great Spirit, and all creation. According to the Scrolls, the bear opens, or pierces, the veil to each new world with its tongue, and it wasn't until I was doing what I'm doing now that I fully realized what that meant. I feel that I'm doing what the Scrolls say; I'm piercing the veil to the next world that will come after the cleansing with my tongue, by teaching people, and warning them of the Earth changes coming, and how they can survive those things. It is Bear Medicine, Bear *knowledge*, that I'm working with on my path of power, and that path has always been organic ... always changing and expanding.

I guess that my uncle, Bo Doge, really knew what he was doing when he named me Sun Bear, almost fifty years ago.

★ ★ ★

I feel that the time for THE PATH OF POWER is now, because, as I said earlier in the book, we're about ten years into the Cleansing today. The Earth changes which were prophesied so long ago are becoming realities. Volcanic eruptions, earthquakes, floods, droughts ... all of these things have developed new and active patterns.

Travelling around the country in these last few years, one could talk to people anywhere, everywhere, and the conversation would often go to the strange weather that a particular area had been having. Areas which had normally been wet were dry, and vice versa. You could have 70 degree weather one day, and 20 degree the next. People wonder what is going on. It's the earth changes happening, and they're happening everywhere.

Many of my visions have allowed me to see the changes coming upon the Earth Mother. I saw years ago that the Earth would begin to withhold her increase .. I've talked about that before ... that one place would be too wet, and another place would be too dry, and that in order for people to survive they would have to watch the weather very closely, and that they would have to be in touch with everything that was going on around them.

What we've been doing, during this time of the Cleansing, is taking people who are ready and willing to open up, and teaching them how they can survive. I often like to call our Mountain the College of the Earth; in a sense it is a living classroom. We not only tell our students about the coming heavy changes; we also teach them how to hear the rest of the story from the elemental forces, from the earth sounds and from the attitudes of our animals.

Medicine people usually know about a natural disaster before it happens. We knew up here, in 1980, that Mt. Saint Helens was ready to erupt, before any scientific organization had made any announcements about it. During the summer of 1982, Wabun had a few days when she felt a great deal of psychic discomfort. She told a few people here, "I think Saint Helens is getting ready to make herself heard again ... I know this feeling". At about the same time, I was walking up on the Mountain and I could feel tiny tremors running beneath my feet, and other people here were smelling light sulphur fumes coming out of the Mountain, by their tents at night.

Within a few days, Mt. Saint Helens began to act up; her dome was building, and there was rumbling, so Wabun had been right. There was no major explosion, but here on Vision Mountain, more than three hundred miles away from the Little Sister, there were sounds and signs and feelings, and we picked up on them. We knew there would be no real danger at this time, and we were right about that part of our feelings, too.

In my medicine I have seen that the people who will survive the Cleansing will be in small groups; they will be living together close to the Earth in love and harmony. They will be both Native and non-Native people, for my vision has told me that we are all human beings living on the same Earth Mother, and that, in order to survive, we will have to rid ourselves of any racist feelings, any arrogance about ourselves, because we're all part of the same universal creation.

At the time of the Cleansing too, I feel, the medicine caves on Vision Mountain may open up for us. They were hidden and sealed by the medicine people here centuries ago, to protect the sacred knowledge inside the Mountain from the encroachment of civilization. Because of some vision quests which have been made up here, because of certain information that has surfaced during those vision quests, I feel I now know the location of one of the major entrances into Vision Mountain. So now, when I feel the time is right, I'll be able to go do the ceremonies for opening up the medicine caves, and then we may be able to work with the forces inside of Vision Mountain.

I feel that the publication of THE PATH OF POWER will give folks a way to look over my shoulder, to see how I've lived my life, and learned my lessons from the Great Spirit. I've tried to put my teachings in here, as well as the story of my life path. I want people to be able to understand me, to come into harmony as I have, because this will help us all to become true brothers and sisters. We have much work to do together upon the Earth Mother at this time.

I feel that this book might also serve to show others that they, too, can have and follow their own visions. It is a very beautiful thing for a person to see his vision coming into physical reality. There are so many people who have had visions or dreams that they've never even talked about, let alone fulfilled. The reason for that, I feel, is that they have kept themselves in prison. They have given away their power.

I also wanted this book to come out now because it will communicate to many people, in many places, what is happening on the Earth Mother right now, and what they can expect to happen. It is important for people to know that there are many others who are working with the natural forces in a good manner.

One of the reasons that I feel so good about my Apprentice Program is that it spreads the word about what is happening, and also provides people with very real tools for survival on every level. It's not enough to know how to plant a garden, without knowing where the rain is. It's a chain-reaction kind of thing. It's not enough to acknowledge the elemental forces without knowing how to get them to respond to you. You've got to know what ceremonies to perform in order to make the right things happen. If you want rain, if you need it for your crops, you have to know how to make a ceremony for that rain. If you want wind, or sunshine, you have to know what you are doing.

Doing these things will take a lot of hard work, and a lot of praying. You have to realize that coming into harmony means coming into a sacred partnership, and you have to do your share. You may go out and smoke your pipe or do a dance or a chant for the Earth Mother and it's just not enough. You must feel what you are doing in your heart; you must *know* that what you are doing is right; and you must be willing to work for the results. Maybe you'll need to smoke your pipe three or four times in a day, and pray constantly before you will get a response from the forces and from the Great Spirit. Sometimes you might need to fast or do a sweat ceremony first. I have a working kind of faith instead of one in which you ask for things and then just sit back and wait for them to come to you.

If you don't make the prayers, if you don't take the responsibility for your share of the partnership in the healing of Mother Earth, then when things get really rough you won't know where to go, or what to do. You won't have any food for your family, or wood to keep you warm or clothes to put on your backs. When it all comes down, the power companies, and the restaurants, and the clothing stores, will all be gone.

★ ★ ★

We've been putting out the same message at Vision Mountain for a lot of years now. The times, I feel, have finally caught up with the message, and, as they have, our methods of communication have become much more effective. We have evolved into a workable alternative to the dominant society, and this fact gives us our power.

Constantly, a growing number of people come to us to learn. There's been a really rapid growth of the Tribe in all respects, especially over the past three or four years, and it's become evident, for that reason, too, that a book about my life would be of value to a lot of searching people.

We have learned at the Bear Tribe to be flexible, accepting and resilient. When people come to join us, we listen to the things that they have to contribute. Shawnodese, who is now my subchief, and director of the Apprentice Program, came here in 1979, with a background in just about every new-age philosophy available. He had some progressive ideas that have helped us in many ways. For one thing, even though I had, at various times in my life, been an *operator* (such as selling real estate or men's clothes) in order to survive, I still had some reservations about being tainted by having a little extra cash. I felt that money was somehow bad. Shawnodese had the idea that money was just energy, and it was how you used it that counted. He took over the bookkeeping for awhile and started writing affirmations on everything having to do with money. He also explained his feelings to us enough times that we began to hear them. Since that time the Bear Tribe has had a very active flow of cash, both in and out, and we no longer fear money but, instead, use it to do and build things that we believe in.

Over the years, too, we've been increasing the background variety of the folks who come here to study and be with us. There are doctors who come now, and lawyers, and ex-military people, as well as those who have spent much of their lives in questioning and questing. This broadening range of people shows us that our message is spreading far beyond those in the "sixties" mind set, and we feel that this is an important step. In our early days we got a lot of people who were looking for a prefabricated utopia. Now we're getting people who are willing to help to build one.

We don't have the answers here for anyone, in the sense that we will tell them how to live their lives; folks need to be more independent than that. They need to be able to teach us some things, too. We've never been a community that tells people when to get up in the morning, what exercises to do, what food to eat, who they have to mate with, and who they ought to marry. That's not our trip. We've always followed, instead, the traditional Native view which is that each person has to go out and speak to the Creator themselves. While they are speaking and listening, they always have to keep in their minds, "How can I best serve my people and the Earth Mother?"

We don't keep a tight rein on people here either. Some other organizations keep really close track of all the folks who have ever come to be with them. We just let the Tribe's medicine work on people, and we hope that the seeds that we plant here will be taken to different places, and grow in the way that's proper for each individual seed.

One of the nicest things people have called me and Wabun is *seed planters*. It's like planting in the garden, in a way. We can have ceremonies, too, that celebrate the planting of spiritual seeds in our brothers and sisters, and we see a larger and more fruitful harvest all the time.

A lot of folks come here feeling that what they're going to learn are the "ground rules" for successful prayer. Some other medicine people will tell you that if you make an offering in the wrong way, if you spill a speck of kinnik-kinnik on the ground while you're filling your pipe, the Creator will be offended, and that you won't have the right to make the prayer. We don't believe that it works that way here, though; that would mean to me that the Great Spirit is pretty vindictive, and always testing you, and I think that the Spirit is much more loving and benevolent than that. When you are making a prayer it is important that you are feeling sincere in your heart. The words don't matter as much as having the right feeling. I don't believe in canned prayers that you can pick up off of a shelf. The more energy you put into a prayer, the more you will get out of it. That's also true with the chants, the dances, the ceremonies.

The Bear Tribe and Vision Mountain have always been very cleansing and healing places for people; sometimes folks get sick when they first get here ... nothing serious ... but maybe a cold that lasts for a few days, and it is a cleansing of their systems. After that, they usually feel better than they've felt in a very long time, and a lot of them will tell us that. The emotional and spiritual cleansings that go on here work in the same way that the physical cleansings do. Even the folks who have left us because they didn't get along too well with our ideas, who may have left having some immediate bad feelings about the place, often write to us later on, and tell us that they later realized how much knowledge of themselves they had gained from being here.

I believe that one thing we've established at Vision Mountain is a safe place where people *can* learn about themselves, and how they relate to the Earth Mother and the Creator, and how all of that relates to their lives every day. When folks leave the Mountain, they take that knowledge with them wherever they go, and I think a lot of times folks go home feeling more comfortable about their surroundings, more self-confident about their own instincts, than they were before they came to be with us.

I think it's important for people who come here to go home realizing that they're not crazy because, maybe, they talk to animals, or their plants, or even rocks, and they seem to pick up a response from those other kingdoms. I know that many folks, in the outside world, make very sure that nobody else knows what they're doing when they communicate with the elemental forces. Communication with animals, with the spirit forces, may come to them naturally, but they don't feel right about it in a world where rationality is supposed to be the key to a productive existence. A lot of the folks who come to Vision Mountain *have* tuned into messages from the other kingdoms, from the elemental forces, and they want *so much* to believe that what's happened to them is real; yet, their rational minds keep nagging at them, telling them that they must be going crazy. These people go along, and maybe one is enraptured because he or she had a vision of a hawk feather lying on the ground; then, later on, he might find that feather in the exact spot where he had envisioned it to be. Someone else might ask for a sign from the wind, and have the wind come to talk to him.

Other folks respond to Earth sounds, even in such noise-polluted places as New York City ... a tree creaks in Central Park, or a pine cone drops, and they say "hello" to it. That's a perfectly natural thing to do. Yet, some of these folks react both with joy and panic inside themselves. They feel that they've found *proof of God*, but, all the time, the society they live in is working to destroy that proof for them. They live in a world of non-believers, and, if they're programmed into it like most folks are, they work hard after a powerful experience of communication with the spirit realms, to finally convince themselves that it didn't really happen ... or that what happened to them had to be some kind of bizarre coincidence ... or that there has to be some *rational* explanation.

A lot of these folks, I feel, stay in a kind of realm of uncomfortable confusion; there's no support for what's happening to them in the mainstream society, and because of that, they sometimes get put into mental institutions, and are labelled schizophrenic or something. We've had a number of people come to us here who have had that negative experience. They weren't crazy at all, you see; they were simply visionary people, but the society that they live in couldn't accept their visions so they locked them up. In the Native way visionary people were honored.

At the Bear Tribe we feel we give those kinds of people permission, in a sense, to believe in those powerful experiences. We don't make them hide their individuality. I like to say at my lectures that there are a lot of *closet tree-huggers* out there, but they're afraid to admit it to each other, and we try to encourage them to do that here. That's why, I think, a lot of people have told us that coming to study with us is like coming home . . . because, for one thing, we *all* hug trees up here, and talk to the clouds up in the sky. It's our life way.

It feels good, too, to know that we can be helpful to people in that way, that we can help them to understand that they're okay, and that, in a lot of cases, they are just capable of seeing things in a deeper way than their society can accept. I think it's important, both in terms of my vision, and in terms of living in harmony, for other people who may be out there having those experiences to know that they're not alone, and that they're not only okay, but probably in better shape than many of the people who are around them.

★ ★ ★

I want to acknowledge here the fact that the Bear Tribe today is made up of a wealth of contributions made by people who have come to be with us over the years. We don't take the folks who aren't with us anymore for granted; each one of them, I feel, shared and gave a part of themselves to build what we have today, and I'm not talking about a small number of people. I would say that in the past five years we have had about two-hundred people come through here as visitors each year, and a lot more than that have come here to participate in our seminars. All of these folks have learned something from us and, at the same time, they've each given something to us in return, no matter how small, or how large, or how easy to pinpoint that contribution may have been. So while the Bear Tribe today is a relatively small group, we're working with the knowledge and experience of many others.

We're now at a point where we have at least a half-dozen affiliate groups around the country, and at least a thousand people who are supporters of the Tribe, working with us in one way or another. These supporters give their good energy to us; they give us their time, and they help us do much of the work that it takes to make our programs as successful as they are.

Since 1978, we've talked to at least ten thousand people per year directly, and to many more through media coverage of our programs. The Bear Tribe Medicine Society today is a very extensive network, which includes the people who have been to Vision Mountain, or to our lectures or seminars or Medicine Wheel Gatherings, and who really feel the energy and the power of our vision. The network is international at this time. One lady told us recently that she had been talking about the Bear Tribe with a friend of hers who had just come back from Germany; her friend told her that while she was in Germany, she'd heard a lot about us and the work we did there in 1981.

I feel gratified, too, because I have stuck my neck out, and continue to do so by working with non-Native people, when some of my Native brothers and sisters are still stuck in their own racism. This saddens me, to see people who should be presenting a united front for the earth's survival, spending time and energy fighting with and criticizing each other. I follow the rainbow path and respect all teachers and medicine people. I do not accept racism and separatism whether it is being pushed by Native or non-Native people.

If the Native people here are not willing to teach the non-Natives our ways, how can they learn them?

Today I see many more of my people approving of my path and the work that I am doing, although there is still some opposition from the more militant groups around the country.

At our 1982 Bay Area Medicine Wheel Gathering, some militant people came on the closing day and asked to be allowed to speak. We gave them this right. They abused it by laying guilt trips on people who were sincerely trying to learn. Nonetheless, we felt that they should have their right to speak and, when angry people in the audience began to heckle them, Wabun, who is the mistress of ceremonies at the Gatherings, walked on stage and asked the audience to give the woman speaking the same respect that they had given to the other speakers.

When the woman finished it was obvious that many of the participants were either sad or angry about what had been said. Bear Heart went out to speak then and said things that, once again, gave people the strength to go on. Still, the sadness was there, along with tension because some of the other members of the militant group were having a shouting contest with each other while they were ostensibly asking me questions.

Wabun went back on the stage and spoke to the people from her heart about what had transpired. She urged them not to allow these people to disturb the good feelings that we had generated together, but, rather, to come over to the Medicine Wheel site and continue with the closing ceremony with love, faith and trust. Most of the participants did, and it was a very powerful ceremony for them and for the earth.

That whole incident made me sad because it was generated

by blatant racism. My people have to give up their fear and bitterness, just as your people have to give up their arrogance and return to a respect for the Earth Mother. Anyone who tries to separate people from each other is just trying to take their power from them.

Shortly after, we received a letter from Steven Foster and Meredith Little, founders of Rites of Passage and the School of Lost Borders, that made us feel much better. I would like to share it with you here.

Our recent attendance at and participation in the Northern California Medicine Wheel Gathering has moved us to write this letter. Peoples of all ages and heritage, a thousand strong, came together in peace and harmony to celebrate our love for Grandmother Earth. We want to honor the great heart of Sun Bear and the beauty of his vision.

Sun Bear's Gatherings can be seen as a sign, a portent of what is to pass. Here is a 'way' almost everyone in their right mind can agree to. Here is an opportunity for generations of families to gather, for elders to be honored, for mothers and fathers to celebrate their parenthood, for the sick in spirit to be healed, for kids to be blessed, for lovers to find each other, for all of the children of the earth to lift up their hearts and be renewed. As the people of our modern world continue to seek new ways to heal old wounds, more and more will come to the Gatherings in the years ahead.

Despite the diversity of traditions and ethnicity that are found at a Gathering, there are remarkably few 'incidents'. The pervading aura of good will is largely due to Sun Bear's acceptance of all, and his willingness to share his vision. Unlike many modern celebrities, he is not always center stage. Those with whom he shares the limelight are invariably enriched and empowered.

Doubtless there will be times when different cultures confront each other. There is often pain involved in the letting go of personally cherished forms and convictions. Sun Bear, Wabun and Shawnodese's way of dealing with this pain is indicative of the quality of their heart energy. They are willing to acknowledge the uniqueness of each person's way, regardless of heritage or religious persuasion. Truly, the essence of Sun Bear's vision is universal. It operates according to the cosmic laws of LOVE — which is another name for the Great Spirit.

We prefer to be optimistic. With the help of love working through us all, Grandmother will be spared great pains, and the human race will not be eradicated. This will come about through the efforts of men and women of great heart who are willing to demonstrate their vision on earth for the people to see. Thank you Sun Bear, and the Bear

Tribe, for the demonstration of your vision. We will take heart from you and go to our own people and give away to them what we have learned.

When Native brothers and sisters come to our Medicine Wheel Gatherings to teach, some of them tell us afterward that they feel good about the work that the Bear Tribe is doing to bring all of the races together. It's our own sort of assimilation that is going on; we're trying to assimilate folks back into the realm of natural humanity, and I see it working. That's all part of bringing back the vision of the Medicine Wheel to the Earth Mother, and the Native people who work with us today feel good about this vision, because they realize how crucial it has become at this time. The Medicine Wheel, I feel, is helping my brothers and sisters to see that life is a circle, and that you can't undervalue anything on the Earth ... that it's all part of the life system, and that if one part of it is broken down, it affects all of the rest.

At the Gatherings, at Vision Mountain, I feel we give folks a very good sense of ceremony, and that's important, because I feel that ceremony is one of the richest ways we human beings can give back to all of the other kingdoms some of the energy that they're constantly giving to us. It feels very good to lecture to some people, and find out six months later that a group we talked to has been having full moon ceremonies, or Medicine Wheel Ceremonies, or changing of the seasons ceremonies on their own. Often, they write to us or let us know in other ways that we helped them to get started on that path. There's a woman in Seattle, Washington, for example, who we've worked with a lot through the years, who has now built a woman's moon circle that meets monthly, and it's a very powerful thing.

We probably don't even know how widespread our effect on people has been, but we hear about it all of the time; it's been a number of years since the publication of THE MEDICINE WHEEL, and not a week goes by that we don't get letters from people who are just discovering it, and who say that it is helping them to get onto their own path of power.

We also know that out of those first two hundred people who came through the Bear Tribe, many of them now have their own land bases and communities, and some of them base what they do on what they learned back at Medicine Rock, and the other early base camps. They may not be doing things the same as we are or on as large a scale as we are, but they were, nevertheless, touched by my vision, and they've kept the vision alive in many ways.

It has been really amazing to us at times, that so many people have been touched by our work to help heal the Earth Mother. It's because we are working with a universal truth, and it comes to us from the Creator.

★ ★ ★

The Bear Tribe is like the bear, one of the few animals that works to heal itself, and so is Vision Mountain. When we first came to live here there were a lot of other people who lived up on the Mountain, and many of them were not living in harmony with the land. The Mountain has either taught those folks to walk in balance, or it's asked them to leave, in one way or another. Most of the people who didn't respect the land have moved off Vision Mountain, and, as the land has come up for sale, people who are in harmony with what we're doing have purchased most of it. So we feel that our Mountain is protected.

Shawnodese recently said that he'd seen more varieties of snakes on Vision Mountain than he'd ever seen in his life, and some of the animals that are coming here now are ones that you wouldn't normally expect to see around here, like the wolverine that a student saw during a vision quest. That is the first wolverine that I've heard of in this part of the country, and it is significant for us because the native people called the wolverine the "little bear." It is very private and peaceful — it never bothers you — but if its territory is invaded, it has been known to conquer even the grizzly bear. We've seen many more deer on the mountain this year, and in the summer the red hawks circle, sometimes six or eight at a time, and they sing out to each other. It is very beautiful.

During the summer of 1982, on Vision Mountain, one of the rattlesnakes I mentioned earlier in the book made its appearance up on the rocks. It had come out to sun itself near a group of our apprentices. We made our prayers and offerings, and we told our brother that we loved him, but that he would have to go live a little further off in the woods, for everybody's peace of mind.

Shawnodese took a long forked stick, and he gently pinned the rattler against the ground; then, picking up the brother with his two hands, one placed firmly behind its diamond head, the other around its mid-section, he started to put it into a sack so that he could take it to a more remote spot on the Mountain.

While Shawnodese was holding the snake in his hands, a yellowjacket buzzed around him, and stung him on the wrist. He didn't flinch; he didn't let go of the snake to swat the wasp or rub his arm. That's called concentration; he was into his power, and his purpose.

Life is like that rattlesnake and that bee sometimes. You can let the small things get you into trouble, when you are holding the power of the universe in your hands.

The snake was put into a sack, and it now lives somewhere near us on the Mountain; we feel that we're living in harmony with it.

If there's a piece of advice that I feel I can give to my readers at this time, it is *don't give away your power, or use it in the wrong places. Don't let the little thorns that prick you every day become too much of a distraction. Remember what your purpose is. Remember that the power of the Creator can be a part of you, and you can love it, and it will work with you.*

Like brother rattlesnake, though, during the Cleansing, that power can and will be awesome, and it can turn on you. The situation Shawnodese found himself in on that summer afternoon illustrates a point; life is going to be full of crucial choices. You need to know which ones you should make.

This whole book, and all of our other work, is a message about a different way of looking at the world and the Great Spirit's creations, a way available to anyone who chooses it. We see brother rattlesnake as a good thing at Vision Mountain; in the same way, we see the power of the Cleansing as a very good thing. I told you earlier in the book about the time that I was bitten by a rattler, and I felt its power surging through me. While I certainly don't recommend that experience for anybody else, it was a very good experience for me. I've told you, too, about the gifts brother rattlesnake has given me for making rain.

You can see the power of the rattlesnake as a bad thing, I suppose; that's the accepted way of looking at it. That's why some folks shoot so many beautiful snakes on sight. But to me to hold the power of the Creator in your hands is a wonderful blessing. It is not, by any means, a usual occurrence; it is a very rare one. It's a gift from the Great Spirit, as is all life, if you know how to tune into its power and its love.

ABOUT THE AUTHORS

Sun Bear, a person of Chippewa descent, is the medicine chief of The Bear Tribe. Publisher of the magazine *Wildfire,* he is also a lecturer, teacher, and author of four previous books: AT HOME IN THE WILDERNESS, BUFFALO HEARTS, THE BEAR TRIBE'S SELF RELIANCE BOOK (with Wabun and Nimimosha), and THE MEDICINE WHEEL: Earth Astrology (with Wabun).

Wabun (born Marlise Ann James), his medicine helper, holds an M.S. from the Columbia School of Journalism and is a consultant to The Bear Tribe. She has written articles for numerous magazines and is the sole author of THE PEOPLE'S LAWYERS, and the co-author, with Sun Bear, of the books listed above. She is currently working on several new books.

Edward Barry Weinstock holds an M.F.A. in creative writing from the University of Arkansas. He teaches at Tidewater Community College in Chesapeake, Virginia. He is the author of THE WILDERNESS WAR: The Struggle to Preserve America's Wildlands; A POEM IN YOUR EYE: An Introduction to the Art of Seeing, Through Poetry; NEW GOTHIC RESTAURANT: Traditional and Experimental Fiction; and has had selections appear in NEW CAMPUS WRITING, NEW WRITING, *Style* magazine, *Metro* magazine, and *Many Smokes.* He is at work on another book.

photo: Ralph Busch   photo: Desiree Eden

For further information about Sun Bear, The Bear Tribe, lectures, the Apprentice Program, Medicine Wheel Gatherings, WILDFIRE, our catalog, our other books or projects write:

THE BEAR TRIBE
P. O. BOX 9167
SPOKANE, WASHINGTON 99209

If you wish a reply, please enclose a stamped, self-addressed envelope. Thanks for your interest.